Key Concepts in
Creative Industries

Recent voulmes include:

Key Concepts in Tourism Research
David Botterill and Vincent Platenkamp

Key Concepts in Sport and Exercise Research Methods
Michael Atkinson

Key Concepts in Media and Communications
Paul Jones and David Holmes

Key Concepts in Sport Psychology
John M.D. Kremer, Aidan Moran, Graham Walker, Cathy Craig

Fifty Key Concepts in Gender Studies
Jane Pilcher and Imelda Whelehan

Key Concepts in Medical Sociology
Jonathan Gabe, Mike Bury and Mary Ann Elston

Key Concepts in Leisure Studies
David Harris

Key Concepts in Urban Studies
Mark Gottdiener and Leslie Budd

The SAGE Key Concepts series provides students with accessible and authoritative knowledge of the essential topics in a variety of disciplines. Cross-referenced throughout, the format encourages critical evaluation through understanding. Written by experienced and respected academics, the books are indispensable study aids and guides to comprehension.

Key Concepts in
Creative Industries

JOHN HARTLEY, JASON POTTS, STUART CUNNINGHAM,
TERRY FLEW, MICHAEL KEANE & JOHN BANKS

Los Angeles | London | New Delhi
Singapore | Washington DC

Los Angeles | London | New Delhi
Singapore | Washington DC

SAGE Publications Ltd
1 Oliver's Yard
55 City Road
London EC1Y 1SP

SAGE Publications Inc.
2455 Teller Road
Thousand Oaks, California 91320

SAGE Publications India Pvt Ltd
B 1/I 1 Mohan Cooperative Industrial Area
Mathura Road
New Delhi 110 044

SAGE Publications Asia-Pacific Pte Ltd
3 Church Street
#10-04 Samsung Hub
Singapore 049483

Editor: Chris Rojek
Editorial assistant: Martine Jonsrud
Production editor: Katherine Haw
Copyeditor: Lotika Singha
Indexer: John Hartley
Marketing manager: Micahel Ainsley
Cover design: Wendy Scott
Typeset by: C&M Digitals (P) Ltd, Chennai, India
Printed by CPI Group (UK) Ltd, Croydon, CR0 4YY

Library of Congress Control Number: 2012939378

British Library Cataloguing in Publication data

A catalogue record for this book is available from
the British Library

ISBN 978-1-4462-0288-3
ISBN 978-1-4462-0289-0 (pbk)

contents

key concepts in
creative industries

vi

about the authors

John Hartley, AM, is Professor of Cultural Science and Director of the Centre for Culture & Technology, Curtin University, Perth, Western Australia; and "Serious Brain Power" chair in the School of Journalism, Media and Cultural Studies, Cardiff University, Wales. He is author of *Digital Futures for Cultural and Media Studies* (Wiley-Blackwell, 2012) and Editor of the *International Journal of Cultural Studies* (Sage Publications).

Jason Potts is an Australian Research Council (ARC) Future Fellow; Associate Professor of Economics at RMIT University, Melbourne, Australia; winner of the Schumpeter Prize; and author of *Creative Industries and Economic Evolution* (Edward Elgar, 2011).

Stuart Cunningham is Distinguished Professor of Media and Communications, Queensland University of Technology, Brisbane, Australia; Director of the ARC Centre of Excellence for Creative Industries and Innovation (CCI); and author of *Hidden Innovation: Policy, Industry and the Creative Sector* (UQP, 2013).

Terry Flew is Professor of Media and Communications, Queensland University of Technology, Brisbane, Australia, and author of *The Creative Industries: Culture and Policy* (Sage, 2012). In 2011–12 he headed the National Classification Scheme Review for the Australian Law Reform Commission.

Michael Keane is Professor, Queensland University of Technology, Brisbane, Australia; Principal Research Fellow at the CCI; and author of *China's New Creative Clusters: Governance, Human Capital and Investment* (Routledge, 2011).

John Banks is Senior Lecturer in the Creative Industries Faculty, Queensland University of Technology, Brisbane, Australia; course leader for the Master in Creative Industries (MCI); and author of *Co-Creating Videogames* (Bloomsbury, 2012).

All of the authors are researchers with the Australian Research Council Centre of Excellence for Creative Industries and Innovation (the CCI).

key concepts in
creative industries

introduction

The general field of **creative industries** studies[1] is now well established in higher education in many countries, especially in universities and colleges where there is a component of creative-practice education as well as cultural and aesthetic theory. Together with the study of public policy, economics and business strategy, the creative industries field is an interdisciplinary amalgam that draws from the humanities, the creative arts, technology studies and the social sciences. While this makes for a dynamic intellectual environment, it also results in untranslatability of concepts across different domains, sometimes amounting to mutual incomprehension and bemusement, occasionally even hostility and presumptions of bad faith.

However, there is more to the problem of interdisciplinarity than this. True dialogue occurs only when different parties learn from each other. Cultural, economic, political, artistic, scientific and technological discourses all contribute to the creative industries field of study, and all deploy their own specialist language. This is not simply jargon, but also a kind of embedded capital, carrying a history of debate, development and application within the terminology, without which it is hardly possible to make sense, let alone to make progress in solving problems. This more substantial exchange of ideas is what each domain needs to learn from others, even if the learning process turns out to be painful, argumentative and challenging.

This is the rationale for *Key Concepts in Creative Industries*. Interdisciplinary dialogue needs not only to be translated, it needs to be put to work: conceptually, to develop and test new approaches to a fast-changing object of study; and practically, to assist those with cultural and economic investments in the creative industries – from employment to activism – to make better decisions. How can we gain a better conceptual and analytical grip on real problems and find the right tools for their solution? And how can we develop a common frame of reference and understanding for our analytical language? Such questions face students undertaking courses in these fields, but equally they face academics, researchers and workers in the creative industries, who may sometimes need a guidebook to a terrain that is no-one's home territory.

There is little agreement even on the definition of the creative industries. Economists, regional development agencies, creative practitioners, art historians, anthropologists, government policymakers, business strategists, lawyers and educationalists will all have a different take on the topic, but they all have something to contribute to the analysis. As a result, there are important insights scattered across many domains, using different definitions, conceptual frameworks and methodologies for divergent instrumental purposes.

This general rule applies also to the authors of this book. Each of us brings a different disciplinary perspective to bear on the terms we discuss; and we've all had

---

[1]Words in **bold text** cross-refer to other entries in this book.

our views modified by working with each other and learning from the interdisciplinary field. We do not start from a partisan stance (although we have our preferences and prejudices). We'd like to get beyond some current controversies, to be able to say that the field of creative industries studies now has a robust conceptual toolkit to analyse real phenomena, to marshal compelling evidence, and to solve real problems in cultural life, business strategy, public policy, critical understanding and intellectual advancement alike.

FIX OR FLUX?

To be clear, what follows is not a set of definitions. It's more a history of ideas. Why does a book that explains *concepts* used in formal study need to worry about *history*? Certain concepts, including most of those covered herein, arise in social life and enjoy a career in ordinary language before being taken up in systematic or scientific analysis. Their meaning changes and adapts in the flux and contestation of lived processes and competing institutions. Further, the same term can retain substantially different meanings in different contexts. All of this is normal in etymological terms – language evolves over time, and words mean what they do only in relation to others in the system. But it is a pain in the neck for science, which has good reason for requiring definitional exactitude, often communicated in mathematical language and in a scientific present tense, where what a concept means is intended to apply universally. Indeed, this is part of what separates the 'exact' sciences from the human and social sciences. Surely, then, a fixed definition is essential, to reduce uncertainty, so that a concept can become part of the conceptual apparatus of a scientific field?

Such a desire is understandable, but it would not lead to understanding the key concepts in the creative industries. It would strip away one of the chief characteristics of such terms – their indeterminacy or propensity to uncertainty and change. The most important concepts are dynamic both historically (in one field over time) and contextually (across different fields). Analysts such as ourselves may strive to reach an agreed definition, so that scholarly work can proceed in a systematic way, and also, importantly, so that the work of different researchers can be compared, but recognition of historical and contextual contingency in the very terms of analysis is irreducible. Thus, in cultural and media studies, the social sciences and even economics (which has developed a much more thoroughgoing mathematical system than the humanities and other social sciences),[2] concepts carry their history with them. What's required of both individual researchers and knowledge domains is a 'history of ideas' approach, *in order* to use concepts systematically.

CULTURE AND KNOWLEDGE

One example will suffice: 'culture'. There are many different definitions of 'culture' in use, arising from different intellectual or disciplinary traditions (Hartley 2011). One definition may literally be incomprehensible in another domain. For instance,

x

[2]See: en.wikipedia.org/wiki/History_of_economic_thought

compare the domain of knowledge of 'the arts' (Arnold 1869) with that of 'complexity science' (Page and Bednar 2007) in the accompanying table, remembering that both are equally intelligible and defensible within their home register.

Definitions of Culture, By Discipline

Who's asking? Domain of knowledge	What do they say? Definition of culture	How do they know? Method of inquiry
The arts	Aesthetics	expression	imagination	Criticism
Anthropology	Customs	norms	practices	Ethnography
Positivist behavioural science	Attitudes	beliefs	values	Experiment
Sociology (quantitative/ qualitative)	Agents	institutions	structures	Empiricism
Structuralism	Relations	meanings	identity	Semiotics/theory
Complexity science	Co-evolution of ensembles of games	Computational modelling[1]

[1]Scott Page, Santa Fe Institute. See, e.g. : www.slidefinder.net/M/Modeling_Culture_Scott_Page_University/28156089/p1

It would be mistaken to attempt to decide which one of these usages is 'right', although it may be appropriate to look for *common rules* across different domains. No field is yet at the stage where it can claim a general definitional formula for such a term as culture (see also Hartley 2011). For the time being, it is appropriate to outline what's at stake in *trying* to define it. The goal is to understand how knowledge is generated, adopted and grown. Here, then, we can see that what a 'key concept' means is determined by discipline (who's asking?) and by methodology (how do they know?) as much as by propositional content (what do they say?). Concepts themselves are part of a dynamic complex system of ideas, and that's what this book seeks to explain: meanings aren't fixed; they're in flux.

This book not only offers a road map to such dynamic usages, but it also shows how a coherent field is slowly resolving itself into focus through this diverse, internationally distributed, multi-discursive and undirected collective enterprise.

CREATIVE INDUSTRIES IN EDUCATION

Higher education around the world has embraced the notion of the creative industries as a domain of study, teaching and research. It extends or combines courses in:

- Communications and media studies;
- Business, economics and regional policy;
- Creative arts (music, visual arts, performing arts);
- Media production (film, television, digital);
- Design (fashion, architecture, interactive design; graphic design);
- Information and communications technology;
- Law (copyright and intellectual property);
- Education (for a creative workforce).

The world's first Creative Industries Faculty was established at Queensland University of Technology (QUT) in Brisbane, Australia, launched by the Premier of the State of Queensland, Peter Beattie, in July 2001. The authors of this book all had a shaping hand in that enterprise, John Hartley as Foundation Dean. Meanwhile, research groups around the world have been active in refining the scholarly approach to creativity, creating a strong readership base for new work in basic (conceptual, modelling) research, as well as applications to specific sectors, countries and problems. Since then, many departments, schools or faculties, and some entire colleges (e.g. the University of the Arts, London), are devoted to the creative industries, as are some secondary schools, e.g. the Queensland Academy for Creative Industries (www.qaci.eq.edu.au).

Creative industries policies have been adopted in many countries, not just advanced or developed economies such as the UK, Australia and European countries, but also in developing or emerging economies, including China, Brazil, Indonesia and Thailand. These developments are fuelling demand for coherent and authoritative educational programmes for students and professionals alike. In short, global education provision is gearing up to the challenge of the creative industries and the need for conceptual guidance is clear.

John, Jason, Stuart, Terry, Michael and John

ARC Centre of Excellence for Creative Industries & Innovation, Australia

The concept of aesthetics in the context of the creative industries pulls in two highly contradictory directions. On the one hand, it denotes a domain of high value. Aesthetic experience is associated with those forms of the creative, performing and visual arts that are produced and consumed at the highest cost, and circulated, sometimes posthumously, at the highest price. But on the other hand, it is a concept of such attenuated authority that there is little agreement on what it means. The dispersal of previously elite creative practice across different media, populations and cultural contexts without restriction of class, income, training or taste-hierarchy means that 'aesthetic' value and judgement can apply to anything from opera to egg-cups, or indeed eggs.[1] There are now no widely agreed criteria for deciding on whether a given object, event or form qualifies as aesthetic, or to what degree.

Aesthetics, then, denotes both high (cultural) value and no (conceptual) value all at once. Thus, the notion of the aesthetic underlies a good deal of publicly funded artistic and cultural endeavour. But it has become almost impossible to use the concept itself to determine what level of funding should be applied.

The diffusion of aesthetic values across complex domains of experience and forms of work means that 'authority' – even that of Aristotle or Kant – cannot determine what those values are in any given case. Ironically, the only mechanism available to perform that function at societal scale is one that is often understood to be the very antithesis of aesthetic values: **markets**. The aesthetic dimension of myriad products and performances inevitably underlies their market value. Very large global corporations base their business model upon the appeal of beauty, and not just in the lucrative fashion and lifestyle markets or the creative industries more generally. Apple is a prominent example in the technological field, with a strong aesthetic ethos that is shared among its customers and users as well as its executives.[2] Thus a critical or philosophical term that has been used in the past to ascribe value to experience has become so diffused and complex that it cannot be defined. Its value can only be determined in the marketplace.

This seemingly contradictory situation is a symptom of a historical process, not of conceptual confusion, whereby the determination of 'taste' has shifted from producer status to consumer choice. In the first place this entailed a 'loss' of critical authority; an abandonment of the universal claims of philosophical critique (Kant) to a recognition of the claims of individual preference (psychology). As a result, aesthetic criteria ceased to be looked for *objectively* in the work or artefact, and began to be explained *subjectively* by reference to the spectator or user.

But this was not the end of the paradigm shift; only the beginning. Aesthetics migrated out of both public art and individual psychology to the economy, the

---

[1] See http://eggartguild.org.

[2] See: http://appleslut.com/blog/computers/some-thoughts-on-apple-aesthetics

market and popular culture. Some saw in this historical trend, which has proceeded in fits and starts since Western industrialisation took hold in the nineteenth century, as a cultural decline (T.S. Eliot); some have seen it as an outcome of cultural democratisation (Hartley 2009). Either way, over the period of modernity from the eighteenth-century Enlightenment to the current era of global networks, the concept of the aesthetic has migrated from cultural value (determined by critics and philosophers) to market value (determined by price).

Oddly enough, in countries where public or philanthropic support for the arts is practised, i.e. countries with arts councils and national arts or cultural policies that entail the expenditure of public funding on the arts, this migration to the market is seen in terms of 'market failure' (Caves 2000; Throsby 2001; Towse 2010). Unregulated markets, driven by demand alone, generally haven't returned enough income to the earlier forms of aesthetic expression to sustain their (often very costly) productive apparatus, especially those connected with philosophical and critical traditions, i.e. 'high' culture, 'serious' music, 'fine' arts, 'contemporary' dance and the like. This is the justification for governments, high net worth individuals (HNWIs) and private companies to step in and pay for what the audience won't: aesthetics.

Thus, in economic terms, 'aesthetics' have become what is called a *public good*. It has become axiomatic that these are 'undersupplied' in a demand-based market. In other words, their production needs to be supported and subsidised by the public purse, even though demand for the *type* of aesthetics so produced remains persistently below the cost of production. Even affluent audiences can't afford the full cost of opera or orchestras, for instance. As a result of this policy assumption, the high, serious, fine and contemporary arts are treated as 'non-rival, non-excludable' public goods. Non-rival means that more than one person can enjoy the good. Unlike the consumption of a packet of crisps, which are used up in the act of consumption, non-rival goods are not used up: just because I have bought a work of fiction in print or media form, doesn't stop you from enjoying it too. This is a major characteristic of the arts, but it also underlies commercial media markets. In other words it is not necessarily a feature of market *failure*; often quite the reverse, as J.K. Rowling's net worth attests. 'Non-excludable' means that no-one in a given population can be excluded from using the good. The higher its aesthetic status in this system, the more universal that population is understood to be: 'goods' like *King Lear*, the *Mona Lisa*, the Parthenon, or Beethoven's Ninth Symphony, it is argued, 'belong' to humanity. Consequently, there is strong pressure to keep such aesthetic treasures 'free' – both generally available and cost-free to experience – or at least to subsidise access, and to recoup cost indirectly, usually by a combination of taxation and tourism.

Thus, 'aesthetics' may appear to be an abstract, philosophical concept, but in the creative industries it is a major *coordinating mechanism* for combining:

- A *production apparatus*, which includes the practitioners and organisations in the specific craft, and their education, training and upkeep;
- *Works*: the 'textual' or object/artefact element of creative enterprise;

- *Demand*, including non-market *patronage* by philanthropists, or educational institutions who pay for students to attend plays but not musicals;
- A *regulatory* or state-sponsored component: tax-dollar subsidies and state-owned agencies such as opera companies and significant parts of the GLAM sector (galleries, libraries, archives, museums).

'Aesthetics' coordinates these activities when each element of the value chain is seen as a public 'good': the production apparatus, the work itself, and the experience of that work can all be subsidised by public funds. In order to achieve such a level of planned coordination, 'market failure' has to be assumed throughout, even to the extent of using the public education system to train (persuade) populations (**audiences**) that aesthetics is a component not of consumption but of citizenship.

The logic of aesthetics as a public good has produced at least one unintended consequence, almost the reverse of 'market failure', for those **creative cities** lucky enough to have gained possession of iconic works in that system. The *cultural* value, and the presumption of a right of *universal* access to and enjoyment of such works, has resulted in a major boost to tourism in 'world cities' with a decent hoard (often gained by imperial plunder). In a city like London, most of the top tourist attractions (apart from the London Eye) are visited to enjoy 'market-failure' public-good experiences. In 2010 for instance, all of the top ten UK 'visitor attractions' were in London, and included five museums, two art galleries, a castle and a cathedral.[3] Between them the top 20 attracted nearly 50 million tourists. Most of the venues are free to enter. This public subsidy for aesthetic experience is then justified as an 'investment' in the market-based tourism industry. Thus, the public and private sectors are fully intermeshed; running through both of them, like steel reinforcement, is the concept of aesthetics.

Over in the market economy proper, aesthetics plays an equally important but less strategically coordinating role. Here, whether something counts as art, and the scale of its aesthetic value, are both determined by consumers and price, rather than by institutional location. Thus, media 'art' can only be recognised in arrears, as it were, after the event, when the market has determined what succeeds and what is forgotten. 'Classic' films, albums, television series or fashions become so by usage, not by naming them as art in advance. In the marketplace, aesthetics is a component of consumer choice, not a distinctive feature of producer identity. As a result, aesthetics in the creative industries should be seen as a component not of critical philosophy but of social learning. It is one of the values in play in the '**attention** economy' (Lanham 2006) within 'social network markets'. A feature of the creative industries is that they form a social network market (Potts et al. 2008a), where choices are determined not directly by price but by the choices of others, especially high-status celebrities. The value of an item is not intrinsic, nor even related to the individual taste of the consumer; it is relative to how strongly others value it, and the status of those others. This is why imitation (social learning) is so important in the creative economy – a choice of frock by a certain celebrity or

---

[3]Source: ALVA statistics: www.alva.org.uk/visitor_statistics.

high-status consumer may send sales of that style through the roof; a beautiful garment may be forgotten because Twiggy's stylist picked the next one on the rack. Here, aesthetics are certainly in play, but 'consumer choice' is not 'free' in the way that economists like to imagine with their model of the rational but needful and desiring individual. People choose what others choose; they learn about that through media; their choices are guided by others but nonetheless express aesthetic values and identity – you are (provisionally) what you wear. Interestingly, this is a market system that can easily sustain anti-market values. A critical, countercultural, anti-capitalist 'aesthetic' is a recognised – even looked-for – element in market-leading art, music, literature and drama, and may be able to command a premium price (e.g. artworks by Banksy).

Thus far, this entry has sought to treat aesthetics as a *system*-value rather than one belonging either to individuals (aesthetic judgement, as in philosophy from Aristotle to Kant) or objects (as in modernism and 'art for art's sake'). However, the philosophical treatment of aesthetics is itself influential in contemporary cultural systems, not least by popularising the idea that individuals *ought* to make judgements about what constitutes beauty, and therefore that they can recognise beauty in nature or the arts, and thence cumulatively form 'good' taste.

In fact, where critical judgement about aesthetic value was once the preserve of experts – literary, art and music critics – it is now democratised and dispersed like everything else. Immanuel Kant may have decreed that aesthetic judgement requires an understanding of what is beautiful by reference to the disinterestedness of the spectator, the universality and necessity of the judgement, the non-utilitarian 'purposiveness' of a work, the genius of the artist, and the aesthetic (as opposed to rational) 'idea' being communicated.[4] But very few people have a clue about how to apply such a rule-book to the flux of life, or how to produce an ordered or coherent set of aesthetic judgements ('taste') out of their application. Time was when such rigours were deputed to the expert critics in specialist magazines. People at large have valued art (to the extent that they did) according to its evaluation by critics – Ruskin, Pater, Eliot, Leavis … all the way to Robert Hughes (*TIME Magazine*) and Waldemar Januszczak (Channel 4), who reinvent the elite tradition for the popular media.

But now, people have to internalise the critical process of judgement and taste formation by themselves; for which DIY (do-it-yourself) effort, nevertheless, they still need guidance and training. This 'social learning' component of aesthetic judgement is *also* marketised. *How* to respond aesthetically is cleverly encoded into advertising and into objects themselves. Journalistic reviews and entire media platforms such as fashion, lifestyle and events-listing magazines are devoted to it. At a slightly slower frequency, educational programmes and textbooks are on hand to assist (Davies et al. 2009). This is one of them.

---

[4]The Internet Encyclopedia of Philosophy: Kant's Aesthetics: (see: www.iep.utm.edu/kantaest).

If you encounter the word 'agency' in the creative industries, it is likely to be a noun, referring to an *advertising agency* (firms such as WPP, Omnicom, Publicis), or a *government agency*, e.g. regulators such as the Federal Communications Commission (FCC) in the USA, State Administration for Radio, Film & TV (SARFT) in China, the UK Office of Communication (Ofcom) and the Australian Communication & Media Authority (ACMA). Similarly, an 'agent' is most likely to be thought of as someone representing or acting on behalf of someone else, as in *literary agent*, *music agent*, *talent agent*, etc. Here the terms 'agent' and 'agency' gain their meaning from one particular discourse, that of the law. The legal concept of agency seeks to regulate the actions of two types of actor, known as 'principals' and 'agents', in their dealings with third parties, allowing agents to represent or act on behalf of principals. A literary agent acts for an author in dealings with publishers, regulatory agencies act on behalf of the government and advertising agents act on behalf of retailers. Thus, in common usage, 'agency' denotes a firm or other form of corporate organisation: it's a thing (a legal entity) not a person.

But if you come across the word 'agency' in social theory, it is more likely to be a verb, denoting human action, both individual and collective. There is a well-known pairing of concepts in sociology that considers the relations between 'structure' and 'agency'. This problem has figured in the work of many classic social theorists, including Simmel, Elias, Parsons, Wittgenstein and Bourdieu, and is a founding problem in the study of contemporary culture (Williams, Hall), because there is uncertainty about the *causal* role of one side of the pairing (agency) as against the other (structure), and the extent of that determining role in specific circumstances. In other words, how much of what we observe in social life can be attributed to the way people act (on their own behalf), and how much to the brick wall against which they're banging their heads? In this context, 'structure' denotes a system of embedded or systematically patterned human arrangements (e.g. class, gender, ethnicity), social institutions (e.g. marriage customs, religion, culture) and historically developed forms (e.g. the law, markets, infrastructure) that determine the scope of action that is open to any individual human being. 'Agency', in contrast, denotes the capacity of those individuals to act independently or autonomously according to their own choices. This apparently simple pairing has in fact been the occasion for irreconcilable political controversy, because it connects with – and may act as a proxy for – differences between collectivist and individualist political traditions, especially Marxism and free-market approaches to human agency.

On one side of the debate, the free-marketeers pursue the doctrine of 'methodological individualism', where *action* is primary. Analysis begins with the choices

5

made, and ensuing actions of, human agents who are in principle free to make those choices in their own interests. This presumption is axiomatic in positivist social sciences including economics, which is based on the notion of individual rational choice as the motivating force for the entire economy. A classic political statement of this position was made by British Prime Minister Margaret Thatcher: 'There is no such thing as society. There is living tapestry of men and women and people …' (1987). The Thatcherite position was not simply that individuals are responsible for their own actions, but also that 'society' *has no agency* of its own – it cannot be at 'fault', nor can 'problems' such as homelessness or unemployment be solved by 'society'. The individual who relies on government handouts is, in effect, taking money from their 'neighbour' (Thatcher 1987). The political implication was that it was morally beneficial to the individual for the government to pursue a radical reduction in the welfare state.

On the other side of the debate, collectivists pursued the doctrine of *historicism* or *materialism*, where *structure* is primary. Analysis begins with the operations of structural determinants that shape, limit or cancel out the agency of human individuals. The classic statement of this is by Karl Marx: 'Men make their own history, but they do not make it as they please … The tradition of all dead generations weighs like a nightmare on the brains of the living' (1852: I). The implications of this perspective are: (1) that people may cloak their actions in historical or even farcical guise (the French Revolution in the garb of Rome; the English Revolution in that of the Old Testament) when what they are actually doing is creating something new (bourgeois society) – such that motivations for action may display not 'rational choice' but 'false consciousness'; (2) that 'Men' (humanity as a whole) make history, not individuals; (3) that 'circumstances' are not of people's own making. Scope for action is 'given' – and that's a 'nightmare' for those who want a transformed future.

The practical outcome of this approach for Marx is *class* politics, because individual action, whether political (e.g. the actions of Napoleon III) or economic (e.g. action by what Marx calls 'knights of industry') is rejected as a mechanism of change. Instead, he saw the motive force of history at this time as the class ascendancy of the bourgeoisie, of which any individual may be seen to be a mere 'agent' (representative). Further, where the 'agent' of history and thus of change is a class and its organised instruments of action, effective action requires individuals to subsume their personal capabilities into organised forms. Here, **institutions** connect agency and structure, taking the form of political parties and labour unions in particular, backed up by equally institutionalised cultural organisations, from working people's associations for education, music and welfare, etc., to popular media such as the 'pauper press' of the nineteenth century, which spoke on behalf (as the *representative agent*) of the 'productive' or 'working' classes (Thompson 1963). The point of all this was to confront structural inequalities with a collective agency that might hope to produce *structural change* in favour of these classes, where individual and unorganised actions could not.

The persistent political stand-off between agency and structure was understood as a problem for social theory itself. Anthony Giddens proposed the influential concept of 'structuration' – human action that is shaped by and in turn shapes social structures – as a reconciliation or integration of the previous opposition (e.g. Giddens 1979; see also Sewell 1992). Not only is structure a product of action, and action determined by structure, but the agents involved may *know* that 'structuration' is part of the process of action – they are *reflexive* agents who adjust their actions to conform to 'given' structures as they encounter them. Furthermore, 'structure' is a space–time phenomenon, not a static edifice. That is, it changes all the time. It is built by past actions and is in dynamic interaction with current actions. Indeed, it could be said that 'structure' doesn't exist except through agency. In this way, Giddens introduces two new terms into the consideration of structure and agency. They are: **knowledge** or reflexivity based on both 'discursive' or explicit and 'practical' or tacit consciousness; and **evolution** or constant micro-level adjustments that accumulate and enable macro-level transformations over time.

The introduction of knowledge and evolution into the equation opens the way for another way of reconciling the opposition between human agency and social structure, this time through the figure of the **entrepreneur**. Entrepreneurs in the Schumpeterian tradition are individuals who catalyse change in structural arrangements through their own energetic agency. Successful entrepreneurs are the ones who can turn 'given' structural constraints into **innovation**, and the routine reproduction of structures into their transformation. They do this by 'seeing' an opportunity that arises *within* the structure–agency relationship, by creating new values and finding ways to appropriate some of them, and then by exploiting their ideas in a practical venture (often but not always a firm), to which others will also need to be committed (Davidsson 2008: 76–7). Thus entrepreneurial *agency* may be transformational of inherited *structures*, which explains Schumpeter's notion of **creative destruction**, because the adoption of the new will be at the expense of regularities and patterns – the *rules* (Dopfer 2004; Dopfer and Potts 2008) – inherited from past structures, themselves the product of myriad embedded actions.

In this respect, as makers of new rules, new 'ways of seeing' and doing, entrepreneurs share many individual characteristics with artists, including the social function of imagining and bringing into existence – structuring – the experience of the new. They are change agents at the organisational level, or 'cultural intermediaries'. The first theorist of this connection was in fact Joseph Schumpeter (Swedberg 2006: 250). This insight, which points to the essential role of both artists and entrepreneurs as dynamic agents of change, has been developed more systematically in evolutionary economics and complexity theory (Beinhocker 2006; Herrmann-Pillath 2010; Potts 2011). Unlike the 'rational' subject of economics, entrepreneurs and artists both rely on 'intuitive choice' – or what is now termed 'inductive reasoning' (Beinhocker 2006: 138–9) or 'bounded rationality' (Gallegati and Richiardi 2011: 38–9). Here, agency depends on making choices in conditions of low information and high dynamism, which require not the calculation of all possible choices but working from observed cases to general abstractions, often through the mechanism of storytelling or 'narrative reasoning' (Hartley 2009: 119–21).

From this insight, the importance of adaptability to change in conditions of uncertainty comes to the fore, leading to a new emphasis on *agent learning* in economics.

Thanks to complexity mathematics and computational power, learning can now be modelled in real-time experiments using *game theory* (Arthur 1999). Thus, the introduction of the concept of adaptive learning requires a new focus on the *choices of others*, because others' choices convey information that can modify an agent's own choices and behaviour. This insight goes against the 'methodological individualism' of positivist approaches to agency, because it requires agents to operate in 'social networks' (some 'small-world'; others large-scale technological networks). Social networks invite collaboration and 'crowd-sourced' choices, involving both copying and innovation (Ormerod and Bentley 2010). In other words, individual choice is not the 'cause' that sets agency in motion; choice – and with it reason – is an *outcome* of socially networked processes.

The **creative industries** can be characterised as 'social network markets' (Potts et al. 2008a), where a new kind of agency is emerging: that of the 'entrepreneurial consumer' (Hartley and Montgomery 2009), where **consumers** as well as producers are endowed with entrepreneurial (artistic) agency, as in the fashion industry, where wearers are themselves risk-taking 'novelty bundlers' (Potts 2011), choosing ensembles and situations in which to create new meanings using both emulation (copying) and innovation. Thus, the **evolutionary** approach to agency has had to move beyond firms, and beyond the previously static and passive conceptualisation of consumers, to grasp the dynamics of social network markets in which *all* the agents (not just the so-called 'producers') are both determining and determined by the choices they make in the networked system. Such a model favours 'bottom-up' rather than 'top-down' understanding of social organisation, regarding what would previously have appeared as a 'given' structure 'weighing like a nightmare on the brains of the living', as a *self-organising system*. How such a system actually works is the subject of intense experimental work among computer scientists, economists and game theorists, with some predicting that a combination of game simulation and agent-based modelling (i.e. machine and human agency) may 'become the basis of a future science of social systems' (Arai et al. 2005: 12).

It will be clear by now that the concept of agency itself is subject to an open, adaptive, evolving order, which seems to have come full circle, because now it is possible to ascribe *agency* to *things* (rather than only to persons), as at the start of this entry. But now, *things* can *act* in complex social systems as autonomous agents, not just as representatives of principals. The idea that 'actors' (rather than natural persons) are part of the working apparatus of 'networks' derives ultimately from formalist semiotics (writers like Propp, Greimas and Todorov: see Hawkes 1977), where 'agents', often magical, are drivers of certain elements of stories, folktales, or myths in language networks. It is currently most strongly associated with the work of Bruno Latour (2005), who elaborated actor–network theory (ANT) to explain scientific processes. An example of the Latourian approach in practice is Gay Hawkins' (2009) study of the career of *bottled water* as an 'agent' in contemporary biopolitics (see also **networks**). Similarly, Hartley (2012b) found that *Vogue* USA (September 2011) had discovered (constructed) an *agent of redemption* for 'beleaguered' fashion designer John Galliano, who had just been convicted of anti-Semitic, anti-Asian hate speech. That agent was Kate Moss's wedding dress.

Human attention is the scarce resource of the creative industries. Economics traditionally studies how a society allocates scarce resource; however, many of the resources that characterise the creative industries are not scarce. Content certainly is not scarce; it is increasingly abundant and available. Richard Lanham writes: 'information is not in short supply in the new information economy. We're drowning in it. What we lack is the human attention needed to make sense of it all' (2006: xii, 7–9). This idea of attention scarcity can be traced back to the work of economist Herbert Simon, who observed that:

> In an information-rich world, the wealth of information means a dearth of something else: a scarcity of whatever it is that information consumes. What information consumes is rather obvious: it consumes the attention of its recipients. Hence a wealth of information creates a poverty of attention and a need to allocate that attention efficiently among the overabundance of information sources that might consume it. (1971: 40–1)

Michael Goldhaber argues that a new theory of economic value is needed, because attention would replace money. In an article about his 'attention economy' thesis in *Wired* (1997), Goldhaber proposes that: 'As the Net becomes an increasingly strong presence in the overall economy, the flow of attention will not only anticipate the flow of money, but eventually replace it altogether'.

This gives new meaning to the idea of *paying* attention, which is what users and **consumers** do. Attention is a social practice or behaviour; people pay attention together and to each other, and in the context of the creative industries it is crucial to understand 'attention dynamics': how to attract and retain it; how to convert it into commercial and social value; and how **networks** facilitate attention-seeking practices, whether amateur (blog posts, tweeting or uploading videos to YouTube), or professional (e.g. online news media, publishers, games and app developers, and performers).

Thus, consumers are confronted by a rapidly growing information and content glut. YouTube's official FAQs claim that '48 hours of video are uploaded every minute, resulting in nearly 8 years of content uploaded every day' (www.youtube.com/t/faq). How do users decide what to watch, let alone which apps to purchase and download? How should they allocate their limited attention? The rapid growth and success of Google is understandable in the context of the attention economy, as its search engine and related services provide attention tools and filters. Content-creators struggle to win consumers' attention for their offerings by adopting strategies to optimise their standing in search results. But these attention economy dynamics are not especially new for the creative industries: writers, performers, animators and filmmakers have always laboured to win precious attention for their creative offerings.

attention

9

Lanham tells us that the traditional knowledge and wisdom of the humanities, which he calls 'arts and letters' (2006: 14), can inform thinking about how people allocate their attention. The creative industries are not just characterised by attention economic dynamics; Lanham's point is that the craft skills and knowledge of stylistic devices and rhetorical figures, which are central to many creative industries disciplines, inform us about the getting of attention. Lanham suggests that the human capital and productivity in this new economy might be found 'in the literary and artistic imagination, the power to take the biogrammar we inherit and spin from it new patterns for how to live and to think about how we live' (2006: 9). He describes the contribution that creative industries can make to an attention economy environment as:

> The arts and letters, which create attention structures to teach us how to attend to the world, must be central to acting in the world as well as to contemplating it. The design of an object in such a world becomes as important as the engineering of the object. The 'positioning in the market' of an object, a version of applied drama, will be as important as either one. (2006: 14)

Lanham argues that the contemporary attention economy is characterised by peoples' ability to oscillate and switch between different modes of attention or two kinds of economy that he calls 'stuff' and 'fluff'. This foregrounds consumers' and users' agency – their actions and behaviour as they engage in attention practice, learning and sharing the skills and knowledge required to effectively navigate attention economies. He describes videogamers, as they oscillate between attention states to play, as 'acute and swift economists of attention'. Lanham observes that is not just professional game developers who are economists of attention as so too are the players: 'Parents may not need to worry so much about their children when they play video games. They may be training themselves for a new economy' (2006: 17).

Lanham's version of the attention economy is very different from Nicholas Carr's (2011) concern (see **consumer**) that many of the social network platforms and tools associated with the Internet, including Google, are 'making us stupid'. Carr's worry is that internet culture shortens and narrows our attention span and concentration. Lanham, on the other hand, suggests that the question of attention in this new economy should not be so quickly reduced to an opposition between the short span associated with internet culture and the deep concentration that Carr associates with more traditional forms of high literary and artistic culture. Lanham tells us instead that people are learning how to oscillate and switch between modes of attention. This is close to Tyler Cowen's argument that Google 'lengthens our attention spans … by allowing greater specialisation of knowledge' (2009: 54–5). Both Cowen (2009) and Lanham (2006) emphasise the cognitive and behavioural challenge of coping with an attention economy. The idea of social network markets (Potts et al. 2008a; Hartley 2009) – that individual consumers' choices are determined by the choices of others – is closely related to Lanham's 'economics of attention'.

One way we deal with the uncertainty generated by information overload is to learn from others' choices and behaviour. And this social learning is at the very heart of the attention economy. If we are uncertain about which apps should be prominently displayed on the home screens of our digital devices, we just copy and adopt what others are using. This social network market phenomenon can be seen in websites such as David Sparks' blog *MacSparky* (www.macsparky.com). Sparks writes about the best tools and workflows for getting work done with Apple products and regularly includes a 'Home Screens' feature which covers prominent and creative Mac users' favoured apps and workflows. The 'Home Screens' articles include a screenshot of the featured user's smart phone or tablet home screen, and briefly describe the chosen apps and how they contribute to the user's daily workflows. This is the attention economy at work and Sparks is an expert navigator. He provides guidance on how to succeed in a rapidly changing work and leisure environment – how to be productive. What note-taking or outlining or mind-mapping app should feature on our devices? Sparks guides our choices by showing us what other prominent users are choosing and using.

In Lanham's terms, Sparks is a consummate economist of attention. He gets that the scarce resource is not information or content in and of itself but attention. As with many other high-profile bloggers and podcasters, Sparks' success reveals an important aspect of attention economy dynamics – the celebrity phenomenon that follows a power law principle (see **complex systems**). A small number of high-profile celebrities manage to attract and in some cases retain a significant proportion of the available attention on particular topics or issues.

Evolutionary biologist Mark Pagel (2011) helps us to understand that how we have evolved as humans is fundamental to these attention economy and social learning behaviours. Indeed, Pagel argues that the human species has invented a new kind of **evolution** based on ideas and their cultural potential. He describes this as a social learning in which our attention can be not only called to something but we are 'able to select, among a range of alternatives, the best one, and then to build on that alternative, and to adapt it and to improve upon it'. He calls this 'cumulative cultural adaptation'. The attention economy and social network market behaviours are best understood then as an evolutionary selection and adaptation mechanism. Pagel also comments that these attention and social learning behaviours are fundamental to our creativity and to the very 'nature of our intelligence as social animals' (2011).

Attention economy dynamics in the context of the creative industries then should not be approached as banal marketing fluff in which we now find ourselves wasting valuable attention on 'shallow' online social networks. As a form of social learning, the creative industries attention economy is a way that we 'select the best ideas – we copy people that we think are successful, we copy good ideas, and we try to improve upon them' (Pagel 2011). By paying attention and copying humans we contribute to creating and innovating, and one of the places people learn to do this is the creative industries.

Copying is at the core of attention economy dynamics. By observing what other people do and then selecting from the best of others' innovations and ideas, we do not have to pay the costs associated with innovating or finding solutions ourselves. Pagel (2011) argues that evolutionary selection has shaped us to be copiers more than innovators. Moreover, the generative mechanism for creating new ideas through this process of copying is random. Over a population exercising their choices, largely by copying others, the outcomes of these choices, and therefore the commercial success of a specific apps, is also random. Pagel tells us that: 'Any process of evolution that relies on exploring an unknown space ... and trying to create connections ... and ... new ideas that explore the space of alternatives that will lead us to what we call creativity in our social world, might be very close to random' Furthermore, he suggests that the digital attention economy of platforms such as Facebook may well move us towards becoming even more random copiers.

Alex Bentley et al. (2011) locate random copying at the very heart of the attention economy and social learning. They foreground that what we now know about human behaviour, informed by advances in behavioural economics and evolutionary psychology, calls into question the classical economic 'rational choice theory'. We are often far from rational thinkers acting in ways that maximise our best interests. The choices that we make at a *population* level appear to be random. However, the crucial point Bentley et al. make, which both evolutionary psychology and recent behavioural economics tend to overlook, is that we are fundamentally social creatures:

> Yes we can be lazy thinkers, and yes, we have Pleistocene brains, but a large part of our success during the Pleistocene and since then is attributable to what we do with those around us, to learn from and influence each other so naturally that we hardly notice it. (2011: xi)

Referring to research in the neurosciences on mirror neurons on the brain, Bentley et al. tell us that our brains are structured to intuit and empathise with each other's intentions. At the most fundamental levels of our brain we are social creatures and we are 'wired to copy ... Other animals don't come close to our speed of learning by imitation, retaining what is learned, and pulling information together from widely separated locales within the brain' (2011: 30).

The creative industries, especially with the widespread changes and uptake of digital media such as social network platforms, increasingly provide the connective tissue for these networks of social influence, social learning and cultural **evolution**. Attention economy dynamics and behaviour concern the connected and social ways in which we increasingly make and share culture.

Audience

The creative industries have a peculiar relationship with audiences, because the creative industries constitute a peculiar type of market, one where *supply precedes demand*. The familiar mantra of 'giving the public what it wants' is a corporate self-delusion, because the general public cannot want anything, least of all experiences they haven't had yet, such as enjoying a specific story, song, sight or sensation. No-one 'demanded' Shakespeare's plays or *The World of Warcraft*, the latest pop sensation or reality TV format, Flickr or Vimeo, before they were created. This is why creative productions rely on reviews and word-of-mouth *after* the release of a title; and why a single negative review can kill a million-dollar investment overnight. To make the matter more complicated, some creative industries – those in the public sector – are sustained by patronage and subsidy rather than by audiences directly. 'Demand' for their services and output comes from *funding agencies* not consumers.

In principle, then, it is not the case that productions are created for audiences; audiences are brought into being by productions. Here we may observe a general characteristic of the **creative industries**: the economic axiom known as Say's Law applies, that 'supply creates its own demand', because creative *novelties* must always exist prior to demand for them. Thus the creative industries are not only 'social network markets', they are also 'novelty bundling markets' (Potts 2011: Chapter 14); the audience chooses novelties from among a repertoire on offer. Pop music (top 40), fashion brands, magazines (e.g. *Vogue*), and festivals all function in this way (Potts 2011). A consequence is that some members of the audience become **expert** (although still amateurs in economic terms) in making choices compared with others, and may themselves enter the market as 'choice entrepreneurs'. Domains as varied as fashion, music, technology and politics all spawn passionate consumers who signal their own choices via blogs, reviews and personal practice, thence to become start-up businesses in their own right. Perez Hilton (celebrity gossip) is a good example; as is Tavi Gevinson, who started her own fashion blog (*Style Rookie*) in 2008 at the age of 11. Its popularity (a reported four million readers) attracted fashion designers and magazines. Tavi's resulting profile enabled her to gain paid work as a columnist and to launch her own online teen magazine – *Rookiemag.com*.[1] Tavi is an 'entrepreneurial consumer' (Hartley and Montgomery 2009); continually switching between 'audience' and 'entrepreneur' in a career that combined her own personal identity formation, competitive signalling of her expertise in novelty choices, and entrepreneurial action to secure a new niche market; all before she turned 16.

The term 'audience' has clearly evolved considerably beyond its origins in drama and performance. There is also a fuzzy line between the concept of 'the audience' and other classes of collective subjectivity, e.g. the consumer, public, citizen, visitor, spectator or tourist. Thus, tourists may visit a city square where a festival based in medieval civic and religious custom is the main attraction, there to become part of the audience for elaborate and thrilling performances for which they may not have to pay directly, but which nevertheless sustain that city's culture and economy. And it is worth noting that this combination of civic observance, spectacular pageantry, festive atmosphere and commercial hard-sell is no recent phenomenon: it goes back to medieval fairs and calendar events such as St Bartholomew's Fair and

audience

---

[1]See: www.thestylerookie.com/; rookiemag.com/; and wikifashion.com/wiki/Tavi_Gevinson

the Lord Mayor's Show in London (Hill 2011). Its legacy can be seen in the Jon Stewart (*Daily Show*)/Stephen Colbert (*Colbert Report*) 'Rally to Restore Sanity and/or Fear' in Washington DC in 2010; which attracted a quarter of a million people – the audience-turned-activist in a rally-cum-comedy festival.[2]

If demand does not drive supply, then what agency *does* determine what gets served up to audiences in the creative industries? Even before creative producers get in on the act, the primary driver is often assumed to be **technology**. However, in the creative industries, it is important not to get carried away by 'technological determinism'. Technology is essential, but it doesn't turn people into audiences. What lies at the bottom of all empirical audience research, whether commissioned by media corporations, state regulatory agencies or academic research bodies, is *uncertainty* about how this vast but unknowing and unknowable body achieves **agency**; specifically (but by no means only) the agency of *choice*.

Whether productions and even companies prosper or go bust depends on audience choice. But at the actual moment of so-called consumption, when these life-or-death choices are made, the audience is not constituted as a consumer (an agent of rational economic choice) at all. It's not engaged with the economy, but with play, language and social interaction, and it is experiencing all this within the context and location of other sense-making, sensation-seeking, socially related cultural identities (from the family to the festival). Embedded in the practices, institutions and meaning-systems of everyday life, this is the human dimension of audiencehood. It explains why there has been such a vogue for in-close observation of the situated audience, using anthropological and ethnographic methods, which see it as part of culture, not commerce, and certainly not 'caused' by technologies. Even if technologies, industries, business plans, platforms, forms, productions, marketing and regulation do influence audiences, that impact is dissipated across a cultural field where complex causations intersect, and where people are attending to many things as well as 'being' or 'doing' audience. Their subjectivity is not constituted by such influences, which are artefacts of industrial and institutional organisational purposes. They are things being done *for and to* populations, not *by or with* them, as Charles Leadbeater (2009) has evocatively put it.

The organism known as the audience was always to some extent a fantasy – a desirable other – imagined from the outside by others, whether they sought to enslave, entertain or emancipate it. It's an ideal type; more of a *hope* than a *thing* (Hartley 1992). Thus, audiences remained somewhat out of the reach of those who sought to control them, even through the most militant decades of industrial capitalism, media monopoly, state control, neoliberal market forces, biopower knowledge complexes, mass persuasion based on propaganda (whether commercial advertising and PR or political – and military – campaigns), globalisation, and

---

[2]See: www.articles.latimes.com/2010/oct/31/nation/la-na-stewart-rally-20101101; and www.comedycentral.com/shows/rally_to_restore_sanity_and_or_fear/index.jhtml

any other top-down, command-and-control model of human organisation you might wish to name. Even through the most intense period of manipulation and enforcement of these attempts to 'produce' new, compliant, docile and biddable versions of the audience that were convenient for and in the image of the institutions and powers that sought to know, govern and profit by them, human identity, meaningfulness and relationship – in short, culture – were not fully captured. In practice, during the industrial-analogue era, this meant that audiences were always to some extent protected from the purposes of the producing institutions and their attendant discourses of control and conformity. No matter how insistent the advertising, many consumers failed to buy the product, or the ideology of consumption.

The idea of the audience as an *effect* of media technologies has suffered another blow in the era of digital and interactive media. Oddly enough, it took further advances in technology to make it clear to everyone (not just to a small band of 'audience activists' and semioticians) that the audience was always 'active' in ways that capitalism, critical and governmental discourses alike had failed to apprehend. Now the 'active audience' wasn't just 'making' *sense* of what was served up to it, it was making content of its own. The question of audience agency shifted from 'reception' to production, and the ideal-type of the audience member shifted from individual consumer to socially networked user (Papacharissi 2010).

Consequently, the concept of the audience for the creative industries is not at all the same as that for the broadcast or live entertainment industries out of which they have emerged. The whole question of agency is altered; rendered uncertain and undergoing transformation. What Raymond Williams long ago identified as a 'deep contradiction' (1974: 30) between the *centralised production* of media and the *privatised reception* of it, is being rebalanced. Now, the emergence of what might be termed privatised *production* has impacted on the concept of the audience by integrating it with the more recent notion of the *user*.

Users add *productive agency* to the concept, enabling audiences to be seen as co-subjects in the overall process of creative productivity. Thus the audience is part of a system of distributed and multi-nodal expertise, contributing to the long-term career of a given product or form. This function for audiences was first described in the context of fan cultures (see works by Henry Jenkins, Matt Hills, Will Brooker etc.) and 'cult' fiction (works by Sarah Gwenllian Jones, Alan McKee, Brett Mills etc.). Here, the remaking of the fictional world of broadcast shows by fans has become a major branch of practice and scholarship in its own right (slash fiction, 'fanfic' etc.), and in series such as *Dr Who* and its spin-off *Torchwood*, it is clear that the programme makers draw from fan culture in the ongoing narrative arc of the series itself, with the audience as a character and agent in the show's diegetic universe. Although gamers would not see themselves as audiences (since their default mode is play not spectatorship), this brings audiences and players into very close alignment, especially as many actual persons will belong to both communities (Banks 2012). Even J.K. Rowling has been drawn into this dimension. With the completion of the book and film series in 2011, a good way to sustain the *Harry Potter* franchise was to let the fans join in too, which was duly announced with the *Pottermore* website and Twitter account.[3]

This extension of the concept of audience into neighbouring domains is not confined to fans and gamers. In the leisure field, audiencehood and tourism are increasingly interdependent in the growth of 'experience-based' tourism, with certain places attracting visitors because of their associations with charismatic screen experiences. But this phenomenon carries over to the realms of citizenship and global politics, when certain cultural *values* – for instance environmental and human-rights consciousness – can be brokered into niche businesses, for instance 'extreme' and 'dark' tourism.

The proliferation of different types of audience experience means that it is increasingly problematic to speak of 'the' audience at all. Culturally, audiences are now so fragmented, multivalent and specialised that they no longer add up to a coherent 'mass' audience. Technologically, the 'long tail' (Anderson 2006) has allowed 'micro-audiences' to gather around specific pleasures – a phenomenon exploited by emerging bands, whose music may be self-broadcast on YouTube or Myspace, and whose fan-base may be tiny in any one place but sufficient globally to sustain sales and thus a band's professional career options. Audiencehood and citizenship converge and coalesce when the devoted fans of an activist entertainer such as the British comic Stephen Fry – who boasts a popular website and 2.75 million followers on Twitter[4] – form themselves into an effective lobby group in relation to causes supported by Fry, especially those related to gay and mental health rights, purposefully linking identity politics, entertainment values and the democratic process.

Thus the model of the audience in the creative industries has evolved from passive consumer to creative producer as a result of the clash of two systems: technology-driven 'affordances' that have enabled consumers to become users; and culture-driven 'identities, relationships and meanings' that can now be expressed directly as well as through representative proxies on-screen. The audience is thus the point of intersection of cultural and economic values in the creative industries. This 'emergent' form of audiencehood is then available as a resource for further entrepreneurial opportunity in both business and social enterprise (Leadbeater 2008; Shirky 2008).

Audiences are now fully integrated into technological and productive systems, dispersed across many fields and yet, at the same time, of global scale. In many cases the term 'users' may be more accurate. In any case, new methods of research and analysis are necessary to understand how they work. Methods derived from computer science, complexity mathematics and evolutionary theory are gaining ground in the study of the creative industries, in order to be able to model, sample and visualise the computational scale of audience choices, productivity and culture.

---

[3]See: www.guardian.co.uk/books/2011/jun/23/pottermore-website-jk-rowling-harry-potter
[4]See www.stephenfry.com/; twitter.com/#!/stephenfry

The creative cluster is a relatively recent addition to the economics of cultural and media industries. Clustering has spread with the international take up of creative industries policy during the first decade of the twenty-first century. The attractiveness of this approach to regional development is aptly illustrated by an annual forum called Creative Clusters, convened in the UK from 2002 to 2008, which promotes itself as a network of creative industries experts.

The creative clusters legacy dates back to the 1970s in Europe and the USA, a decade in which urban regeneration began to utilise post-industrial space. However, the provenance of clusters derives from the British economist Alfred Marshall's account of 'industrial districts' (1890: Bk IV, Ch X, Par 12). Marshall coined this term to describe clusters of businesses in particular locations, especially concentrations of specialised small firms. A century later, Michael Porter (1990) introduced the business cluster concept into the policy mainstream. Porter defined a cluster as a geographically proximate group of interconnected companies and associated institutions in a specific field based on commonalities and complementarities. Prior to Porter's intervention economic geographers had promoted concepts such as the industrial district, new industrial spaces, territorial production complexes, network regions and learning regions. The concept that came closest to winning the support of government prior to the advent of the 'creative cluster' was 'innovative milieu' (Camagni 1991). A key idea here was the role of innovative small and medium enterprises (SMEs) and their networks, both formal and informal (Fingleton et al. 2007); and also the idea of 'collective learning', which was found in work on regional innovation systems, the latter generating what Lundvall et al. (2007) have called 'interactive learning'. In the main these terms celebrate increasing returns and 'learning economy' effects (Krugman 1991; Belleflamme et al. 2000).

The common factor in all variations on the theme of clusters is *localised external economies*; in other words the benefits of co-location to businesses competing in similar markets but cooperating in the development of similar knowledge. Storper describes external economies as 'complex outcomes of interaction between scale, specialisation, and flexibility in the context of proximity' (1997: 27). These accrue in several ways. The primary attracting factor is pooling of skilled workers. In large 'regional' creative clusters such as Hollywood, these include technical workers (programmers, animators and film crews), core intellectual property creators (artists, writers, designers) and cultural intermediaries (entrepreneurs, business facilitation services). Ideally, a cluster will attract workers with specific and specialised skills, lowering the human capital search costs of firms within the cluster. The presence of similar firms produces incentive for other business to establish specialist services to these firms, complementing the value chain of production and in many cases facilitating marketing and distribution. In turn, this enables firms to concentrate on core capabilities, which improves average productivity and the competitive advantage of all firms within the cluster. From an economy of scale perspective infrastructure, utilities, transport, and other business requirements and institutions can be more efficiently supplied to a cluster, again lowering average costs and reinforcing the global competitiveness of firms within the cluster.

Historically, clusters of media, artistic and cultural communities have developed organically, often slowly. A prototypical form of the cluster is a scene; for instance, a geographically proximate community of writers, musicians and artists (scenes now play out largely in online networks). The value of scenes to a city's cultural economy is well illustrated in Elizabeth Currid's (2007) study of New York City. While a scene is essentially informal in nature, formal consolidation as a *cultural quarter*, *cultural cluster* or *creative cluster* depends on coordinated action. Places that attract creative activities are identified and earmarked for conversion or regeneration. Questions of how effectively cultural and creative clusters might be planned and coordinated remain largely unresolved. Despite a paucity of hard evidence to validate success factors, a great deal of policy focus is currently directed towards championing such initiatives.

Quarters are often regarded as clusters although these forms of agglomeration pre-existed the current interest in creative clusters (Roodhouse 2010). The concept of the cultural, art or entertainment district emerged in the USA and Europe, drawing on the residual energy of 1960s inner-city protest movements, which by the 1970s and early 1980s had an established identification with urban locales (Mommaas 2009). The most cited examples are Soho and TriBeCa in downtown Manhattan in New York, where the concept of the loft as a combined living and working space emerged. In the past, cultural quarters emerged spontaneously; for instance Paris' Left Bank and Latin Quarter, and Manchester's Northern Quarter. In recent times urban regeneration strategies have endeavoured to fast-track quarters, often making use of disused factory space.

One the one hand, the dominant rationale for quarters is urban regeneration with attendant criticisms of gentrification (Zukin 2010); on the other hand, creative clusters, mostly in media and technology sectors, are directly targeted at fostering innovation in high-value markets. However, this is not to suggest there is necessarily a hard distinction between cultural and creative clusters: broadly speaking, however, a cultural quarter or cultural cluster is inclined towards consumption activities (galleries, lofts, coffee shops) whereas a creative cluster tends towards production (SMEs, start-ups); in practice, terminologies are used interchangeably and hybrid cultural creative clusters are common. Clusters also vary in respect to age and function: accordingly we can see evidence of emergence, growth, decline and transformation.

The term 'cluster' is both useful and confusing when applied to the creative industries. Usually a cluster implies a spatial co-location of activity; from the perspective of innovation and regional studies literature, such co-location takes advantage of shared resources and indicates a desire for innovation effects (see Mommaas 2009). In respect to creative industries policy three perspectives on clustering are evident. The first emanates from the initial foray of the UK Department for Culture, Media and Sport (DCMS) into mapping of creative business and employment in 1998, which was predicated on the observation that creative activities and businesses tend to form (cluster) in specific places. Accordingly, employment growth in creative industries

SMEs provides a means to map geographical concentrations. An econometric tool sometimes used is location quotient (LQ), which provides a measure of relative concentration derived from national employment statistical repositories. The location quotient of a particular industry, for instance design, measures whether the industry or industry sector has a higher or lower share than the national average. An LQ greater than 1 indicates an above average proportion of employment in a given industry in a given area. However, it does not provide any information about the absolute size of the industry in that area (Fingleton et al. 2007). The second way of designating creative clusters is the geographical agglomeration of businesses, resources and activities in particular spatial locations, which often act as a kind of branding: e.g. Hollywood, West End, SOHO, and Southbank. Mommaas (2009: 53) says that creative clusters can be differentiated according to their form of organisation; for instance those organised around the autonomous arts (the artistic professions), those that are more applied and entrepreneurial (design, fashion, media) and those that pertain more directly to technological, scientific or economic notions of creativity. The third use of the term creative cluster is aspatial and derives from Singapore. Kong (2009) notes how the 'creative cluster' is the defining nomenclature for industrial groups; hence Singapore identifies three broad policy groupings – arts and culture, design and media – within which are specific industry sectors.

As the 'cluster' became popular in regional development strategy, the strategy of cultivating external economies entered into the cultural economy, paving a way for a new generation of scholar-consultants to offer their services to urban planners. As a mechanism for attracting creative human capital and investment, the term promises much. In regions seeking transformation, clustering is a relatively low-cost model of social renewal and strategy of aggregating creative labour. The larger and better known clusters have grown organically and tend to enjoy spillovers from cognate industries; in turn they produce spillover effects into other industry sectors. Successful regional clusters such as Hollywood and Silicon Valley are driven by soft factors of embedded knowledge and skills. Their products often have a global presence, brand recognition, and can command high prices. The down side is that an excess of clusters in the same region can lead to negative externalities: according to Fingleton et al., 'local competition for sector-specific factors may intensify, creating shortages of key skills, specialised inputs, and appropriate office space' (2007: 65). Those with a high concentration of similar firms, or poorly governed clusters, can lead to reliance on low-value products; often this translates into a business strategy supported by profit from tourism, rents and land speculation.

However, not all forms of cultural production benefit from proximity; in the age of instantaneous online global communication, knowledge can be shared without recourse to physical co-location. Studies have tended to focus on inputs to and spillovers of benefit *to* culturally oriented clusters that contribute to sustainability. Later work on co-location and spillovers *from* creative businesses of benefit to other sectors (Chapain et al. 2010) has shown that these are unevenly distributed across the creative industries. Advertising and software firms, more than other creative businesses, tend to co-locate with high-tech manufacturing and knowledge-intensive business services (KIBS), although other sectors which provide content and cultural experiences show some significant co-location. What this research suggests is that those creative sectors that are focused on downstream business-to-business services also tend to co-locate with sectors that use their services, and that this can lead to spillovers based on creative supply. On the other hand, those creative sectors which are focused on producing final consumption goods and services tend to be more disposed to spillovers based on demand: in Cardiff, television and production companies' strong demand for technology and digital services supports the growth of local digital clusters (Chapain et al. 2010: 34).

Likewise many so-called creative industry clusters are engaged in the production of standardised goods and services; that is, the emphasis falls on 'industry' more so than 'creative'. This is particularly evident in developing countries where clusters have taken advantage of outsourcing opportunities from countries where the cost of labour is high (see Keane 2012). Many developing countries have transformed from agriculture and labour intensive industries (such as textiles) to assembly-based industries and high-value computer technology industries. The transition, however, to intangible creative industries, marks a recent phase, one that can offer a degree of freedom from manual labour – these industries produce a high proportion of intangible goods and services. The cluster model offers a fast track; in many instances districts are earmarked for development and policymakers respond favourably to cluster proposals as this gives the impression that something is taking place; in other words, the cluster is a physical manifestation of development, absorbing labour and skills. What are often missing, however, is effective management of stakeholders and effective coordination of collective action or labour skills. The case of China illustrates how the strategy of clustering was transferred from the industrial economy, where it was very successful in the 1990s, into the creative economy, where it has been less so. Part of the reason is that the creative economy is heavily geared to intangible goods while clusters, at least in China, are still seen as places where 'things' are produced.

Creative clustering or institutional geographical thickness by itself is not a panacea: spillovers are a result of social capital, willingness to share, size of companies, types of companies and markets (domestic or international) – all these must be developed over time and are subject to factors other than the policy imperative (Gwee 2009). This suggests that the role of tacit knowledge, trust relationships, 'know-who' as much as 'know-how' may play a greater role in making at least some creative industries more 'geographically sticky' than other industries. Important early attempts to grasp this, such as Leadbeater and Oakley's *The Independents* (1999), emphasised the importance of market organisers (such as a commissioning broadcaster) for regional sustainability for a sector composed overwhelmingly by small businesses; a thoroughly mixed economy, connecting the non-commercial with the commercial; and the crucial role of demanding consumers (such as university student populations).

In summary, the creative cluster is a term that has come back into vogue as the regions look for ways to find a sustainable niche in the **creative economy**. However, the sustainability of clusters, whether these are simply geographical concentrations of employment in a given area or purpose-built districts, depends on a range of factors. It is not simply a matter of agglomeration.

Co-Creation (User-Created Content; User-Generated Content)

Media consumers increasingly make and share content. Collaborating with each other and with professional media producers, consumers design, produce, circulate and market media content and experiences. User-generated content and user-led innovation are significant cultural and economic phenomena (Benkler 2006; Jenkins 2006; OECD 2007; Bruns 2008; Shirky 2008; Hartley 2009). In 2006, *TIME Magazine* celebrated 'You' as the person of the year, saluting the millions of people who make media content for social networking platforms such as YouTube and Wikipedia. Our starting point for this phenomenon is that co-creation involves consumers contributing a non-trivial component of the design, development, production, marketing and distribution of a new or existing product (Banks 2012). Value is increasingly co-created by both the firm and the customer (see NESTA 2006; Green and Jenkins 2011: 213).

The value-generating media consumer is at the very core of creative industries discourse. Hartley's definition of the creative industries, for example, foregrounds the combination of 'new media technologies' and 'newly interactive citizen-consumers' in the growth of creativity as the driver of social and economic change (2005: 5). The idea here is that consumers' role in generating content and value is no longer merely a peripheral activity, something that just hard-core fans do, but is increasingly fundamental to the creative industries.

User-created content is not an entirely new phenomenon (see **audience**; **convergence**). Work in the 'active audience' tradition of cultural and media studies reminds us that audiences have never been especially passive, engaging in practices to remake texts for their own ends. Henry Jenkins (2009) recounts that all this did not simply emerge with Web 2.0 digital media platforms. He finds a rich history in the diverse practices of media fans, writing and circulating zines and in various forms of fan-made video, well before the advent of the internet. David Gauntlett (2011a) also acknowledges the cultural history lineages of co-creation in earlier craft traditions. However, the idea of co-creation and associated theories, such as Bruns's (2008) 'produsage' (his term for user-generated content and related practices), Jenkins's participatory and convergence culture (2006), or Shirky's (2008, 2010) accounts of crowd-sourced wisdom, suggest something rather different is occurring in the context of digital technologies and online social network platforms. These shifts blur production and consumption relationships to redefine media consumers as drivers of wealth production and innovative creativity. No longer at the end of the value chain, consuming what is offered up by professionals, consumers now generate value with their activities actively pursued and harnessed by media companies.

Clay Shirky celebrates the coming widespread uptake of these collaborative and creative energies with his clarion call book title: *Here Comes Everybody* (2008). But who *is* 'everybody'? Is it everyone on earth; or everyone participating in these collaborative forms of co-creative media making and sharing? Or is the term restricted in practice to a relatively narrow elite of privileged 'teched up and well connected' users? What are the implications of media businesses and platform owners, e.g. videogames developers and YouTube, seeking to harness and profit from these activities? In other words, does 'everybody' include organisations and firms as well as natural persons? If consumers and users are indeed creating value through these activities then what rights do such consumers have to that content? What obligations do media companies have to these users? Furthermore, how do these emerging practices impact on the jobs and employment conditions of media professionals (see **creative labour**)?

Such questions do not dismiss the importance or significance of user-created content. They prompt us to move beyond marvelling at the phenomenon of co-creation and to start exploring and interrogating the nature and characteristics of these activities. For example, when Bruns (2008) proposes that the role of consumer has 'disappeared' in the context of produsage, should we accept this proposition at face value? Participants who have purchased and enjoyed the *Harry Potter* movies and books can sign-up for the online *Pottermore* experience and contribute content (perhaps a story). But should we assume that this co-creative activity means that such participants are no longer consumers (see **audience**)? We need to ask in what industry context is co-creative activity so prominent that it is reasonable to claim the user-participants are not simply consumers. We also need to investigate the broad range of activities that might be described as co-creative – from making the odd blog post or tweet through to radically remaking a videogame.

Critical perspectives on co-creation challenge the perceived populist and celebratory accounts offered by writers such as Jenkins and Shirky. Scholars such as Graeme Turner (2010) do not accept that consumer participation in content creation represents 'democratisation' of media participation. Often coming from a political economy perspective (see **culture industry**), such critiques are concerned that media companies adopt user-created content strategies to extract economic value without recognising their accountability to the users producing this content. For these scholars the more positive and optimistic accounts of user-created content may overlook the power and ownership relationships that structure these co-creative relationships in the context of global capitalism. Tiziana Terranova's (2000) work is often cited to support a claim that user-created content and related online social-network activities may amount to a form of free labour that media companies unfairly exploit (see **creative labour**; see also Andrejevic 2011). So when a videogamer uploads an item of add-on content for his or her favourite game to share with fellow players, it is arguable that the game developer and publisher companies directly benefit from the value of this content and therefore the player is effectively functioning as a form of free labour. Turner argues that in the context of global media consumption and production the scale of user-created content 'is not that significant' (2010: 127). Turner's concern is that the enthusiasm and optimism for user-created content is often not supported by evidence. He comments: 'The political empowerment promised to consumers is largely based on the expansion of consumer choice, the provision of interactivity and the corresponding rise of the produser' (2010: 129). S. Elizabeth Bird notes that, 'True produsers are a reality, but they are not the norm, and can often seem to be so in thrall to big media and technological 'coolness' that they accept the disciplining of their creative activities' (2011: 512).

Yochai Benkler (2006, 2011) argues that the motivations and incentives for people to participate in co-creative activities are significantly non-commercial and non-market. People contribute to co-creative projects because of their intrinsic motivations and communitarian spirit. Starting out from open-source software projects such as Linux, Benkler argues that these co-operative and networked forms of production do not rely on market signals or the market system. The value potential of these co-creative networks, for Benkler, may indicate a genuine limit to the **market**. Here we see an opposition between a social mode of production and the corporate, commercial or market domains. He sees this as a profound change through which 'nonmarket behavior is becoming central to producing our information and cultural environment' (Benkler 2006: 56). Benkler (2011) draws on research from the behavioural and cognitive sciences to foreground cooperative behaviours and intrinsic motivations. Research in these sciences certainly demonstrates that we are more cooperative and less self-interested than some branches of economic and political theory may assume. There is strong evidence that humans have a predisposition to cooperate and that trust, reciprocity and altruism are just as significant behavioural indicators as are assumptions that we are self-interested agents calculating to maximise our material interests. Cooperative and altruistic behaviours are most certainly fundamental to many co-creative activities. But it does not follow that we should therefore privilege these values of cooperation and altruism over market-based, commercial practices. After all, many of the social network platforms that are at the forefront of these co-creative initiatives are commercial enterprises – such as *Pottermore* or videogames.

We need better analytic models of the mechanisms and processes of co-creative media production in all of the diverse forms it might take across various sectors of the creative industries as well as across national and cultural differences. This emerging phenomenon unsettles our understandings of production–consumption relationships. In the context of the creative industries, the idea of co-creation asks us to consider, question and interrogate these emerging dynamic relationships. It suggests that rather than starting from oppositional frameworks in which we assume that we already know the nature of the values and behaviours involved, we instead ask how we can coordinate these forms of collective action for mutual benefit. It would be a mistake at this early stage to assume we already know what the behaviours, values and meanings of co-creativity are. The idea of co-creativity in the context of the creative industries seeks to develop an explanatory model that focuses on the complex interactions between market and cultural domains (see **complex systems**). This co-creative approach shifts explanatory analysis to a study of the interactions between the economic and the cultural domains. This leads to a somewhat different perspective from assumptions that co-creation is either an exchange relation or a production relation in a market or non-market context. Both may be occurring simultaneously with analysis then focused on how they mutually affect and continuously transform into each other (Banks and Potts 2010; Banks 2012).

In the process of co-creating things, people are creating connections and it is these connections that generate value (Burgess and Green 2009; Gauntlett 2011a). But these connections are not only among users and consumers. Consumers also interact and connect with media professionals as they collaborate to create these co-creative experiences. Effective co-creativity also therefore requires the craft skills and knowledge of professionals (see **expert** and **creative labour**).

Co-creativity involves processes of social learning through which we are experimenting with and adapting to the various opportunities and risks associated with these relationships. People are learning from each other by imitating and copying and adapting behaviours about how to create and collaborate through online networks. We all have a lot to learn about how these emerging forms of co-creative cultural production are working. From a creative industries perspective this is not a static or closed situation in which we can pre-emptively and clearly identify what the motivations, incentives and behaviours are. Instead, and this is perhaps also why these emerging practices are so fascinating and challenging, co-creation potentially redefines our understandings of what markets are and how they operate in relation to social and cultural networks (Banks and Potts 2010; Banks 2012). These are most certainly markets because exchange occurs, but it is social connections and recommendations, access and attention that perform the coordinating function, not just price.

Competition

This is a concept that usually drives a stake between cultural studies, where it is one of many forces at work in the unfolding cultural order, and economics, where it is the fundamental mechanism by which social order arises, even in the domains of arts and culture (see Cowen 1998; Cowen and Kaplan 2004). There is a manifest tension between different views of competition, on the one hand as 'regrettable', i.e. something that is seemingly necessary, like security locks on doors, but that would not exist in an ideal world; and on the other hand as a effective, efficient mechanism of allocating scarce resources that cannot be improved upon, even by intelligent design.

However, neither of these two views – the 'Marxist' view of a regrettable force or the 'neoliberal' view of an ideal mechanism – actually captures the reality of *competition as a process* by which novel ideas compete with existing ideas, sometimes winning and sometimes not, but all the while as an institutional process for coordinating new ideas into an existing order. From this perspective, competition is an essential mechanism in cultural and media processes, as well as cultural and media studies, which concern themselves with change and, in another language, that is what competition in an economic sense covers.

It should also be recognised that just as competition between theatre groups or movie studios ultimately benefits audiences, so too does competition between all producers in markets ultimately benefit *consumers*. Theatre groups, like all other producers, do not like competition, and will do whatever is necessary to eliminate it. Competition benefits consumers, and it is in their name that economists sing the praises of competition and urge governments to enact legislation to foster competition and to punish anti-competitive behaviour. It is for the benefits to consumers, audiences, and citizens that competition policy and legislation exists, not for the benefit of business or industry.

Like all sectors, competition is critical to the efficiency and vitality of the cultural and creative industries. This is so because competition is an effective *process* to induce *progress* through the entry of new ideas. Without competition, the creative industries go the same way as do other industries when similarly protected, namely toward stagnation and largely for the benefit of producers who enjoy the rents that the absence of competition furnish. It is *consumers* who are the main beneficiaries of competition, through lower prices and increased variety of choices; *new entrants* to the supply of creative goods and services also benefit from the presence of effective competition. For the most part, it is only existing producers who dislike competition and thus seek protection – or monopoly.

Nevertheless, the logic of promoting competition in the cultural and creative industries (Seaman 2004; Potts and Cunningham 2008) is usually overshadowed by another competitive market consideration: namely the prospect of large-scale *market failure*. Baumol and Bowen's (1966) 'cost disease' argument is a prominent mechanism, in which due to productivity gains in other sectors wages are pushed up in all sectors including the creative industries, thus making them ever less competitive. But other types of market failure have also been proposed (Throsby 1994; Caves 2000). Consideration of the benefits of competition in the cultural and creative industries is thus often dominated by discussion of the impossibility of effective competition due to market failure. Cowen (1996) has sought to explain why the cost disease is not an effective argument because it ignores entrepreneurial developments such as new business models. Despite this, there remains little serious concern with the promotion of competition in cultural and creative industries.

Competition works in two ways:

1 As *price competition*, where existing suppliers of creative output compete on price (or other terms) to provide the most value at the least cost for the same item.
2 As *evolutionary competition*, where producers, for example artists or writers, compete to expand their market by developing and introducing new goods or services (Schumpeter 1942).

In both cases (these often occur simultaneously) the mechanisms of competition – in the form of cultural, social and legal institutions that form the formal and informal rules of (market) competition – constitute a process that works to select the most appropriate producers for a task, as decided by consumers. In this way, competition occurs when various producers seek to make ever better offers to consumers about what might best meet their needs and wants. The producers who win gain market share, and vice versa. Producers like competition only when they win, but mostly they don't like it; but consumers benefit no matter who wins.

Note two key points. First, competition is a *process*, not an end state. It is a process of *selection* whereby those with better ideas or more efficient businesses gain market share while those with higher prices or less attractive offerings lose market share. Second, that process benefits *consumers*, not producers. These two points signal why students of creative industries should not think of competition as a derogatory term or institution. Competition underpins the operation and advance of the creative industries because, more than many industries, the sector depends upon the creation of continuous flows of novelty to meet consumer demand.

The process of competition occurs as economic agents interact subject to particular 'rules of the game'. Competition is thus a rule-governed process with **institutions** (i.e. population adopted rules) that can be changed through cultural, social, legal and political means. The mechanisms of competition (i.e. the 'market' and the cultural norms, social expectations and laws that support it) are institutions that facilitate the replacement of existing ideas with new and better ideas or ways of doing things (Loasby 1999). Competition is thus the *evolutionary process* by which progress happens. Without competition, progress is retarded.

Similarly, competition is not the antithesis of *cooperation*. Competition is often a highly cooperative activity, as groups of people, businesses and networks work together in order to successfully compete. The 'fiercest' market competition typically goes hand-in-hand with the most extensive and highly developed cooperation, such as between two television channels or fashion houses, each of which are massively cooperative and collaborative undertakings, but are engaged in highly competitive markets. The opposite of competition is not cooperation, but rather *monopoly*, as for example when there is only one television channel. Monopoly is bad because it leads to higher prices and lower output, thus imposing costs on consumers; producers of course like monopoly for the same reason. Monopolies transfer 'economic rents' from consumers to producers, resulting in a net welfare loss. Like all industries, the creative industries also weaken when they tend towards monopoly market structures or industrial organisation (from the perspective of consumers).

Competition involves both success and failure. Businesses or individuals competing in creative industries markets are in effect competing for the 'votes' of consumers, whether they vote with money or attention, implicitly ranking competitors based on who can meet their needs or best solve their problems. When a producer fails and loses market share, it is consumers who benefit. It is obviously true that competitive failure obviously means job losses and business collapse for some, but it equally implies new job creation and business expansion for those who were successful and gained market share. Consumers like competition for the same reason businesses don't, namely it is the process that ensures that producers are providing the best they can possibly provide. Competition ensures that they are not padding prices to extract rents, or even when new services or technologies are difficult and risky to develop, that firms still have an incentive to try, i.e. to 'compete' to offer and develop these.

Cowen (2002) explains how **globalisation** (i.e. market liberalisation and global competition) in cultural and creative industries has been a net benefit for consumers, and also for many cultural and creative producers. The consumer argument is simple: increased variety and lowered cost, as per the two processes of competition above. But this also benefits *some producers* as well, particularly those under protectionist regimes constrained by limited local markets who could not previously specialise to the extent that their art demanded. Globalisation is a competitive shaping force on the creative industries that benefits consumers everywhere, and also benefits some producers who can gain by competitively tapping into global markets to enable creative scale economies of specialisation.

Market failure, in theory, is the economic concept that describes situations where *perfect competition* is violated. This means the existence of *externalities* (including 'spillovers') not captured in property rights. In practice, it refers to situations when producers have *market power*. What are the 'degrees of competition' in creative industries markets? In a *monopoly*, there is only one producer of the creative good or service; with *perfect competition*, there are many such rival offerings. *Oligopolistic* market structure means a small number of producers who can potentially *collude* to behave like a monopolist. Market failure of this sort occurs in media markets, for example, when there is only a small number of media production or distribution channels. Two responses to competitive (market) failure are *regulation*, or *deregulation*. The first is to legislatively force the producer to do what the market wants, which of course must be decided by the legislator, i.e. to enact specific new regulations on incumbent producers. The second is to deregulate, which in practice means to allow new entrants. The first seeks to reduce price by law, but has the effect of stultifying innovation. The second seeks to increase **innovation** by reducing barriers to competition.

Richard Caves (2000) examines the particular *costs of competition* in creative industries markets as analysis of what economists call 'transactions costs', which are the various costs of using a market. Information gathering and contractual monitoring costs, for example, are transactions costs. Caves argues that the creative industries, by doing new and novel things as a matter of routine, and due to the problem of contracting input resources on this basis, are particularly beset with transaction cost concerns. He shows how this shapes the structure of the creative industries in particular ways, for example leading to prevalence of winner-take-all phenomena (see De Vany 2004), to significant risk aversion in contracting, and significant resources devoted to signalling to deal with uncertainty.

Competition in creative industries implies that the sites of creative production, by the competitive market processes of entry and exit, will be those with the greatest *comparative advantage* in production. Comparative advantage is the core idea in the economics of trade (Cowen 1998, 2002). It means that production will gravitate to the places with the lowest 'opportunity cost' of production (assuming entrepreneurs can first figure this out). This keystone of economic reasoning has important implications for the local and global structure of creative industries under competition. By implication, a region or nation should specialise only where it has a comparative advantage, then trade for the rest. This means that regions will specialise on the production side. This logic applies to all goods and services, not just creative industries. Consumers of course don't need to only consume locally produced creative output, but producers will come to specialise in order to exploit economies of scale and scope, including the positive spillovers from industrial **clusters** in this competitive market process.

With respect to competition, policy is appropriate in creative industries where it promotes effective entry and exit behaviour of producers in order to benefit consumers. In practice, this means limiting *trade protection* (e.g. tariffs or quotas on cultural imports, which are sources of competition); minimising *industry policy* (e.g. granting monopolies or industry support favouring incumbents); and maximising *innovation and competition policy* (e.g. market discovery, Bakhshi et al. 2011). The purpose of competition in creative industries is to set up institutions that incentivise producers to do best by consumers, which typically means developing new ideas.

Complex Systems

Analysts, strategists, theorists and policymakers regularly encounter problems whose inherent difficulty or unpredictability is due to the 'complexity' of the relevant systems domains. This is invariably because they are composed of a great many distributed interactions, or because they are subject to adaptive, emergent or otherwise surprising outcomes. These are called *complex systems*. The internet for example is a complex system, as are markets, innovation systems, languages, and indeed almost all cultural and social systems. Climate is a complex system, as is media preference, brain function, terrorism, fashion and global finance. Complex systems are everywhere, but we've only just discovered them in the past few decades. Crucially, it turns out that the creative industries are full of them.

Complex systems theory (or complexity science) is a development of modern mathematics and computer simulation has emerged in the past few decades as one of the major frontiers of modern science across a vast domain of applications, including analysis of the creative industries (see www.complexity-creative-economy.net/, McNair 2006; Mitleton-Kelly 2006; J. Johnson 2010; Potts 2011) and increasingly of public policy too (OECD 2008). Key ideas from complex systems theory that have reached popular usage include the notions of 'the edge of chaos', 'order out of chaos', 'tipping points', 'the butterfly effect', 'small worlds', 'phase transitions', 'power laws' and the theory of 'emergence'. Many interesting phenomena in creative industries can be better understood when viewed from the perspective of complex systems theory. This includes things such as fashion cascades, winner-take-all markets, the emergence of new genres and styles of design, 'crowd-sourcing', and the general unpredictability of success and failure in the creative industries.

Complex systems theory is a general (although not unified) analytic framework that helps explain many of the interesting and peculiar dynamic processes commonly observed in the creative industries as the result of the inherent 'complexity' of many aspects of the creative industries. Our purpose here is not to offer a technical primer on complex systems theory; there are many such highly readable accounts (e.g. Kauffman 1995, 2000; Watts 1999; Strogatz 2001; Barabasi 2002; Miller and Page 2007; Vega-Redondo 2007). Instead, the meaning of complex systems theory can be elucidated in relation to other general analytic frameworks. These include the theory of *linear systems* (used in physics), *equilibrium* or *closed systems* (used in economics), and *developmental systems* (used in anthropology and sociology). Complex systems theory offers a different view on the structure and dynamics of the sorts of socio-cultural and economic systems that compose and affect the creative industries.

Linear systems have a 'linear' relation between cause and effect. Small changes in inputs cause small changes in outputs and vice versa. Complex systems do not often have this property: instead small changes in initial conditions or inputs can cause large changes in outputs, and vice versa. This renders complex systems unpredictable. The reason for these non-linear responses is due to the 'complex' structure of interaction, adaptation and feedback. A small change may get amplified, resulting in a cascading consequence of effects. A fashion cycle often proceeds like this. Or a small change may occur in a system that is poised near a phase transition or 'tipping point', leading to large-scale structural change from a seemingly minor input change. Such properties make policy and control of complex systems often very difficult.

Equilibrium systems are stable from within and only change due to an 'exogenous shock'. Economists model markets as such. A marble sitting at the bottom of a bowl is a physical example of an equilibrium system. An isolated and fully institutionalised cultural system might also be modelled as such. Complex systems are *disequilibrium* (or dissipative) systems in that they maintain their order and structure only by continuous flows of energy, information or ideas from without. Life, for example, is a complex system in this respect, where equilibrium literally means death. Disequilibrium systems also change from within (this is the connection to evolutionary systems, and Schumpeter's re-conception of economic systems in terms of **creative destruction**). Disequilibrium systems have far more complex and unpredictable dynamics than equilibrium systems.

Complex systems dynamics tend to be evolutionary, not developmental (see **evolution**), but more importantly because of *adaptation* and *emergence*. Adaptation means that local actions are governed by adaptation to local circumstance, rather than some overarching development plan, and thus the specific local conditions can have a large effect on the dynamics of the system. Emergence means that in consequence of such adaptation, new properties and systems can emerge that were entirely unpredictable from any knowledge of the component elements. These emergent properties then become new 'laws' of the system, upsetting the supposed developmental path. This is why complex systems are mostly impossible to predict, even with very detailed information on initial states or high levels of controlling power. The 2011 'Arab Spring' is a good example of emergence due to social network media interacting in very specific local circumstances, leading to unplanned revolutionary change.

A complex system is not the same as a complicated system. A complex system can be very simple (such as a coupled pendulum), and many highly complicated systems (e.g. tax systems) are not actually complex systems. What defines a complex system is *distributed feedback* and *emergence*. A complex system is composed of a set of *elements* and a set of *connections*, where connections carry information and feedback. Complex systems tend to form spontaneously, or to *self-organise*. Complex systems are usually the product of evolutionary processes. Planning usually produces a complicated system, rarely a complex system. Complex systems in turn are usually the product of self-organisation.

Second, the dynamics of complex systems are governed by local *adaptation* to specific inputs, but where that adaptation then carries further information to other elements, who in turn adapt, and so on. Complex systems are thus distributed *adaptive* systems that can change in response to new information, or new constraints or opportunities, through a decentralised process of local adaptation and mutual re-coordination. No one is actually in control. There is no central agent directing the process of change. A global process of change in a complex system typically comes about through many localised adaptations and changes that are mostly small but sometimes large. In other words, complex systems 'evolve' (see **evolution**), and are only rarely changed by 'revolutionary' means. The dynamics of complex systems are best described as a local process of distributed adaptation, resulting in what is called self-organisation. This self-organisation is a theory of how high-level *order* can arise without the guidance of a central agent or plan, but simply through the mutual feedback and adaptation of distributed independent agents (Ormerod 2005; Beinhocker 2006).

Third, complex systems display sensitive dependence to *initial conditions*, and are therefore impossible to predict. Complex systems are driven by feedback, so even minor changes in that initial local state can have ramifying consequences on the overall system as these small initial differences magnify through, for example, an evolutionary process. This explains why movies, music and most fashion trends are mostly *impossible to predict* due to sensitive dependence to initial conditions, resulting in winner-take-all feedback (De Vany 2004). This also explains why fundamental uncertainty is such an endemic component of creative industries. As film mogul Sam Goldwyn put it: 'No-one knows anything!' In turn, that's why **creative destruction** is such a prominent feature of creative industries' structure and dynamics. A related point is that complex systems are often subject to *phase* *transitions*, or switching between several macro-states based on the cumulative interactive effect of its interconnections. This can be observed when the underlying technological foundation or dominant business model of an industry abruptly shifts, as for example with digital music or newspapers.

Fourth, complex systems give rise to *emergence*. Emergence is the process by which new ideas or elements are produced by the re-combinatorial dynamics of adaptation and self-organisation. Complex systems are thus systems of interacting elements with the potential to generate new elements entirely through those interactions. These new elements then become part of the new system, and so on. An example here is the technology of search engines. These were initially freestanding web navigation tools but as these were embedded in elements such as other websites or apps, search became something that machines could do, which changed the structure and dynamics of those newly affected practices, firms, technologies, markets and industries. That's emergence.

Fifth, complex systems often generate 'power law' outcomes. A power law is an analytical statement about a statistical distribution between the frequency of an event and some underlying causal attribute. A power law outcome (complex systems) differs from normally distributed outcomes (equilibrium systems). A power law occurs when the frequency of an outcome is a power function (in the algebraic sense) of a description of that situation. Power laws occur in consequence of feedback and adaptive response leading to amplification. A power law implies that a distribution is *scale-free*. It behaves the same at every scale, and thus has infinite variance. Human height, for example is not a power law, but a normal distribution. Most adults fall between 4 to 7 feet tall. There are no people who are two inches high, or 29 feet high. Variance is finite. But human income and wealth is a power law, as are most natural phenomena. Some earn nothing, some thousands, some earn millions and billions. There is no such thing as 'average income', or the average movie or song, or even the average earthquake. Variance is infinite. Creative industries outcomes seem to be described by power laws everywhere we look (De Vany 2004; Bentley 2009). *Creativity is a power law*. The implication is that because only complex systems generate power laws, the creative industries are best analysed as complex systems.

How do you do complex systems analysis? There is a rapidly growing body of tools and theory of complex systems. These include multi-agent simulation modelling; network theory; dynamical systems modelling, scenario analysis and 'stress testing', and even data mining. Generally these are specialist skills still much in the province of mathematicians and those trained in dynamical systems or computational statistical analysis. These are increasingly packaged as software programs (for example Matlab). Yet as of writing, the best way to do complex systems analysis from within the creative industries remains to have a good idea about a possible complex systems effect, and ideally some data to seed simulations or some already researched effect to explore, and then to team up with a complex-systems trained researcher. That's not necessarily such a bad division of labour.

Complex systems theory is at base a challenge to 'received' ontology and to 'common sense' imagination. It suggests that the world is not necessarily as it analytically seems – closed, linear, in equilibrium and developmental – and instead may be complex. The most obvious practical implication of 'complexity thinking' in creative industries is to forget prediction and planning. Instead, embrace adaptation and *experimentation*, and also constant alertness to possible sources and sites of emergence. The complexity perspective favours 'fast learning' and 'rapid adaptation', and mostly eschews top-down long-range planning and control.

At base, complexity theory undermines the rule of **experts**, or the supposition that for every problem someone knows the solution (if only we can find them). Complexity theory is a scientifically rigorous statement to the effect that the future is mostly unpredictable and that that will always be so. Its main contribution is to explain why this is, namely interactive feedback and dynamics from sensitive dependence to initial conditions in the context of multiple attractors and emergence. The challenge for creative industries is to integrate the complexity framework and develop new strategic and policy models based about this new view of the world, or what Stephen Wolfram (2002) calls 'A new kind of science'.

Consumer

The consumer is at the very heart of the creative industries. Employment, wealth-creation and innovation that these industries generate are all predicated on consumption; people buying various creative products, services and experiences. What is distinctive about a 'creative industries' approach to this concept? First, note that the entry is called 'Consumer' not 'Consumption', because the **agency** of the consumer – what consumers do, with and through products as well as with each other – is central to a creative industries approach (see **audience, co-creation**). This is not to marginalise the professional producers, who remain crucial to the **creative economy** (see **expert**). Nevertheless, consumers are no longer simply at the end of the value chain; they're part of a **network** of **productivity**.

Axel Bruns argues that the productive activity of consumers, which he calls 'produsage', is now so significant that 'the role of "consumer" and even that of "end-user" have long disappeared, and the distinction between producers and users has faded into comparative insignificance' (2008: 2). While Bruns helpfully foregrounds the productive agency of consumers, abandoning the term altogether may create further problems. In fact, produsage and consumption coexist: for instance the consumption of telecommunications services and the devices that allow consumers to produce their own DIY media content.

Marxist theorists such as Theodor Adorno and Max Horkheimer (1979), associated with the Frankfurt School critique of capitalism, criticised what they viewed as the capitalist domination of the cultural sphere, at the time when cultural production and consumption became increasingly integrated in the capitalist system. These thinkers argue that the industrialisation and commodification of culture result in uniformity and sameness rather than any cultural freedom of increased consumer 'choice'. Their target is mass culture and mass society. This critique, however, offers a very restricted understanding of cultural commodities and overlooks the extent to which such commodities genuinely meet and fulfil human needs for meaning and enjoyment (Dunn 2008; Flew 2012).

Further, as David Hesmondhalgh (2007: 15–17) observes, by reducing culture to a singular logic of commodification, such approaches overlook the complexity and diversity of logics functioning across different types of cultural production. It does not make sense to reduce the consumption of videogames and popular musicals, for example, to such a singular logic. The assumption that such cultural commodities also directly reflect and transmit an underlying dominant capitalist ideology is also deeply problematic (Garnham 1990: 34). One may think that these are old debates involving by now quite discredited ways of thinking about cultural consumers. Nevertheless, these critiques regularly reassert themselves in various forms. For example, Jeffrey Sachs (2011) argues that America's mass media culture is among the fundamental causes of the tendency to let **markets** run rampant over social values. As Flew notes, the view that commercial markets debase culture has been 'an underlying influence on the development of national arts and cultural policies' (2012: 63) (see **culture**).

Commodification-of-culture critiques tend to reduce consumers to the role of manipulated, misled dupes, and therefore they systematically underestimate consumer activity and **agency**. A cultural industries approach rejects such theories of the deluded consumer by theorising consumers as social agents who gain identity, meaning, pleasure and knowledge through consumption, which itself is expressive of social relationships. But is this more complex and differentiated idea of consumer culture also endorsing a form of consumer*ism*? Has identity been reduced to buying cultural commodities; has personal choice been reduced to attenuated 'consumer sovereignty'? Responding to such a proposition depends on how we understand the consumer and consumer choice. As is evident in various entries in this book that draw on the idea of social network markets (Potts et al. 2008a), the fact that consumers make choices does not necessarily turn them into the narrowly conceived, utility-maximising individualist of economic theory. The very act and practice of choice requires close attention to what others are doing, especially in the context of cultural consumption. How people exercise choice and the significance of the choices that they make are important questions that should not be reduced too quickly to a critique of consumer choice. Further, the very technologies of cultural production and consumption remain active, continually transforming what it means to be a consumer and to exercise choice.

Thorstein Veblen's idea of 'conspicuous consumption' (1899) tells us that spending on cultural products is a way of displaying membership of a particular class. Decisions to buy and wear a particular brand and style of jeans or to purchase tickets for a cultural performance such as a play or a concert, are not simply about our enjoyment of the cultural content. By consuming cultural products people

consumer

33

signal their social position and standing. Sociologist Pierre Bourdieu also conceptualises culture as a field of class distinction and domination. Bourdieu conceives of cultural consumption as expressing positionality within a social system of class relations. He writes: 'A class is defined as much by its being-perceived as by its being, by its consumption – which need not be conspicuous in order to be symbolic – as much as by its position in the relations of production' (1984: 483). A weakness of Bourdieu's approach is that it ultimately emphasises social structure at the expense of social action (see **agency**). As Robert Dunn notes, Bourdieu provides a richly theorised elaboration of Veblenesque consumption as social positioning, but neglects the 'actual practices of social actors. Bourdieu brackets the processes of consumption in favor of an analysis of its *effects*' (2008: 63). Perhaps a more important aspect of Veblen's theory is that 'conspicuous' consumption entails observing and emulating others – it is a social learning dynamic. It is this understanding of consumption as a process of social learning that should be fundamental to any creative industries approach (see **attention**).

Anthropologist Daniel Miller (1995) provides important accounts of consumption and commodities as meaningful for individuals and social groups. Miller describes how consumption is a practice through which goods are invested with meaning and value by being recontextualised in the context of people's everyday lives. Here, think of the various cultural commodities that you have purchased that take on value and significance due to how they have entered the fabric of your life and matter to you. Miller's (1995: 21–7) work challenges assumptions that consumption is an acquisitive individualism that represents a loss of authenticity.

We know that a defining characteristic of cultural consumption is quite fundamental uncertainty about the value and quality of specific products in terms of demand (Caves 2000). The creative industries continually produce new creative products and consumers generally lack knowledge of the products in advance of actually consuming them. Which pair of jeans should one purchase? To which film should one commit viewing time and a purchase decision? Our response is to observe and learn from others, which is a fundamental principle of the social network market approach. Our choices are influenced by others when we consider what films are the most popular, when friends and acquaintances tell us what is the current 'must watch' television programme, and when we heed critics and reviewers whose recommendations we have previously found helpful. In short, individual choice is determined by what is often called word-of-mouth; and therefore it is a social practice. As Hartley argues, the point is not to reduce self-realisation to shopping, but to observe that self-realisation and with that the growth of knowledge are available, and exercised socially, '*within* commercial democracies' (2009: 10–11).

The challenge here is not to celebrate commercial culture and consumer choice but to better understand the dynamics and characteristics of consumer action and productivity so as to 'promote the development of "consumer entrepreneurship" within a complex system of market based self-actualisation' (Hartley 2009: 12–14). It would be a mistake though to reduce this to a narrowly individualising comprehension of consumer choice. Self-actualisation in this context requires the scaling up of consumer-users' capacity to learn from each other the **digital literacy** needed to produce as well as to consume cultural content and so to contribute to the growth of **knowledge**.

In developing this understanding of networked consumers, Hartley foregrounds the introduction of massive computing power into the consumer environment. However, all of these networked actions and choices leave digital traces, and corporations such as Amazon, Apple and Facebook carefully track, monitor and analyse those data. Mark Andrejevic raises important privacy concerns about this corporate data-mining and what he calls 'the facilitation of monitoring-based regimes of control' (2011: 612). He argues that marketers and advertisers are using 'interactive environments to subject consumers to an ongoing series of randomised, controlled experiments'. Andrejevic then cites *Wired* magazine editor-in-chief Chris Anderson (2008) to note that the size of databases fundamentally changes how researchers think about and use data: 'its descriptive power is replaced by a generative capacity' (2011: 614). Andrejevic writes that marketers will use data-mining techniques to engage and enlist consumers:

> for the purpose of brand management, constituting myriad data points whose online activities and interactions generate 'actionable' findings available exclusively to those who mine the databases. If the Internet is supposed to be the great equaliser, the rise of super-crunching in the data mine reintroduces asymmetry in the form of the database. (2011: 615)

But the asymmetry may be constituted by the very terms of Andrejevic's analysis. For him, 'actionable' and 'data-mining' are *done to* consumers, rather than a practice that they are themselves learning and doing. What if networked consumers might also wield the power of data crunching and associated analytics? A creative industries perspective does not assume that future consumers will be manipulated and submissive dupes of data-mining corporations.

A creative industries perspective reappraises the role of the cultural consumers in driving creative enterprise and culture. This approach recognises the creativity of the commercial sphere and identifies the possibility of achieving emancipation and creative freedom through commercial environments rather than by opposing or resisting these domains. Consumption is not treated as a behavioural outcome and effect of corporate manipulation. Instead:

> consumption needs to be rethought as action not behaviour, and media consumption as a mode of literacy: that is, an autonomous means of communication in which 'writing' is as widespread as 'reading'; something that was never possible during the era of broadcast, one-to-many, passively received 'mass' communication. (Hartley 2009: 14)

The implications of reconceptualising consumers and consumption in terms of complex and networked **productivity** and **agency** are profound and far-reaching. Hartley argues that consumers now need to be:

> imagined as being able to 'make a deal' – to agree on an exchange that may also require a continuing relationship – based on some level of calculation of advantage to themselves, as well as paying money or attention to the provider. It's a two-way transaction (dialogue) in a complex network of choices (meaning system). (2009: 48)

consumer

There are big questions in all of this about 'big data' (Boyd and Crawford 2011) – questions and challenges about privacy and the terms of access to data. The creative industries are important because they provide enabling social technologies for networked consumers to learn and play and experiment. And it may also be through such networked choice making that we will innovate and navigate our way towards solving the pressing challenges of big data. It is also in these ways that consumers will contribute to the growth of knowledge.

Convergence

Convergence is at the heart of many of the changes associated with digital media, and these changes profoundly impact cultural production and consumption across the creative industries. Indeed, it is arguable that the growth in the creative industries has coincided with, if not been driven by, the technological changes and cultural transformations associated with convergence. Convergence came to prominence when computers, telecommunications and broadcast media converged technologically and thence industrially in and after the 1990s. Cunningham and Turner write that 'convergence is customarily used to describe the dissolving distinctions between media systems, media content and the resulting trade between systems' (2010: 3). They suggest that convergence has three dimensions:

- *Technological* convergence in which digitisation enables the conversion and distribution of content across multiple formats and platforms;
- *Industry* convergence occurs when media and communications industries merge and form alliances as media conglomerates, e.g. Disney combines film and television production, publishing, merchandising, travel, and theme parks into one of the world's top five media conglomerates. Entirely new types of converged conglomerates have emerged, such as Google (McPhail 2010);
- *Policy* convergence is required, often across multiple ministries, by those who seek to regulate these rapidly changing industries.

Many of the developments associated with convergence are global (see **globalisation**), and this confronts national governments and policymakers with serious and pressing challenges as they seek to regulate at the national and local levels.

Graham Meikle and Sherman Young draw on the example of WikiLeaks to demonstrate that convergence usefully describes and explains 'the complex media environment that we now inhabit, an environment built on both broadcast and broadband' (2012: 2). WikiLeaks played out across diverse media forms and platforms – networked digital media such as blogs, YouTube, Facebook and Twitter; but also traditional creative industries including news organisations, television and radio. They observe that the case of WikiLeaks 'highlights how the convergent media environment is characterised by both contestation and continuity – new actors and old industries, contending modes of distribution and visibility, complex assemblages of networked digital media' (Meikle and Young 2012: 10).

Although covering the important economic and policy dimensions of convergence for creative industries, Meikle and Young emphasise the everyday uses of networked, digital media; they describe how people use Facebook, iTunes, Google, Wikipedia and the BBC iPlayer to navigate the contemporary convergent media environment. An important point they make, however, is that focusing on digitisation may be a mistake when trying to understand convergence 'because the digitisation of media content is now so pervasive and so firmly established that the term is unhelpful as a general label' (2012: 3). Instead, they foreground the significance of the **networked** nature of contemporary media, that enables complex communication relationships, especially 'two-way communication' (2012: 4). In a convergent media environment, people explore new ways to interact with and to share media. Convergence means that: 'for many people, the media are no longer just what they watch, listen to or read – the media are now what people *do*' (2012: 13) (see **co-creation**).

Henry Jenkins explores these participatory dimensions of convergence in a much-cited book. Jenkins starts from the straightforward proposition that convergence concerns 'where old and new media collide, where grassroots and corporate media intersect, where the power of the media producer and the power of the media consumer interact in unpredictable ways' (2006: 259–60). He defines convergence as:

> the flow of content across multiple media platforms, the cooperation between multiple media industries, and the migratory behavior of media audiences who will go almost anywhere in search of the kinds of entertainment experiences they want. Convergence is a word that manages to describe technological, industrial, cultural, and social changes depending on who's speaking and what they think they are talking about. (Jenkins 2006: 2–3)

Media are increasingly delivered across various 'transmedia' platforms and in varied formats. Digital technologies have transformed the music industry with people now listening to music on devices including mobile phones. Some people also buy their music online via Apple and Amazon, and personalise their listening experience by making playlists using tools such as iTunes. People also now read newspapers, magazines and novels on mobile devices such as Kindles, iPhones, and iPads. They watch film and television shows and follow sporting events on various devices. This shakes up the business of making and selling media. Media businesses grapple with the opportunities and challenges of cross-media and trans-media as they seek to deliver compelling and commercially successful offerings of the same content across various platforms (Gray 2010a).

Governmental regulators and policymakers struggle to identify and respond to the varied threats and opportunities of convergence. The various policy challenges

convergence

of licensing powers, ownership restrictions and content rules are crucial (Meikle and Young 2012). But media policy in the context of convergence should not simply be about top-down regulatory regimes. More significantly, the policy challenge involves juggling and balancing relationships among media industries as they seek economic opportunities that create jobs with responsibilities to citizens in a globally networked digital environment (Meikle and Young 2012: 198-200).

The shift from a vertically defined regulatory environment in which television, film, newspapers and radio are silos to a more horizontal convergent dynamic in which content is distributed across traditional platforms and social media such as YouTube, Facebook and blogs, as well as to mobile devices, raises pressing challenges for finding a regulatory balance between government, industry and user interests and expectations. Kate Crawford and Catharine Lumby propose, however, that the very changes associated with convergence, such as more active and participatory users, offer an opportunity to develop a new and adaptive policy framework. This would shift from top-down content regulation by engaging users as participants in the process of developing policy and regulatory responses:

> We suggest that it is critical to see government, industry and media users as key stakeholders who must work together in the future governance of media content. By cooperating, the three groups can increase opportunities for the identification of truly harmful material and the enforcement of criminal law. They can share the responsibility of governance of media content in an era where the share volume of material outstrips the capacity of any government or corporation to pre-vet all material. (Crawford and Lumby 2011: 4)

Their proposal for convergent media governance seeks to adapt to the opportunities and complexities of the convergent environment.

These various formulations of convergence are not simply about the effects of digitisation. Jenkins (2006) reminds us that convergence concerns the *cultural* implications and potentials of these changes. His approach to convergence is cultural as it concerns what people increasingly *do with each other* as they collaborate to make and share media, and it is about the meanings, values, and identities that both shape and emerge from this process. Jenkins is very clear on this – while he starts from digital media technologies, he concentrates on the cultural dimension:

> I will argue here against the idea that convergence should be understood primarily as a technological process bringing together multiple media functions within the same devices. Instead, convergence represents a cultural shift as consumers are encouraged to seek out new information and make connections among dispersed media content. (2006: 3)

By emphasising the active, participatory role of consumers, Jenkins helps us to see that convergence also 'occurs within the brains of individual consumers and through their social interactions with others' (2006: 3). But in the effort to foreground the cultural dimension and thereby avoid all the problems associated with technological determinism (see **technology**), Jenkins may too quickly abandon the task of figuring out the relationships between these technologies and the participatory media consumers. The materiality of technologies such as mobile devices, PCs and server farms go missing from his account of convergence. The question of technology needs to be reformulated, such that it does not imply reducing culture to technology. Instead, we need to consider the nature of the dynamic relations between technology and culture, and these relations should be at the core of any effort to understand convergence.

Nick Couldry argues that Jenkins' (2006) *Convergence Culture* over-generalises and thereby fails to focus on the specific range of practices that constitute convergence cultures. Although he agrees that transformations of the contemporary media environment indicate shifts in the economics and organisation of cultural production, Couldry questions Jenkins's assumption that *fans* exemplify the wider media audience (Couldry 2011: 490–3; see Meikle and Young 2012: 6–7). He questions Jenkins' claim that democratising and empowering consequences will follow from these changes. Jenkins' important work on convergence culture helps to identify significant transformations in the conditions of media production and consumption. Traditional ways of producing and consuming media for established industries such as television, newspapers and music are profoundly changed by the possibilities of engagement and interactivity offered by networked, convergent digital media. Nevertheless, criticisms such as Couldry's suggest that we need rich empirical research about the diverse forms of convergence, to test claims about their emancipatory potential.

In considering such criticisms and questions, however, we should remember that convergence continues to be central to the creative industries. Cloud-computing practices and infrastructures through which users access services and data, regardless of their location or device, for example, are a significant trend in convergence culture. Vic Gundotra, head of Google's social media, told the 2011 Web 2.0 summit in San Francisco that 3.4 billion photos had been added to Google + (Google's competitor to Facebook). Apple's iCloud service enables users wirelessly to sync and integrate apps and content (from music to photos to documents) across their various devices. The important point here is not so much the amount of digital content that is being shared and distributed, but more an observation about emerging behaviours. We are in the process of learning and sharing how to work and play and make in the context of convergent media networks and environments (Burgess and Green 2009). Convergence is central to how we access, share, make and manipulate media content, and it will therefore continue to be a pressing topic for any consideration of the creative industries.

Creative Arts

The English word 'art' derives from a Latin root meaning 'to fit together; join', evident in words such as *arm*, *artisan*, *artefact* and *articulate*. The question of what constitutes creative art might therefore be rephrased as: 'What has historically been called the creative arts, by whom and when?' For example, an *artefact* is something that is 'made to fit' in both a practical and aesthetic sense (Bohm and Peat 2011: 263). The sense of fitting is demonstrated by the existence of canons. Throughout history, art – as well as knowledge – has preserved traditions and reinforced power: as in what is 'fit and proper'. The focus from this perspective is a model or standard of fitness that can be emulated (see **culture**). This leaves a key role for gatekeepers.

Jack Goody dates the emergence of 'art' to the post-medieval period: 'An art market gradually emerged in the Renaissance, where each prince or republic wanted the best artist' (2010: 14). Historians characterise the birth of the modern artist from among communities of medieval craftsmen as a deliberate stepping away from the demands of clients and patrons towards a refuge in 'autonomous creativity' (Sennett 2008: 72). As lay markets increased for creative works, 'artists' became free to choose their subject.

In the main, historical accounts privilege a hierarchy of art, design and media in which art represents something original and unique, either for sale or display (see **aesthetics**). While **design** has its precursor in craft, it is perhaps best seen as a 'process' that leads art into the marketplace. The arrival of the modern media in turn provided the means of distribution. O'Connor (2011) argues that arrival of 'the art industry' had its roots in the rapid growth of new cities in Europe in the eighteenth century. The art industry would be further recharged by politics and nation building in the twentieth century. This was a century that witnessed the invention of **cultural policy**.

While the Western understanding of creative arts is often regarded as foundational, a wider historical scan reveals otherwise. In ancient China, a work of art was both an object of admiration and a means of delivering philosophical ideas. As elsewhere, art was concerned with the relationship between 'the beautiful, the good and the true' (Mou 2009: 1). Creative arts were central to court life but were also a dynamic part of social life. China was among many non-European territories to have prosperous cultural markets in which art was traded for popular as well as elite consumption (Clunas 2004; Keane 2007). The existence of a block printing press by the Tang Dynasty together with the centrality of Buddhism stimulated the development of literature. As in the classical Western tradition, the artist was intent on illustrating relationships between culture and nature (art imitates nature).

Performing arts have played a central role in all cultures. Artists have 'articulated' the relationship between their works and society and in doing so they have institutionalised specific disciplinary procedures and artistic conventions. The terminology of art practices – genres, styles and conventions – has in turn shaped the institutionalisation of training, the conditions of work, perceptions of value and the marketplace for such works. The fitting of the work to the genre, to the format, to the market is often pragmatic. Moreover, the process of *not fitting* can lead to a counterclaim: 'You do not understand me', as Sennett notes, is 'a not entirely enticing selling point' (2008: 66).

A more contemporary conception of art is that the fit between culture and nature is redefined moment to moment, in ongoing acts of creative perception (fit for purpose). For instance, in the European Enlightenment tradition the artist is cast as a person able to stand at a distance from society and to raise questions about established relationships and conventions through his or her work. Although nature might still be a 'divinely ordained' system there was a role for 'man' – especially artists and geniuses – to apprehend that system (Watson 2006: 555). As mentioned above the Renaissance led to the institutionalisation of professional arts forms: high among which were architecture and design.

In most professional training institutions today the term creative arts is broadly understood as certified professional art forms: e.g. performing arts, music, dance, visual arts, creative writing, film and television production. In this sense the creative arts provide the skills and training for people wishing to enter into the creative industries. Architecture and **design** are sometimes admitted into the creative arts; at times they are dismissed as essentially functional activities.

Cultural (and arts) policy is often regarded as a means to protect artists from the uncertainty of the market by providing institutional supports that channel both aesthetic creativity and collective ways of life (Miller and Yudice 2002: 1). What is now called 'creative industries' are activities and enterprises through which individuals or businesses earn income from art, culture and entertainment pursuits, and more significantly in relation to the concept's diffusion globally, through pursuits that are not directly contingent on creative inputs. A critical perspective on the **internationalisation** of the creative industries maintains that it is 'at best a catch-word, if not a logo, clubbing together distinct categories such as "skill", "talent" and "innovation" which masquerade as an affinity to the world of artists but with no real evidence of the labour and imagination that goes into art-making' (Bharucha 2010: 22).

Within many contemporary policy debates the creative arts are juxtaposed to the creative and **entertainment** industries; that is, the creative arts are viewed as a 'pure' form of symbolic production whereas the creative industries are deemed fundamentally commercial. Such separation is problematic, not only because the arts serve to provide inputs into the creative industries, but also because the arts are themselves 'big business' and many people work across arts and creative industries sectors. That is, they might receive art subsidies in some activities but are also engaged commercially in other activities; for instance a member of a symphony orchestra might do session work on commercial film scores.

The dominant term found in cultural policy documents prior to the emergence of the creative industries is 'the arts'. Comparative studies of arts policy in many countries reveals that governments invest in the creative arts for a variety of reasons. Governments have sought to provide citizens with access to 'exemplary works', as defined by history (e.g. opera) or by critical acclaim (new work by emerging stars). This access is often justified as a cultural right or a citizenship claim; in the past access to such exemplary cultural forms was not universal: the working classes and the poor could not afford or were said to lack the capacity to recognise the value of such art forms. In the policy field creative arts programmes are a key element of social services, indicative of what George Yúdice calls 'an expanded role for culture'. Creative arts are 'no longer restricted to the sanctioned arenas of culture' (Yúdice 2003: 11).

The 'creative arts' in the 'pure' account were thought to engender artistic freedom or autonomy. This perspective has a legacy in the flowering of bourgeois society in Europe in the eighteenth century, when the ability to exercise taste was deemed to be restricted to those who had sufficient income for leisure and education (O'Connor 2011). The uneducated were thought not to have the capacity to make judgements of taste and were more likely to be attracted to popular pleasures.

More significantly, in many accounts, and most notably that of the Frankfurt School during the 1940s and 1950s, 'industry' produced standardised works that pacified its consumers, who were thought to be unaware of underlying messages. In contrast the critical and 'creative arts' were illuminating (if one knew how to understand them). From this standpoint it is clear that tensions have existed between what is deemed popular and what is considered 'meaningful'. The counterclaim to this is that many canonical creative works were originally produced for popular consumption (e.g. Shakespeare's plays) and many instances of pop culture have attained the status of classic (e.g. the Beatles).

An analogous account is that commercial culture limits autonomy because the products are ultimately constrained by the dictates of formats, genres, censorship and advertising. However, this perspective on the autonomy of the artist is challenged by several accounts. Andersson and Andersson (2006) differentiate the creative industries in worlds of 'arts' and '**entertainment**'. Entry into the world of arts is monitored by actions of curators, cultural lobbyists, interest groups, critics, sponsors, politicians and bureaucrats. Many entrants come from educational institutions specialising in fine or performing arts. This difficulty of entry reflects what Bourdieu (1998) has called 'cultural capital' and the ever-changing relationship of would-be cultural producers to power structures: for instance, economic gatekeepers and cultural aficionados. Conversely entry into the 'world of entertainment' requires navigating different gatekeepers: brokers of entertainment, critics and consumers. For instance, I might have a script for an action movie: it has to fit the conventions of the market in order to find producers and investors; in time it will be tested in the market by critics and audiences. In the world of entertainment it is evident there are many elements to achieving a creative outcome.

Conventions are maintained by gatekeepers but are often set by the state. State intervention in 'art worlds' takes many forms; these include open support, censorship and suppression. In fact conventions, subventions and interventions are linked. Subventions represent the many ways that government provide funding for artists according to designated criteria; for instance whether or not the work reflects government social campaigns.

In 1982, Howard Becker drew attention to multiple environmental factors that allow creative ideas to be conceived, executed and distributed (Becker 2008). In regarding art production as collective activity, Becker identified how visual 'art worlds' are populated by various agents whose activities are essential to the production of works that are deemed to be 'art': judgements are made by connoisseurs, critics, peers and consumers. Aside from these obvious members of the field, an expanded list of persons associated with visual art worlds would include workers who make canvasses and supply paints and frames; impresarios who mount exhibitions, curators, auctioneers and even caterers; landlords who rent studios and work spaces; cultural bureaucrats who administer public funds; and policymakers who define boundaries of expression.

Becker's sociological approach is at variance with many accounts of art which privilege the originality of the creator; for instance, the celebration of stylistic breakthroughs. The world of arts, moreover, is frequently sustained by a myth of the 'individual creator', the aura of the autonomous artist. Sennett, among many others, has voiced suspicion of the concept of originality. While he says that 'art seems to draw our attention to something that is unique or at least distinctive', he believes that originality is a 'social label'; it conjures up an image of sudden appearance, arousing wonder. And yet all art, even avant-garde expressionism, is based on existing foundations and tradition. The work of great artists and major thinkers sets the 'terms of reference' (Sennett 2008: 79). In the first instance one might have an idea; however, this must fit standards or conventions in order to be evaluated.

In conclusion, the significance of the creative arts has now moved beyond debates over who deserves recognition as 'creative': these judgements are adjudicated by both arts funding bodies and commercial peer groups; for instance the Creative Arts Emmy awards are conferred for excellence in technical achievements in television production. The description 'creative' is also loosely conferred on people working in the advertising industry, whether or not their output is mundane or imaginative, whether it follows a client's brief or is the execution of an original idea. **Digital literacy** and **co-creation** have complicated simplistic assumptions that creative expression requires training in art academies or long periods of apprenticeship to a master. While the aura of the creative artist has diminished, the output of writing, performing and producing content for consumption has increased. The creative industries may defer to the professions (see **expert**), but successful artists are discovered outside the confines of 'art worlds'.

Creative Cities

The year 2009 was a tipping point in the history of human habitation. From that year, a majority of the world's population live in urban areas. Each month, five million city dwellers are created through migration or birth, mostly in Africa, Asia and the Middle East. By the end of the century, it is predicted, this process may settle down with about 75 per cent of total population living in cities (Saunders 2010). This epochal urbanisation means that how creatively people live in cities, and the creativity that cities facilitate, will become an increasingly central global issue.

Arjun Appadurai identifies contemporary **globalised** flows of finance, people, technology, media and meanings, respectively, as the financescape, ethnoscape, technoscape, mediascape and ideoscape (1996: Chapter 2). These are often not under the control of national governments. It is cities and city-regions that lead in the generation or coordination of such flows. Thus, cities have come to be seen as drivers of modern economies. This has given rise to a burgeoning literature on established 'world' or 'global' cities (New York, London, Paris, Los Angeles, Tokyo), but also the emergence of comprehensive indexes that lay out the claims of second- and third-tier cities as they increasingly plug into these global flows and power economic growth.[1]

Accompanying these developments has been a growing focus on the quality of lived experience in cities and the sectors and activities that facilitate it. This is where the creative industries come in. But it also should be noted that creative cities will grow in importance, paradoxically, as more and more culture, creativity and communication moves online. Cultural production will continue to be even more digitally created and delivered on multi-platforms as barriers to entry and transaction costs on digital platforms are lowered. Cultural production will be engaged with globally while also being narrowcast within and to increasingly targeted niches. Such 'global narrowcasting' is the emergent form in which culture will be produced and consumed into the future. But cities will become an anchorage point for this increasingly global and mobile culture, with locative dynamics that secure culture's real-time, real-life embodiment. The question of 'quality of life' in burgeoning cities will bring the consumption and production side of the agenda closer together around the phenomenon of the 'produser' or producer-user (Bruns 2008) (see **co-creation**).

Note where almost all the current and future urbanisation is occurring: Asia, South America, Africa and the Middle East. Cities in these regions face a quite different set of circumstances from those that have preoccupied the canonical 'city writers' within the Western tradition. Major city-regions of the twenty-first century will not necessarily be cultural production centres on a core-periphery model, with a small number of world-cities exporting to the rest of the world. They will consolidate according to polycentric models such as the geolinguistic regional model (Sinclair et al. 1996). Peter Hall apologised for his almost exclusively Western focus (with the singular exception of Tokyo-Kanagawa) in his book *Cities of Civilisation* (1998: 23). Yet, given that most of the largest cities in the world are now or will be non-Western in the near future, it is hard to imagine a successor to Peter Hall, in a twenty-first century survey of 'cities of civilisation', excluding cities such as Shanghai, Mexico City, Mumbai, Rio or Lagos.

'Creative cities' is a concept that requires some initial unpacking, as close, but different, meanings are attributed to it. There is a venerable tradition of analysing 'the city in history' and 'cities in civilisation' which takes a very broad view of the

44

---

[1]For examples see: www.worldcitiesculturalaudit.com; and www.lboro.ac.uk/gawc/

urbanisation of humankind, while celebrating the achievements of certain leading cities. The writers who have distinguished themselves in this tradition – for example, Mumford (1961), Jacobs (1961), Hall (1998) and Sassen (1994) – often combined urban studies, city planning, architectural history, and the history of technology with passionate commitment to the sustainability of 'great', 'world' or 'global' cities, and the creative and innovative environments they furnish. 'Creative' in this tradition means the generalised flourishing of human potential. This tradition intersects with the second tradition when topics such as creative industries in cities, or conditions for a flourishing creative workforce come up, but these specific uses of 'creative' take their place in the much broader contexts of general conditions of city dynamics.

There is also a tradition that claims the more specific sense of 'creative' cities and it is this tradition that we concentrate on for the purposes of understanding the concept. It has a shorter history than the other tradition and it is helpful to approach it around a central problem – are the motive forces for the growth and success of creative cities based principally on production or consumption?

This understanding of creative cities is drawn from many discipline fields: urban studies, urban planning, architecture, design, media communication, and cultural and economic geography. The corpus consists of major historical and analytical work (e.g. Scott 2000, 2005); work that is focused on urban planning (e.g. Montgomery 2007); and work that is concerned with place-competitiveness (Landry 2000; Florida 2002). The latter type is often policy-oriented, and also quite technical when it engages with urban zoning regulations, architectural design, and statistics on city-region hotspots in the global economy. But it can be highly rhetorical, with place competitiveness and downright hucksterism displayed by civic officials as they jostle to put their city on the map.

Increasingly ubiquitous place competition not only draws on rigorous academic research and analysis but also, in the hands of many of its practitioners, is driven by the need for both hard economic and symbolic capital. Yet this strong element of ranking and tiering contrasts with approaches where every city can have its day and be creative. In the battle for city profile, there is a tension between the established pantheon of truly world-leading cities and the approach that offers, with appropriate strategy, policy and programmes, virtually any city the opportunity to bootstrap itself into contention as a creative city (see Hartley et al. 2012).

An easy balance between production and consumption is presumed in, for example, this definition from cultural economist David Throsby:

> The concept of the creative city describes an urban complex where cultural activities of various sorts are an integral component of the city's economic and social functioning. Such cities tend to be built upon a strong social and cultural infrastructure; to have relatively high concentrations of creative employment; and to be attractive to inward investment because of their well-established arts and cultural facilities. (2010: 139)

Beneath Throsby's appealingly balanced vision of the creative city lies a dynamic debate. When Richard Florida reversed the accepted economic development strategies employed by countless governments and councils throughout the developed world, he insisted that city growth strategy can be based on 'building a community that is attractive to creative people' (2002: 283). Variations on that approach have been developed by Charles Landry (2000), who champions policy interventions by providing 'toolkits for urban innovators' that give municipal authorities reason to consider a hitherto hidden or neglected resource. This burgeoning 'industry', in its rush to advise almost any prospective city, no matter how unprepossessing, is such that 'the Creative City idea has now become a catch-all phrase in danger of losing its meaning' (Wikipedia, 'Creative city').

This approach contrasts with the production-centric accounts of writers such as Sassen (1994), Scott (2000, 2005), Storper and Scott (2009) and Curtin (2007), who seek to account for the effects of **globalisation** on creative production in cities. Scott asserts that the 'origins of urban development and growth in modern society reside, above all, in the dynamics of economic production and work' (2006b: 2). Refuting consumption-centric claims, Storper and Scott warn that 'Recourse to amenities-based theories as a guiding principle for urban growth policy is ill-advised because their theories manifestly fail to address the basic issues of building, sustaining and transforming regional ensembles of production activities and their attendant local labor markets' (Storper and Scott 2009: 164).

The production-centric school of thought has made an important contribution to our understanding of the dynamics of global cultural flows, and it currently dominates the academic literature. But it cannot be the last word on the matter, as consumption-centric accounts play a key role for smaller or non-metropolitan cities; the ones that are catered for by consultants such as Florida, Landry and Montgomery. In addition, there are new attempts to reconcile the differences, with 'cultural city audits'[2] and 'creative city indexes' (Hartley et al. 2012) that combine production and consumption elements in assessing creative places. Creative cities develop in complex, organic ways. Despite this, and despite the dangers of template-driven, or 'cookie-cutter', approaches (Oakley 2004; Gibson and Kong 2005), cities the world over go on promoting place competitiveness through strategies, policies and programmes.

One such city is Beijing. This is no municipal council boosterism. This is nation-statecraft at its most purposeful. The intent of the Chinese authorities is for Beijing to become nothing less than a global 'media capital' as well as the political capital of an emerging superpower. For Michael Curtin (2007), there are three essential elements for a media capital: industrial infrastructure driven by the logic of accumulation; human capital driven by trajectories of creative migration; and a successful management of the forces of socio-cultural variation. In a context where entrepreneurial Shanghai and global Hong Kong display the 'forces of socio-cultural variation' (2007: 23) more readily than the political capital, the development of Beijing as a media capital is hampered, even as industrial infrastructure and creative migration are proceeding apace. Despite state-sponsored investment in Beijing as a creative capital, there are also considerable obstacles to be overcome if it is to be successful.

Seoul is the most wired mega-city in the world, with around 80 per cent of the population having broadband and personal computers. Superfast broadband and digital saturation are everyday affordances. Online, Seoul netizens are globally

---

[2]See www.worldcitiesculturalaudit.com/

connected but come together in highly communal, locationally specific *bangs* (ubiquitous communal online social spaces). Storper and Scott's 'large-scale agglomeration' occurs in games and film, national-cultural assertion is strong, but also the new conditions of 'produsage' (production–consumption blurring) are played out through massive social investment in user-generated content and Web 2.0, a hyperactive blogosphere (Ohmynews), massive multiplayer online games (MMOG) (Choi 2010). This is all mediated by the Korean language which is bound to act as a locative moderator of global-local flows. Seoul offers a large-scale prospect of overcoming the production–consumption divide.

It would be hard to think of a greater contrast to Peter Hall's examples of culturally creative cities than Lagos. Lagos is projected to be the fastest growing city in the world, exploding from 288,000 in 1950 to 14 million in 2009, to 23 million by 2015. Lagos is one of the most chaotic, least planned mega-cities, and yet out of it has grown the newest major film industry in the world: Nollywood. Evolving out of an informal economic base reliant on pirate networks that have gone commercial, with absolutely no state subsidy or other support mechanisms, Nigerian video is low-tech, low production quality, high-volume filmmaking servicing mostly the urban poor. If we can think of innovation in this way, Nollywood's achievements, in the words of Ramon Lobato, make Lagos 'the innovation capital of the world' (Lobato 2010: 337).

Creative cities ideas have given rise to the widespread perception that the prototypical creative city is represented by inner urban milieux – dynamic, bohemian, innovative and ultramodern – while that which exists outside, particularly the outer suburbs of large cities and smaller towns in predominantly rural landscapes, are dull, static, and culturally backward. The case of Aotearoa New Zealand makes this perception difficult to sustain. The successes of filmmakers such as Peter Jackson; the best practice screen infrastructure he has built in Wellington through his company WETA; design-led innovation into manufacturing and tourism; leading strategies for cultural and eco-tourism – these are all examples of world-class creativity on a very small national population base (4.3 million), with only three cities of any size. In stark contrast to Florida's vision of a highly mobile, footloose creative class based on the strength of weak ties, New Zealand is experienced – at least by those reported by Smith (2010) – as a 'giant creative village, in which social connectedness, trust and a sense of belonging form an ideal framework for creativity to flourish'.

Creative Class

While it may appear that the concept of the 'creative class' appeared full-blown in Richard Florida's influential *The Rise of the Creative Class* (2002), it has a much longer lineage. Richard Barbrook (2006) has identified 78 separate concepts, from Adam Smith's 'philosophers' in *The Wealth of Nations* in 1776 through to Leadbeater and Miller's 'pro-ams' in 2004, which claim to be describing a new class of labour or leader that typifies the present or heralds the future. This includes the most famous class analysts, Marx and Engels, as well as Weber's bureaucrats, Taylor's scientific managers, the Fordist worker, Schumpeter's entrepreneurs, Wright Mills' power elite, and Whyte's organisation man. That takes us about up to the 1950s.

Then there was a wave of concepts focused on grasping the implications of postindustrial society. Peter Drucker's (1959) 'knowledge workers' and Daniel Bell's (1973) 'knowledge class' have proven most resilient, while Barbrook has found an early glimpse of the blurring of production and consumption in the 1969 use of the term 'produsumers' (taken up later as prosumer or produser – see **co-creation**). The contemporary period has given us a plethora of terms for the knowledge-intensive economy and virtualism: symbolic analysts, netizens, digerati, immaterial labourers, new independents, the cognitariat. What is especially fascinating is that Barbrook splits his list of concepts into the new ruling class, the new working class and the new intermediate class. Florida's creative class turns up in all three lists. Florida is putting his concept forward to explain new leadership, the everyday workforce and those who link between classes, all at once. What exactly *is* the creative class?

Florida distinguishes between a 'Super-Creative Core' and the 'creative professionals'. Those in the Super-Creative Core are responsible for 'the highest order of creative work' (2002: 69); this group includes creative producers and designers, and IT entrepreneurs. Creative professionals comprise a much larger group and are essentially coterminous with knowledge-intensive workers (high tech, finance, legal, healthcare, business management and academic researchers). Florida estimated that together these two components of the creative class made up about one-third of the US workforce and produced half of the nation's wealth.

Using detailed data on the geographic disposition of standard occupation codes (SOCs) in the United States, Florida asked where there is a greater occurrence of such a creative class. To explain such differences, he used data from a variety of other official sources (for example, where patents are held, the qualifications held by a city's workforce, and the qualities of diversity in a city's population). He found that higher concentrations of the creative class correlated with three crucial factors: *technology, talent and tolerance* – the 'three Ts'.

Florida neatly reversed the usual economic booster strategies employed by governments and councils throughout the developed world. Instead of inward investment to build industrial-scale production infrastructure and capacity, he has famously promoted the idea that city growth strategy can be based on 'building a community that is attractive to creative people' (Florida 2002: 283). The 'creative class', by virtue of their lifestyle-based locational choices, drive city renewal and growth. The argument is that 'places with a flourishing artistic and cultural environment are the ones that generate economic outcomes and overall economic growth' (Florida 2002: 261) not because of the economic muscle of the cultural/creative industries but because of their high-tech workers' pulling power. The worker does not follow the industry; industry follows the worker.

Florida's work has attracted strong and sustained criticism. But it is undeniable that his focus on creative occupation counterbalances the usual dependence simply on industry statistics in regional development debates. His insistence on 'creative' capital rather than the more generic 'human' capital has focused attention on the creative worker in mainstream policy debate in ways no other contributions have. The generic argument is made by Charles Landry (2000) that cities have one crucial resource, people, and that human creativity 'is replacing location, natural resources and market access as the principal key to urban dynamics' (quoted in Throsby 2010: 139). But Florida insisted that generic human capital was too imprecise a category to capture his understanding of 'urban dynamics' and instead has put the creative class centre stage (Florida 2005: 6). Florida and other urban consultants champion policy interventions that give municipal authorities reason to consider a hitherto hidden or neglected resource. This has, at the very least, democratised and diversified the creative cities 'discourse' to the extent that it is no longer the exclusive preserve of the historical pantheon of global cities like London, New York and Paris. Also, Florida's politics are clear. He warns that, post 9/11, the USA runs the risk of seeing a flight of its most precious asset and wealth-creating engine and the loss of inward migration of new members of the creative class because of its punitive, restrictive and biased war on terror (Florida 2006). Having said this, it remains the case that important academic commentary runs against Florida. It is often argued that the definition of the creative class is far too broad at one-third of the US workforce to allow it to work as anything more (or less) than the consumption and lifestyle choices of the urban middle classes.

There is a way to account for the creative workforce that is far wider than simply those who work in the **creative industries** (see **creative economy**), but still based on a defined set of creative occupations rather than dissolving that specificity into a formula such as 'anyone with a degree who works in knowledge-based services'. That lack of specificity is reinforced with Florida's concluding acknowledgement in *Rise* that the creative class lacks 'class consciousness'. While he calls for such consciousness to allow those so designated to assume their role as leaders of the future networked society, it is hard to imagine class solidarity when the bohemian artist is being pushed out of her urban loft by the gentrifying tastes of bankers and lawyers and the other much better paid 'creative' professionals. The width of Florida's definition of the class has added to confusion over who are the winners and losers in what Storper and Scott (2009) call *amenities-based* models of urban growth. Such a model can displace policies aimed at the creative *workforce* and its sustainability through production-oriented initiatives (Cunningham 2011). The consumption-oriented focus on discretionary expenditure by the creative class favours white-collar professionals rather than artistic bohemians and risk-taking entrepreneurs. While it might appear that Florida is explaining the role of creative industries in economic growth, actually he is telling us something about what creatives do at leisure, but not what they do at work.

Florida's focus on tolerance among the three Ts (talent, technology, tolerance: 2005: 7) allows him to embed progressive politics in his research. But it has proven difficult to sustain analytically. The lack of causal or even a strong correlation between cultural diversity/openness and economic growth has led Florida and his team to step away from a strong adherence to tolerance as a driver (Storper and Scott 2009: 165). Some thought that Florida's 'tolerance' was stereotyped and did not extend to those who could not participate in his vision of inner-urban, modish, bike-riding connoisseurs of nightclubs and restaurants, the night-time economy and funky urban street life (Oakley 2004; McRobbie 2005).

On the more central policy question of whether cities can reinvigorate themselves and become economic powerhouses through investments to support cultural consumption by urban professionals, the evidence is equivocal, and the picture is muddied significantly by a propensity to conflate evidence that city governments have adopted 'creative class' strategies with evidence that they have worked as a form of urban economic policy (Peck 2005). Evans (2009) has questioned the focus in such accounts on cultural consumption rather than cultural production networks, arguing that consumption-led strategies will always be dependent upon public subsidy of middle class lifestyles. Storper and Scott (2009) have criticised the neglect in what they term 'amenities-led' models of urban development of endogenous growth factors that lead some cities to become creative hubs, and the difficulties of transferring these factors from one city to another. Finally, the focus on inner cities as hubs of creative talent in major cities neglects the extent to which a growing proportion of the creative workforce in major cities, like the workforce generally, is located in suburbs rather than inner cities (Collis et al. 2010). Even in the much-discussed case of New York, there has been an accelerated suburbanisation that will need different analytical tools for its relationship to creative industries to be properly understood (Hammett and Hammett 2007).

Nevertheless, the impact of Florida's creative class thesis on urban policy in the 2000s was substantial and cannot be gainsaid. Peck observed that 'in the field of urban policy, which has hardly been cluttered with new and innovative ideas lately, creativity strategies have quickly become the policies of choice, since they license both a discursively distinctive and an ostensibly deliverable development agenda' (2005: 740). By commencing this entry with a litany of previous claims that have been made about new classes and new configurations of labour, it may look as if we are intent on diminishing the newness of Florida's 'class of the new'. It could be read differently – that, shorn of the proselytising zeal, Florida's work is enhanced by being placed in a strong lineage of identification of the emergent forces shaping labour and market power. The lineage, after all, is populated by some of the major names of Western intellectual life, and many of their 'identifications' have been prescient and vindicated. Contemporaneously, it sits in the tradition of searching for an adequate empirical base to investigate broad claims about the 'culturisation' of the economy (see **creative economy**). Moreover, it is consistent with, and indeed generative of, much business and management debate in terms of recruiting and managing knowledge workers today (Thrift 2002: 201).

More sober accounts of **creative labour** acknowledge that much of the early creative industries discourse bought into such boosterism unreflectingly; but at the same time that it is necessary to deal with significant changes in labour markets and relations. If Florida's indexes, correlations and causal propositions have been debunked, the message is that we must work out better ones. If Florida's lumping together bohemian and banker reduces the specificity of each, we must analyse the relations between creative and knowledge sectors (see **creative economy** and **information economy**), rather than collapse them. If the notion of a creative class that has no 'class consciousness' contradicts such a central analytical category, we must consider how the creative workforce and its interests and contribution should better be represented – to itself, to power, and to contemporary society.

Perhaps the greatest challenge to claims about the creative class lies in its being hollowed out from its 'creative core'. The deep financial crisis confronting especially the West since 2008 has generated claims that the creative class is a 'lie' (Timberg 2011), based on the difficulties faced by workers in threatened industries like writing and publishing, journalism and video retailing. Florida's (2011) answer, pointing to steep rises for other members of the creative class, reminds us of the continuing empirical as well as theoretical and policy challenges the concept embodies.

Creative Destruction

Creative destruction is a term that fascinates because it seems to be an oxymoron – a term that clashes opposites together. It is a 'key concept' because of the extraordinary levels of change occurring in the media and in cultural production and consumption, and because of the opportunities as well as downsides of these changes. The idea of the creative industries is tied to notions of change and transformation. Creative destruction is central here, as it goes to the question of what drives economic and social change in capitalist societies, and where such mechanisms are taking us.

According to Wikipedia, 'creative destruction' is 'a term originally derived from Marxist economic theory which refers to the linked processes of the accumulation and annihilation of wealth under capitalism'. The idea is powerful because it insists that 'accumulation' (progress, greater good for the greater number, etc.) and 'annihilation' (business failure, environmental degradation, etc.) are mutually constitutive forces. It thus has conceptual roots in Hegelian dialectical thought and even, perhaps, in Hinduism, where the god Shiva is imaged as simultaneously destroyer and creator, as well as in other mythical creator-destroyers, from ancient Greece (Hermes) to native America (Coyote) (Hartley 2012a: 199–214). But its major protagonists were Marx and Engels, who analyse capitalism as in continual crisis:

'In these crises, a great part not only of existing production, but also of previously created productive forces, are periodically destroyed' (1848: 226). The Marxian tradition has continued in the work of such contemporary writers as David Harvey, Marshall Berman and Manuel Castells. Harvey, a geographer, stresses the way in which capitalism attempts to resolve its crises through a 'spatial fix' (2001: 284–311), constantly seeking out new markets, extending its reach and constantly ramping up the rate of innovation, which in this account only means the acceleration of the rate of destruction of established market value and the social values that went along with it.

A fork in the road of capitalist critique, however, occurred with the work of Austrian economist Joseph Schumpeter, with whom the term creative destruction has become virtually synonymous. While often accused of being a stalking horse for neoliberalism, Schumpeter rewards closer attention. Schumpeter (1942) contains a sustained appreciation of Marx and one of the most searching systemic critiques of capitalism ever penned by one of its strongest defenders. Now all of this might have been an elaborate game play, an extended exercise in irony, as his biographer McCraw (2007) argues, but this doesn't invalidate the sense that Schumpeter is enjoining on us the similarities of his critique to that of Marx as much as its differences.

For Schumpeter, capitalism grows the seeds of its own downfall. But the seeds are not grown from its failure – the increasing 'immiseration' of the masses (Wikipedia: 'Immiseration thesis'); decreasing returns to scale – but from its success. Capitalism has delivered remarkable growth in the standard of living of working people, but the capitalist 'engine' drives incessant 'gales of creative destruction' – a metaphor uncannily like Marx's 'all that is solid melts into air' (Marx and Engels 1848). Over time, the culture that long-run capitalism breeds becomes inimical to it. Rationalisation and the erosion of bourgeois spiritual and moral values that gave capitalism its impetus, cost-benefit calculation made the benchmark of all manner of human transaction, the abstraction of stock market rather than real property relations, the routinisation of innovation: it sounds like Marx 100 years on.

Schumpeter's critique offers a radical understanding of the revolutionary dynamism, inherent contradictions and fragility of the capitalist engine without succumbing to teleological closure, or prophesying the future. It is arguable that recognising the 'engine's' fragility assists fundamentally in securing an ongoing role for the state and for government policymaking. Even market-liberal Schumpeter himself accepted such a role, especially the wake of capitalism's near-death experience, the Great Depression, in the 1930s. This perspective can help to analyse the 'culturisation of everyday life' (Lash and Urry 1994) and its implications for creative industries policy, including the breakdown of business models that have served industries like music, film, and publishing, for decades. It can help us beyond the depressing predicament of much debate based on exaggerated oppositionalism: overly enthusiastic optimism versus determined pessimism about the potential of new technologies; fundamental crisis in the longer-term viability of these industries versus the inevitability that hegemonic capital will always triumph.

Instead, we can ask a range of questions which are subject to empirical confirmation or refutation: what are the models? What are the alternative models? What have been their histories and successes/failures? At what *rate* is 'creative destruction' occurring? What are the different impacts in different sectors? The role of policy can then be understood as responding to the place of cultural activity in its wider economic context.

Schumpeter helps us to break down the black box approach to capitalism that cultural and media studies have inherited from cultural Marxism. He insisted on distinguishing monopoly (bad) and big business (not necessarily bad and historically a very efficient driver of improvements in the lot of common people). He placed enormous stress on individual human agency in large-scale economic and social change. He focused on the **entrepreneur** as critical to the emergent process of coordination of resources. He resolutely criticised (neoclassical) equilibrium economics and its impossibly rational subject. His insistence on the centrality of access to finance to keep entrepreneurialism alive is particularly apposite for the creative industries, as they routinely find it difficult to convince financiers of the worth of their plans and assets (although the *Dragon's Den* genre of reality television demonstrates that financiers' caution may well be justified).

The concept of creative destruction has been brought back into creative industries debate through the need to account for the extraordinary levels of change occurring now in the media and in cultural production and consumption. We see similar concepts at work in major cultural thinkers. Raymond Williams' typology of 'residual, dominant, and emergent' culture (1958, 1977: 121–7) emphasises that culture has a dynamic, contradictory and uneven topography. Williams set himself against much structuralist cultural analysis with its homogenising 'spirit of the age' approach, for example in the work of Georg Lukács and Lucien Goldmann. At any given moment, the dominant, or official, mode may have displaced and rendered marginal a residual mode while at the same time being challenged by an emergent one (Potts and Cunningham 2008).

Tyler Cowen (2002) has written a book on creative destruction. A controversial cultural economist who promotes the benefits of free markets, Cowen takes on the 'globalisation = cultural homogenisation' thesis – the idea that globalisation means the destruction of cultural diversity. He argues that cross-cultural exchange tends to favour diversity *within* a society but not diversity *across* societies. Cultural homogenisation and heterogenisation tend to converge over time. And, while globalisation disrupts and may destroy cultural particularity, it also produces innovation, growth and new horizons. Additionally, cultural globalisation is uneven across sectors: Hollywood cinema dominates the world; US television is globally prominent not dominant; stateside print-bestsellers rarely so. Cowen may be criticised for being too relaxed about **globalisation** and the creative destruction it wreaks, but he offers interesting analytical and methodological applications of the concept, he discusses different types of creative destruction, and assesses how much of the 'destruction' that goes on in contemporary capitalist cultural enterprise is actually 'creative'.

McKnight et al. (2001: 4–5) differentiate among four relevant types of creative destruction:

- Traditional *industry structures* (through, for example, lowered entry barriers);
- Traditional *regulatory approaches* (which work less well when internet-based businesses can move out of particular jurisdictions);
- Traditional *competitive positioning strategies* (it is much more difficult to protect industry when it is all digital); and
- *Technological assumptions* (for example, there is much more piracy with fast broadband).

Federal Trade Commission chairman Jon Leibowitz (2009) asks how journalism will survive the internet age: is it undergoing 'creative' destruction or just the 'plain' variety? His answer is the latter because, while the public's demand for the sort of information vital to democracy remains unabated, the business model on which news is delivered has broken down. Sellers of content that is a core public good can't be paid enough to remain in business. There is a fundamental market failure. However, the standard answer to 'market failure' – for government to step in – is problematic because this would compromise the independence of the 'fourth estate'. Whether Leibowitz is right remains to be seen, but clearly the market has not failed to experiment with new models of online journalism, so perhaps his pessimism was premature.

Economist Christian Handke (2006a) proposes a test for telling the difference between creative and plain destruction, in an analysis of copyright erosion in the music industry. Handke is neither an apologist for the industry nor a starry-eyed copyleftist, but he shows empirically that there has been an extraordinarily high number of market entries by small record companies during a severe recession in the German recorded music market. Thus he finds that creative destruction is at work, and one of the consequences of this is that 'isolated attempts to reinforce copyright protection could be misguided. They should be complemented by efforts to promote innovation within the record industry' (Handke 2006a: 29).

Another variant, *self*-destruction, is exemplified in the record industry's series of responses to the threat posed by digital filesharing. In an exhaustive history (and admittedly from hindsight) Steve Knopper (2009) paints a picture of systematically bad decisions by the industry that only made their plight worse. From the point of view of researchable issues in the creative industries, you could not choose a more interesting and relevant field than this: what have main media industries learnt from what Knopper calls the record industry's 'appetite for self-destruction'?

You can see from these examples that there is great scope for analysis of contemporary culture using the concept of creative destruction. It is supple enough to allow for both optimism and pessimism about the changes being wrought by digitisation, **globalisation**, **convergence** and the upsurge of social media. But more important, as we saw with Raymond Williams' conflict-generated cultural dynamism and Tyler Cowen's careful ripostes to big picture theories such as globalisation, it enjoins on us an empirical approach that tracks actual change in its complexity and open-endedness.

Bringing together Schumpeter and Williams (Hartley 2008b), it may be that, if you're at the innovative edge – the emergent-becoming-dominant – you might take the optimistic view, focusing on *opportunities* in creative destruction. That is certainly the emphasis of Schumpeterian analyses of the role of the **entrepreneur**. If you are stuck in the dominant-becoming-residual, you may lament that so much is being lost in the process. For those looking in on a process that may not directly impact them, it may be that the **evolutionary** view prevails – that this is just the way capitalism works. But from the point of those on the political left, it is axiomatic that global capital should be 'civilised' through public policy, to ameliorate social dislocation while also smoothing out the ups and downs of business cycles.

Creative Economy

It is important to understand the basic distinction between **creative industries** and creative economy. The concept of creative industries first emerged in the late 1990s as a model of post-industrial development coupled with urban regeneration. The principal conceptual preoccupations of this first 'wave' of creative industries thinking were to map this newly defined industrial sector in respect of its contribution to jobs and economic value-add, and to set policy directions accordingly. These early, baseline considerations did not seek to account for spillover effects and contributions to other sectors, or to consumption patterns and innovation processes in the wider economy. It was only when analysts began to consider the contribution of creativity to the economy as a whole that the idea of a 'creative economy' emerged, vying with other attempts to rethink the entire economic system such as the 'knowledge economy.' The incoherence of the original definition of 'creative industries' left the boundaries of the category fluid and therefore what was 'in' or 'out' remained contestable, and its relation to neighbouring sectors undecided.

In particular, there was legitimate concern over the promiscuous insertion of a broad definition of software in the original characterisation of the sector (Hesmondhalgh and Pratt 2005: 8). Critics argued that this was done in order to boost its size; it could also be said that it was a function of the outdated standard industry classifications (SIC) codes by which industry sectors perforce were classified. One of the enduring controversies in the field is precisely one of 'boundaries': the extent to which creative industries is beholden to the 'prestige' of information and communications technology (ICT) and thus conflates cultural and information sectors (Garnham 2005). This, in part, can be addressed by empirically testing the interdependence between creative industries and ICT-intensive services, as Chapain et al. do (2010). Another study (Oakley et al. 2008) shows that those trained in what David Throsby (2001) would call the creative core (i.e. the traditional arts) have tended to remain in the arts or 'spilled' into the creative industries, but have tended not to make careers in the wider economy. Detailed statistical mapping work shows that there is more creative employment outside the creative industries than inside them. This raises the issue of creative employment in the general labour markets. Recent research has drawn attention to creative industries value chains and the varied geographical distribution of creative industries. Thus, the concept of **creative clusters** also fits into the general category of spillovers.

While sector-specific issues have not been neglected, there has been quite rapid evolution of policy-makers' interests and a broadening of the remit of government attention to creativity and the wider economy. In the UK, various reviews, white papers and restructures morphed the original 'creative industries' idea into a broader *Creative Economy Programme*.[1] This focused on higher growth businesses, the nature and value of creative inputs into the broader economy, a broader promotion of 'creative careers', and clearer differentiations of economic and cultural goals. The *Cox Review* (2006) recommended a series of measures to refocus, including creativity and innovation 'centres of excellence' in all regions. The *Gowers Review* (2006) and *Hargreaves Review* (2011)[2] both examined intellectual property (IP) law and its impact on how business and society can deal with the tension between, on the one hand, stronger digital rights management and technical protection measures to guard IP against easier ways of accessing and using digital content and, on the other hand, the public-interest value of promoting better access to and sharing – or 'spillover' – of knowledge.

Recent research has shown that spillovers can take the form of knowledge, product and network spillovers (Chapain et al. 2010). Knowledge spillovers, which include flexible, collaborative models of work organisation developed for highly dynamic competitive environments, can influence sectors that engage with the creative industries. Research in Britain has shown that firms that spend double the average on creative industries inputs are 25 per cent more likely to introduce products or services which are new to the firm or market (Chapain et al. 2010: 24). Soon, we will focus on arguably the major supply-side spillover; that is, the supply of creative professionals into the broader economy.

There are also demand-driven knowledge spillovers. Often creative industries, particularly those at the cutting-edge of digital applications such as high-end games, computer graphics and other special effects, and telepresence, demand new and rapid advances in technology which stimulate innovation on the supply side. Innovation studies in Britain have shown that sectors such as advertising, architecture and creative software have high levels of user innovation which may spill over to their suppliers (Chapain et al. 2010: 25).

Product spillovers are a well-known feature of the creative industries (Gray 2010a) – they include so-called ancillary markets for mass entertainment (toys, clothing and household items themed on Hollywood blockbusters) and the ubiquity of music online has made access devices such as MP3 players equally ubiquitous consumer 'must-haves'. Network spillovers can take the form of the presence of a 'creative milieu' (the presence of significant numbers of creative businesses, people and activities) influencing tourism, property values or specialist retail (for example, café society).

---

[1] See www.cep.culture.gov.uk
[2] Gowers: www.official-documents.gov.uk/document/other/0118404830/0118404830. asp; Hargreaves: www.ipo.gov.uk/ipreview.htm

The creative economy can be approached through the concept of the 'creative workforce' (see Cunningham 2011; and see **creative labour**). This can be understood as the total of creative occupations within the core creative industries (specialists), plus the creative occupations employed in other industries, for example designers or media producers working for mining companies or government departments (embedded), plus the business and administrative occupations employed in creative industries that are often responsible for managing, accounting for, and technically supporting creative activity (support). The addition of 'embedded' and 'support' occupations greatly expands the scale of the overall creative workforce in the economy as a whole.

This approach shares some similarities with Richard Florida's (see **creative class**). Florida corralled all white-collar and 'no-collar' workers into the definition of the creative class, even as he helpfully highlighted the importance of studying those in creative occupations in their own right, rather than focusing narrowly on the industries in which they work. The creative workforce approach is a much more constrained categorisation of the numbers of the labour force who can be considered 'creative' creative workforce, while also being much broader than traditional arts and culture. The key finding from this approach is that there are more ('embedded') creatives working outside the creative industries than inside. If we are to understand the creative economy, it is just as important to study the embedded workforce as the specialist one.

These perspectives have been given additional conceptual depth through a school of contemporary thought that seeks radically to collapse the relations between culture and the economy. The concept of the 'culturisation of the economy' has been developed by Scott Lash and John Urry. This idea distinguishes between the 'industrialisation of culture' (Adorno and Horkheimer's original dystopian version of the **culture industry**) and the more contemporary 'culturisation' of industry. 'Ordinary manufacturing industry is becoming more and more like the production of culture' (Lash and Urry 1994: 123). Their 'culturisation' thesis sees not only standard cultural products and services growing as a proportion of the whole economy (as we have seen, that was the starting point for whole idea of creative industries) but also cultural ideas, processes and dispositions being recognised and adopted in non-cultural products and services such as mobile phones, clothes, education (games-based learning), retail precincts (malls as entertainment venues), and so on. This is consistent with the emphasis placed earlier on the 'creative workforce' in the wider economy, as these economic domains need creatively trained people to inform the culturisation process.

John Howkins pushes such claims further with his take on the management of creativity, or 'the economics of the imagination' (2001). Howkins' approach has been influential internationally, especially in China and through his association with the United Nations Conference on Trade and Development (UNCTAD 2008/2010, and see **internationalisation**). He lists creative people's special personality traits, creative entrepreneurship (which unlocks the wealth that lies in human capital), the post-employment job (portfolio career), the just-in-time company and the temporary company, and the network office. In itemising these characteristics, he reinforces Lash and Urry's point that contemporary forms of corporate and enterprise organisation have derived much from cultural or creative business practices. This has also been observed by Ruth Towse (2010), who argues that typical features of artistic labour markets – casualisation, self-employment, the project-based company – are becoming more widespread in the economy as a whole. Chris Bilton (2010) provides a more sceptical, historical and cautious view, arguing from a management viewpoint that the 'heroic', disruptive model of creativity is being replaced with a 'structural' model in which creativity is eminently manageable, thereby running the risk of minimising the unpredictability of creative processes.

Perhaps the outstanding example of the culturisation thesis for business practice is Hollywood. It consolidated by reproducing the dominant Fordist mode of production of its day (from the 1910s) but survived and thrived in the post-war era by pioneering particular post-Fordist production modes – such as the 'package-unit system' (Bordwell et al. 1985), the 'just-in-time' company (Howkins 2001) and complex contingency contracting (Caves 2000) – that have been widely adopted as prototypical and in turn produced major spillover effects for the wider economy. Such business model spillovers have carried through to the present and to everyday, including small business, activity.

While Howkins devotes much of his business analysis to creative industries actors and scenarios, his inclusion of 'science and technology' and 'general software' in the definition of **creative industries** (15 sectors rather than the original 13), and his emphasis on creativity as generic to all humans, makes his notion of the creative economy almost the equivalent of the knowledge-intensive economy. In that sense, his account has similarities to that of Richard Florida (see **creative class**).

The 'cultural economy' school of thought (e.g. Du Gay and Pryke 2002) shows that big concepts such as culture, economy and the social are never stable categories – what counts for them changes over time and therefore their relationships must be established on a case basis, not assumed. But this is not simply another variant of constructivism, seeking to reduce one large category (the economy) to another (culture, or the social). Such constructivism, say the editors of the *Journal of Cultural Economy*, 'yields vanishingly little in the way of understanding how [economies] work' (Bennett et al. 2008: 2). Instead, this school draws on a range of humanities and social science disciplines to analyse the history, emergence and operation of markets, which are assemblages of social, cultural, and technical knowledge and practices.

Creative Industries

The term 'creative industries' was first given policy and industry prominence through initiatives taken from 1997 by the new UK Labour government through minister Chris Smith (1998) and the Department for Culture, Media and Sport (DCMS). A Creative Industries Taskforce published the *Creative Industries Mapping Document* (1998, revised edition 2001). This established a foundational definition: the creative industries are 'those industries which have their origin in individual creativity, skill and talent which have a potential for job and wealth creation through the generation and exploitation of intellectual property' (DCMS 1998: 3). The DCMS definition included 13 industry sectors: advertising, architecture, art and antiques, computer games/leisure software, crafts, design, designer fashion, film and video, music, performing arts, publishing, software, television and radio.

This foundational demarcation of the field has proven resilient, even while attracting great controversy. Above all, it has proven a useful concept. First, it is valuable because it mainstreams the economic value of culture, media and design. It does this through recognising that creativity is a critical input into contemporary economies that demonstrate features of 'culturisation' (Lash and Urry 1994; Du Gay and Pryke 2002), digitisation and highly designed goods and services. While these claims have been criticised (e.g. Dyson 2010) for buying in too fashionably to new economy thinking and its promotion of intangibles, 'weightlessness' (Coyle 1997), and of 'living on thin air' (Leadbeater 1999), the outputs of creative industries were always a mix of high value-added services and manufactured goods.

Second, it brings together in a provisional **convergence** a range of sectors which have not typically been linked with each other. This has been the source of much criticism – the idea that such co-location was driven by the tendentious need to make Britain look a world leader in a field it had defined for and by itself. Nevertheless, it has been the basis on which fundamental claims were made – that the creative sector was far larger than previously thought, and that it was growing at a rate significantly higher than that of national economies generally. Third, the sectors within creative industries – the **creative arts** (visual and performing arts, dance, theatre etc.); the established media (broadcasting, film, television, radio, music); new media (software, games, e-commerce and e-content) together with architecture and design – move from the resolutely non-commercial to the high-tech and commercial. This continuum moves from the culturally specific non-commercial to the globalised and commercial, where generically creative, rather than culturally specific, content drives advances.

This continuum is less coherent than the neat definitions for the arts, media and cultural industries that organise thinking and policy in the field, but it arguably takes into greater account the profound changes wrought by digitisation, convergence and globalisation than these more traditional categories. One of the reasons the idea of creative industries has been taken up so widely is that it connects two key contemporary policy clusters: on the one hand, high-growth information and communications technologies and research and development (R&D)-based sectors (*production*); and on the other, the 'experience' economy, cultural identity and social empowerment (*consumption*).

As would be expected, much research and debate in the ensuing decade and more has been concerned with developing policies and programmes to support the sectors identified as belonging to the creative industries. But there has also been much debate about the coherence of what constitutes the creative industries, as might be expected of a term that was a policy intervention, rather than a rigorously researched academic category. There are thus many attempts to refine, clarify and improve understanding of the sectors in, and boundaries of, the creative industries. For example, the UK National Endowment for Science, Technology and the Arts (NESTA 2006: 55) has proposed four overlapping sub-groupings (but see Hartley 2009: 56–8), based on the various business models employed:

- *Originals* (e.g. fine art) trades on the production of scarce one-offs;
- *Content* is the opposite, creating mass media as widely consumed as possible;
- *Services* such as advertising and architecture are business-to-business, not final consumption or retail; and
- *Experiences* attract people to typically live events (music festivals, theme parks, museums, art galleries).

Cultural economist David Throsby puts forward a 'concentric circles' model, in which the core are the creative arts (literature; music; performing arts; visual arts), because these are 'the locus of origin of creative ideas' (2001: 112). Outside the core are the 'cultural industries' (film, and museums and libraries), the wider cultural industries (heritage services, publishing, sound), and recording (television and radio, video and computer games) and finally related industries (advertising, architecture, design, fashion) based on the degree to which they mix 'pure' creativity with other inputs. The Work Foundation (2007) has produced a different model of concentric circles (but see Hartley 2009: 58–62). The centre comprises the 'core' creative fields including all forms of *original* product. Then there are those cultural industries which attempt to *commercialise* these creative products. Next are creative industries which have intrinsically *functional* applications (architecture, design, advertising). Finally, there are sectors selling an 'experience' that depends on creative inputs (which include theme parks, museums, art galleries). This model avoids the hierarchy implicit in Throsby's circles which, implausibly, suggest that the traditional arts are the principal engine generating the ideas that drive the wider creative industries. And there is indeed a literature defining creative industries as the 'experience economy' (Pine and Gilmore 1999; Andersson and Andersson 2006), which stresses the high degree of intangible value-adding that accompanies the consumption of creative products and services.

Justin O'Connor (2011: 92) conceptualises creative industries as comprising segmentation into 'art-media-design', integrating the original 13 sub-sectors. This dispenses with the topography of concentric circles. Each of these three segments is an industry sector, each mixes cultural and social value, and each deals with tensions between intrinsic and instrumental value. 'Art designates those activities/industries concerned primarily/exclusively with the creation of these expressive-symbolic values' (O'Connor 2011: 92). Media and design, which also create (and circulate widely) content with expressive-symbolic values, nevertheless 'have much more explicit social and political priorities, as design has social and material-functional priorities' (O'Connor 2011: 93). All three are industries, all produce artistic or aesthetic value, all mix cultural and social value, and all have messy, unresolved relations between intrinsic and instrumental (read economic) value, he says. They differ on degrees of functionality. The Dutch Ministry of Economic Affairs (MEA 2006) posits a broader variation on this tripartite model: there are the arts, media and entertainment, and creative business services.

There are, of course, conceptualisations that go beyond the industry-based or sectoral perspectives reviewed here (see **creative economy**). We would propose for consideration approaches that link creative industries to fundamental innovation processes in an evolving economy and thus can be contrasted with the foregoing classifications which are static (see, for instance, Hartley 2009, 2012a; Potts 2011; Flew 2012). How can an industrial sector devoted to media, fashion, craft, design, performing arts, advertising, architecture, heritage, music, film and television, games, publishing and interactive software possibly contribute to fundamental dynamics of economic growth? At first sight, it might seem from a mainstream business perspective, the creative industries are not progenitors of the standard causes of economic growth in developing new technology, in capital deepening, in operational efficiency, in business model innovation or in institutional evolution. Yet many of the people and businesses in this sector are actually intimately involved in all of these things. The creative industries are deeply engaged in the experimental use of new technologies, in developing new content and applications, and in creating new business models. They are broadly engaged in the coordination of new technologies to new lifestyles, new meanings and new ways of being, which in turn is the basis of new business opportunities. The creative industries are not seminal forces of material economic growth, but they are germinal in their role in coordinating the individual and social structure of novelty and in resetting the definition of the normal. The creative industries contribute to process of *adaptation to novelty* and the *facilitation of change*, which by definition underpin the process of economic evolution: they are 'social network markets' (Potts et al. 2008).

This approach is embedded in Potts and Cunningham's (2008) 'four models' of how the creative industries are disposed in relation to the rest of the economy. The first model is based on market failure (principally the publicly supported arts and cultural heritage) and justifies transfers to maintain the sectors' economic viability. The second recognises that many sectors of the creative industries (such as broadcasting, film and publishing) are well-established, mature business sectors – they are 'just another industry'. Their distinctive characteristics are addressed under established regulatory and market-competitive conditions. The third model, however, conceptualises the creative industries as significant not in themselves but as drivers of growth through supplying novelty (such as the need for design solutions) broadly across the economy. This calls for an investment model of policy response. The fourth, innovation, model suggests that the creative industries be seen as a part of the innovation system of the broader economy, originating and coordinating change in the knowledge base of the economy, as much on the demand as the supply side. Hartley (2009 Chapter 2) has reinforced and built on this attempt to grasp the dynamics of the role that the creative industries play in the economy with his schema of four phases (which may be co-present):

- *Creative clusters*: Industry definition; creative outputs; closed expert pipeline;
- *Creative services*: Economy definition; creative inputs; open expert system;
- *Creative citizens*: Culture definition; creative users; open innovation network;
- *Creative cities*: Complexity definition; creative emergence and innovation; self-organising adaptive systems (and clash of different systems).

There have been many criticisms of the concept of creative industries. Indeed, it has been what Cunningham calls a 'globally contestable policy field' (2009). O'Connor and Banks (2009) summarise these as: it promotes a simplistic narrative of the merging of culture and economics and represents incoherent policy; the data sources are suspect and underdeveloped; there is untoward celebration of the liberationist potential of 'creative' labour; and it is guilty of a benign globalist narrative of the adoption of the idea (see **creative labour**, **internationalisation** and **creative economy**).

For critics of the creative industries concept (e.g. Garnham 2005; T. Miller 2009; Oakley 2009; O'Connor 2011), it is seen as a kind of Trojan horse for 'market forces', undermining the case for public support for culture. It could, however, be viewed as opening up the hitherto ossified relation between economics and culture; a relationship no longer limited to questions of the arts and 'market failure' (cultural economics), or of rationales for cultural regulation. Instead, there is a focus on the role of media, culture and communications in generating change and growth in what Schumpeter called the capitalist 'engine'. Engaging with the heterodox school of evolutionary economics can, perhaps ironically, bring us back to many animating questions of our field (see **competition** and **entrepreneurship**): what are the genuine advances in the communications and media sectors (including **aesthetic** advances); how would we measure them; and what have been their impact? These are indeed questions of cultural value, from which the debates have rarely veered. Indeed, the appropriate relations between the economic and the cultural might be best traced as the **evolution** of cultural forms as social and industrial norms themselves evolve.

Creative Labour

Debate about the creative industries has often centred on the significance and contribution of its creative workers in driving innovation and wealth-creation throughout the wider economy. The debate about the significance of creative labour is not only about aggregate numbers of jobs; it also concerns the nature and characteristics of those jobs. The creative talent and capabilities fostered in these industries are argued to be crucial to the success of wider national performance. Creativity and innovation are vital for maintaining 'competitive advantage' in a global environment that sees manufacturing and services 'outsourced' to lower-wage economies. The creative human capital characterising creative workers might also offer avenues for mitigating the effects of 'technological unemployment and inequality', while exploring the potential of new technologies to grow the economy and generate broad-based cultural and social value (Brynjolfsson and McAfee 2011).

Terry Flew (2012) notes that values of autonomy, non-conformity and indeterminacy, which are often deemed to characterise creative processes, exist in tension with the industrial mode of organising the workforce (see also Bilton 2007). The challenge for the creative industries is how to align creative talent to organisational goals through the exercise of 'soft control' rather than exerting traditional managerial imperatives. Critics of labour relations in the creative sector point to corporate practices that manipulatively exploit creative workers' desire for experiences that are genuinely self-actualising; and they point out that in times of economic uncertainty such jobs are insecure or 'precarious'. Perhaps a more interesting possibility that needs investigation is that creative workers are balancing a mix of monetary and non-monetary rewards, including the risks and uncertainties associated with working in a volatile sector. While there are most certainly risks, creative careers can also offer significant cultural rewards, owing to the expressive and non-routine nature of creative work. At a certain level of competence they are often paid well, in part to compensate for the volatility and uncertainty.

While acknowledging the value of creative autonomy, however, critics such as Angela McRobbie (2005) and Andrew Ross (2009) question the individualisation associated with creative workforce identities. McRobbie, for example, argues that labour 'flexibility' is actually capital finding 'novel ways of offloading its responsibility for a workforce'. But at the same time it is also a force for 'self-actualisation, even freedom and independence' (2005: 376). She carefully foregrounds both the opportunities and risks associated with these forms of 'cultural entrepreneurialisation'. Andrew Ross (2009) observes that the policy agendas associated with the creative industries often conveniently overlook altogether working conditions in the sector. Here the category of labour is used by Ross to mount a classic political economy critique of the creative industries. He argues that the push for flexibility in labour markets is driven by capital-owners seeking 'lavish returns from low-end casualisation – subcontracting, outsourcing, and other modes of "flexploitation" – and increasingly expect the same in higher-skill sectors of the economy' (2009: 4). He observes that the idea of work flexibility as a source of autonomy and self-fulfilment is a 'perversion of the original vision of an existence freed from work-life alienation' (2009: 5). These 'precarious employment' conditions, for Ross, while offering an alternative to the 'tedium of stable employment in a large, hierarchical organisation', are also characterised by workers who:

subsist, neither as employers nor traditional employees, in a limbo of uncertainty, juggling their options, massaging their contacts, managing their overcommitted time, and developing coping strategies for handling the uncertainty of never knowing where their next project, or source of income is coming from. (2009: 5)

The critique of precarious labour can become so general and all-encompassing as to lose analytic purchase on the changing conditions of labour that it seeks to understand. Generalising the precarious conditions and experience of marginalised workers such as cleaners and domestic labourers to the status of a common cause with creative cultural workers and professionals is deeply problematic. As Hesmondhalgh comments, 'too many different kinds of work are being lumped together in the same category … [and] this may well undermine the coherence of the critique being presented' (2007: 62). Rather than making an effort to understand labour trends, the goal of critique seems pre-emptively to judge how capital is, yet again, exploiting the surplus value of labour. Such analysis yields no new information.

This problem is especially apparent when Ross applies the precarious labour critique to the 'free labour' that makes user-generated content. He argues that through platforms such as YouTube, Flickr and Twitter, 'the burden of productive waged labour is increasingly transferred to users or consumers' (2009: 22) and asks us to consider what happens to the labour conditions of professional creatives in the context of such user-created content. 'Free or cut-price content', he suggests, is: 'a clear threat to the livelihoods of professional creatives whose prices are driven down by, or who simply cannot compete with, the commercial mining of these burgeoning, discount alternatives' (Ross 2009: 22; see also Banks and Deuze 2009). Here Ross raises an important topic in the context of creative labour: the shifting relationships among professionals and amateurs (see **expert** and **co-creation**). But should we assume that the most significant outcome of amateurs creating content is to threaten the jobs of professionals? It's not a zero-sum game but a rapid-growth ecology, where new jobs are created for professionals to produce and manage the various tools, devices, platforms and software applications that 'amateurs' use to make and share new content. Users may also take advantage of the opportunities provided by co-creativity to develop and refine their own skills and capabilities, and thereby gain attention to become professionals themselves. Flew (2012) observes that well-understood theories of frictional, cyclical and structural unemployment might provide a more straightforward explanation. Jobs are lost and created as industries change, adjust or disappear, owing to profound transformations associated with technological change and the associated changes of consumer preferences and production processes, as can clearly be observed at the moment in the newspaper industry.

While we should take seriously the pressing questions raised about conditions of work in the creative industries, to do this well we need to know more about where creative professionals are finding work and the kinds of jobs they are doing. We need to know more about the capabilities that creative workers are refining to navigate the precarity that scholars such as Ross (2009) and Toby Miller (2010b) describe. For example, how should we understand and measure the **productivity** of creative labour? And how does this workforce respond to the challenges identified recently by Brynjolfsson and McAfee (2011), in which while driving and accelerating innovation and productivity, digital technologies are also profoundly transforming employment and work (see **technology**)?

Our own research centre, the ARC Centre of Excellence for Creative Industries and Innovation (CCI), has developed the *creative trident* approach to measure the creative industries workforce more adequately. It tells us that there has been a systematic tendency to underestimate the number of people working in creative occupations (Higgs et al. 2008). Earlier studies focused on those employed directly in the creative industries (firms with creative outputs). But two further cohorts should be counted, that is 'embedded' and 'support' workers, to make the 'trident' (see **creative economy**). This approach reveals that even while the numbers of creative specialists working in television or the press may be shrinking, employment in creative *services* is growing. To argue that employment in the creative industries as a whole is in decline is simply wrong. Research approaches and methodologies such as the CCI's 'creative trident' demonstrate the importance of understanding the size, composition and characteristics of the creative workforce. This has important implications when considering how creative workers contribute to the broader creative economy, not just to the immediate creative industries sector (Cunningham 2011; Hartley 2012a).

Creative workforce research need not be *opposed* to the labour critiques of the creative industries. Such critiques pose important questions about the changing conditions of work in the creative industries. The problem is that these critical stances often assume they already have the answers, pre-packaged as political-economy opposition to the interests of capital. This tends to foreclose any effort to understand the categories and strategies that creative workers may use as they navigate the opportunities and risks of working in the creative industries. Ross's questions about the challenge of developing sustainable, rewarding livelihoods in the creative industries are so important that they should not be reduced to well-worn rhetoric about exploitive neoliberal agendas. At the same time the jargon of flexible creativity and innovation must not be allowed to obscure or sidestep difficult questions about creative labour. We need to get beyond this 'pro' versus 'anti' impasse, to rethink the categories of labour and work more fundamentally, while observing carefully the actual changes that are unfolding in the economy as a whole. We should pay close attention to the capabilities and skills that workers – including users, consumers and 'amateurs' – are adopting and adapting for effectively working in the context of these dynamic and volatile markets and industries.

Creativity

The pairing of 'creative' with 'industries' may seem to be a contradiction in terms, if we adopt a time-honoured Western European perspective on creativity derived from Kant's **aesthetics** and represented in the ideal type of the 'creative genius'. In fact, the first recorded usage of the noun 'creation' in English is attributed to the Bible and a creator who turned chaos – emptiness, separation and confusion – into cosmos, the sense of order and 'being'. This divine act was secularised in the European Enlightenment into the pattern of dualistic thinking. The Western philosophical tradition, particularly since Descartes, has in the main emphasised 'being', where the work, the artefact, the invention is 'brought into being' by an agent or author modelled on the original divine creator (Hartley 2012b), culminating in the modern sense of intellectual property and emphasising concrete form.

The idea of creation *ex nihilo* subsequently dominates accounts of Western creativity. The fascination with conjuring something out of 'thin air' (Leadbeater 1999), or thinking 'out of the box', suggests serendipity, or in rare cases an act of genius. Isaac Newton felt the force of an apple on his head, so the story goes. What is often left out of this account is that Newton managed to break out of a pattern of thinking about the laws of motion reaching back to Aristotle. His discovery was in effect a refinement of Aristotle's principle that all objects naturally come to rest. Creative insight can therefore be construed in more mundane terms, as variations and modifications of existing realities (Arthur 2009), a perspective that informs much non-Western literature on invention and discovery. From a conceptual perspective creativity represents the interplay between *similar differences* and *different similarities* (Bohm 1996). In many spheres of creative activity a desire for structure prevails; this is often provisional, illustrated by the existence of genres in art, theories in scientific research, and paradigms in the social sciences. There are always opportunities to restructure, to rearrange in more appropriate ways, in doing so to transcend conflicts within and between existing orders. Creativity from this perspective is a process of continuing and never-ending differentiation.

The English verb 'to create' derives from the Latin *creare* 'to produce, to make'. In the thirteenth century it was used to describe a finished product, something that 'was created'; in this context it reflected the Biblical myth of 'divine creation from nothing'. This usage prevailed until the late fifteenth century when the present tense form appeared, albeit still in the sense of the finished work. Rob Pope says: 'the model of "divine creation from nothing" underwrites an aesthetics and a politics of fixed (not fluid) form and absolute (not relative) value' (2005: 39).

Modern references appeared primarily in education and psychological circles. The abstract noun 'creativity' was first recorded in English in 1875 and was found in the early twentieth century in phases such as 'creative education' (1936), 'creative salesman' (1930) and courses in 'creative writing' (1930) (Pope 2005). The modern usage of creativity therefore is a product of the mid-twentieth century and the modern West. It generally implies utilitarian creativity, typified by J.P. Guildford's 1950 presidential address to the American Psychological Association in which he championed the benefits of research into creativity. Guildford went on to devise psychometric tests that were later incorporated into the well-known Torrance Tests for Creative Thinking (Sternberg and Lubart 1999).

Creativity however is not a generic term despite attempts by the behavioural sciences to attribute it to the individual. The 'creative industries' concept is undoubtedly a more pragmatic development, breaking away from the narrow usage associated with divergent thinking and performance tests. It also illustrates how the concept of creativity is taken up in different disciplinary domains. Devised in the Western hemisphere and exported globally, the creative industries initially made its way through British Commonwealth domains (see **creative industries**; **internationalisation**). Significantly in respect to its uptake in developing countries, the creative industries concept embodies a legacy of the rationalist world view; that is, the UK's Department for Culture, Media and Sport (DCMS) definition of creative industries favours product over process, being over becoming. Policymakers designate industry 'sectors'; they formulate strategies to make these 'perform better' and they attempt to 'pick winners'. In most countries and jurisdictions there is a high degree of congruence with the aims of fostering employment, intellectual property, box office receipts and value-adding effects into associated industry sectors.

The root of the creative industries is cultural policy, bureaucratically determined rather than organic and ultimately concerned with outputs that can be counted, compared and evaluated. Significantly, the DCMS definition is decidedly individualised ('those that have their origin in individual skill or talent'). The strong relationship between individualism and creativity (and **innovation**) does have a downside in that it tends 'to disconnect creative thinking and creative people from the contexts and systems which give their innovations and individual talents meaning and value' (Bilton 2007: 3). The key point to note therefore is that creativity is part of a complex dynamic system of feedback, one in which novel ideas and acts may result in creativity – but only in the context of an interaction with a symbolic system inherited from previous generations, and with a social system qualified to evaluate and accept novelty (Mockros and Csikszentmihali 1999). The relationship between the creative industries and creativity has become a divisive issue. The noun form 'creativity' conjures up a range of felicitous associations: some are banal; others are specific and useful. One problem is the credibility of creativity: the adjective form 'creative' is liberally applied to products or works that involve negligible amounts of novelty. Alternatively the term creativity ends up trapped within a closed system as a completely self-referential concept: that is, 'a creative product is creative because it is the outcome of a creative process; a creative process is characterised by its outcomes defined as creative products; the creative person is recognised by her creative products and the creative processes she experiences' (Rehn and De Cock 2009).

Indeed, Williams (1976: 19) highlighted 'an obvious difficulty': the adjective 'creative' places a stress on originality. Almost all current definitions of creativity and innovation agree on the importance of three attributes: newness, value and usefulness. Most attention is accorded to the first, which is often expressed in legal texts, in the economics of innovation, and in cognitive psychology as 'novelty'. The assumption that originality and novelty are fundamental to the creative industries is to some extent ideological. This assumption predisposes us to think that what is old world/old economy is in need of change, and creativity is the means to deliver a better world – for instance manufacturing and processing industries are polluting while **design** is clean.

Despite the general celebration of novelty, the creative industries, as defined globally, are made up of practices, occupations, and commodities that are more often routine, frequently standardised and generally derivative. While this critique deflates the sense of wonder associated with aesthetic creativity and acquisition of cultural capital, it also points to the fact that all creative acts are generative: they enable more variations to emerge. In an industrial sense, variations and adaptations are efficacious rather than serendipitous or leading edge. As noted above, much of what is deemed creative is subject to social or expert judgement. Moreover creative outputs are relevant to culture; as Pope notes, 'we never create anything fresh or valuable in utter isolation' (2005: xvi).

The fashion industry identifies its outputs as creative but success can come from recycling trends and picking the right time to introduce these into the media. Television seems endlessly repetitive. Formats dominate schedules. Genres organise film financing. Creative occupations are problematic. Are pastry chefs and hairdressers creative? What about scientists; shouldn't we consider their outputs as creative even if they spend a great deal of time in labs? Of course, one can always 'fit' more and more pursuits into the cultural and creative industries family by designating core and none-core activities. The problem here is that many core activities listed in such reports simply do not involve novelty; furthermore many show little evidence of originality. They can only be regarded as creative if we downgrade the emphasis on newness and originality.

Indeed, considering all products and services available for consumption in the economy we can observe a continuum: at one end there are those made to a certain preconceived specification; for instance most people would concur that assembly line manufacturing is an uncreative activity. We might choose to include carpet making, garment manufacture and the outsourcing of animation here. At the other end of the continuum is originality, the much-vaunted breakthroughs in style and paradigm; for instance Picasso's cubism, Einstein's theory of relativity and the Tang poetry of Dufu. In the middle and taking up a lot of the territory is 'proficiency' in various forms (which is useful but not so novel) and 'eccentricity' (which is novel but not so useful) (Moran 2009).

Paradoxically, much value creation in the creative industries is due to 'mundane' or 'humdrum' labour, the work of accountants, lawyers and a range of technical staff, located on the boundary where commerce meets art (Caves 2000). Likewise in the realm of research and development 'many technology transfers that were meant to be merely rote applications of one procedure to another become illuminating' (Sennett 2008: 211). In many cases, the bringing together of different elements produces frustration, poor fit and incompatibility. Indeed, the transfer of the idea or technology may generate a different set of problems that need to be resolved. In order to sustain a creative ecosystem there needs to be recognition of the value of diversity, complexity and contradiction (Bilton 2007). This applies to individual as well as collectives. It is important therefore to recognise that ideas occur at the intersection of knowledge and practical domains; the testing out of combinations from adjacent cultural domains and disciplinary fields often results in unexpected results.

Brian Arthur has coined the term 'combinatorial evolution': he says: 'Early technologies form using existing primitive technologies as components. These new technologies in time become possible components – building blocks – for the construction of new technologies. Some of these in turn go on to become possible building blocks for the creation of newer technologies' (2009: 21). Taking the argument further, Stephen Johnson refers to the 'adjacent possible', the idea that new combinations of technologies, of ideas, open doors: 'the history of cultural progress is, almost without exception, a story of one door leading to another' (S. Johnson 2010: 36).

The combinatorial approach was noted earlier, but without Arthur's emphasis on **evolution**, by Margaret Boden (2004) who identified two types of creativity: historical (H) and psychological (P). H creativity implies that an idea is new because someone has not thought of it before. This 'glamorous notion' of invention and celebration of the creative individual makes news. P creativity, moreover, is when something appears to be creative with respect 'to the individual mind'; for instance, I have recombined my ideas in ways that I haven't done so before and I feel this to be new or creative. However, others may well have done so. Moreover, H creativity, while highly prized, is at the best only 'provisional' (Boden 2004: 45) as all ideas are in effect recombinations. Finally, in terms of how creative processes are best managed by those working in creative *organisations*, Chris Bilton draws our attention to a number of generally accepted principles (2007: 6):

1 Such organisations tend to tolerate diversity, complexity and contradiction;
2 Creative thinking is less likely to result from individual genius (the H-creativity mentioned above) but from combinations of different kinds of thinking;
3 The creativity of an idea goes beyond the content of the idea to the way that it is developed presented and interpreted;
4 Creativity thinking takes place neither 'inside the box nor outside the box but at the edge of the box';
5 Boundaries and constraints are necessary to enable the creative process (this principle is particularly relevant to countries that might want to over-regulate creative industries or censor creative ideas);
6 While singularity of vision is often celebrated in success stories of creative entrepreneurs it is important to take account of diversity, compromise and collaboration;
7 Summarising the views expressed in this entry, creativity is ultimately embedded in a cultural context.

Cultural Policy

An argument can be made that the origins of modern cultural policy lie with the French Revolution of 1789. When the revolutionary government transferred the royal art collections from the Palace of Versailles to the Louvre, and moved other historically significant art works from the palaces of the nobility to the new public museums and galleries, it set in train the idea that artworks were the property of the nation-state – its cultural patrimony or common cultural heritage. This was consistent with an opening up of culture to the whole population that would be a feature of modern societies, and the transformation of cultural institutions, such as galleries, libraries and museums, into instruments of collective civic and cultural education by the state for its citizens. Cultural policy in its more contemporary forms took shape in the second half of the twentieth century. In Britain, the first chair of the Arts Council of Great Britain (established in 1946) was the famous economist John Maynard Keynes. Keynes saw the purpose of an arts policy as being to promote creative excellence, with government providing a limited financial and infrastructural scaffolding to underpin this, while maintaining an 'arm's length' relationship from the arts themselves. Keynes saw the arts as a higher-order social good, believing that if capitalist economies could be made to work without cycles of boom and slump, there would be scope to enable greater public access to the arts and **culture**, so that the whole of society could enjoy the arts and culture as part of a better life (Flew 2010).

In France, the formation of the Fifth Republic in 1958 commenced a fertile period for cultural policy development. The first Ministry of Culture was headed by the writer Andre Malraux, whose broad trajectory for cultural policy identified three major tasks. First, the concept of *heritage* saw a role for the state in distributing the 'eternal products of the imagination' (Looseley 1995: 36) throughout the national population, through museums, galleries, libraries and other public exhibition spaces. Second, the state had an ongoing role in promoting the *creation* of new artistic and cultural works, using public funding to provide support for artists and cultural workers. Finally, the objective of *democratisation* constituted an activist role for cultural policy in redressing socio-economic inequalities by cultural means. An ambiguity has existed in the latter concept, around the question of whether cultural policy primarily involves bringing great works of art to the masses, or promoting a more diverse range of forms of cultural expression, including community-based arts and culture (Looseley 1995). Such a vision of arts and cultural policy as being concerned with heritage, creation and cultural access and diversity was highly influential with UNESCO, which developed various policy manuals and protocols for the development of national cultural policies, particularly in the developing world (Mattelart 1994).

The concept of **creative industries** is both connected to cultural policy discourses and disruptive of cultural policy as it has typically been theorised and practised. The creative industries paradigm challenges many of the traditional assumptions of cultural policy. It proposes that both commercial and state-supported forms of cultural activity are wellsprings of **creativity**, and therefore worthy of attention from a policy perspective. There is not an artificial line drawn between the arts and the media industries, or between tangible and digital content, on the basis of one being perceived to have more cultural value than the other. While not saying that all creative industries sectors are the same, or have similar policy requirements, the creative industries debate nonetheless opens up for critical scrutiny claims that are made about the cultural value of one activity as compared to another (Holden 2009).

The appropriate scope and breadth of cultural policy is a subject of ongoing debate, not least because expanding the domain of cultural policy beyond the arts inevitably brings it more into the realms of commercial markets and industry development. The cultural economist David Throsby (2010) has identified cultural policy as being a form of public policy that is applied to the production, distribution, consumption and trade in cultural goods and services. While this refers to *explicit* cultural policies, Throsby also observes that there are *implicit* cultural policies, which include policies developed in other domains that nonetheless have cultural impacts, including economic policy, trade policy, urban and regional development policies, education policy, and policies towards **intellectual property**. Ruth Towse (2010) has argued that the traditional concern of cultural economics with market failure, or the limits of commercial industries as cultural providers, also need to be balanced with consideration of government failure. In particular, Towse also makes reference to principal-**agent** problems in cultural policy, arising from the arm's length relationship of funding agencies to those in receipt of government support, which makes it difficult to track the effective use of funds without appearing excessively to interfere in the autonomous spheres of **art and aesthetics**.

A more expansive account of cultural policy was developed by Tony Bennett (1992), who drew upon Michel Foucault's (1991) concept of *governmentality* to argue that cultural policy, broadly defined, has been a central element of modern forms of government. Bennett proposed that culture was best understood as 'a historically specific set of institutionally embedded relations of government', aimed at transforming how populations behave socially (1992: 28). For example, the nineteenth-century museum or the early twentieth-century public broadcaster aimed to inculcate a common national culture and a way of 'thinking the nation' among its citizenry. By contrast, twenty-first-century cultural institutions assist with managing the implications of more culturally diverse national populations through cultural policies of multiculturalism. Yúdice (2003) has extended this understanding of culture as a social resource to draw attention to significant government and private investments in cultural institutions, and activities designed to achieve goals not traditionally associated with cultural policy, such as economic innovation, community development and urban regeneration. A distinction is sometimes made in cultural policy between the 'core arts' (music, performing arts, literature and visual arts), and other sectors. This is what is known as the *concentric circles* model of the cultural sectors (Throsby 2010), where cultural value and creativity are most concentrated in the core arts, and emanate outwards to film, media, publishing, fashion, advertising and design. Craik et al. (2000) identified four key domains of cultural policy:

- *Arts and culture*, including direct funding to cultural producers, support for cultural institutions, and the funding of cultural agencies;
- *Communications and media*, including support for film and broadcast media (both publicly funded and commercial), as well as policies related to new media technologies, publishing, and intellectual property;

- *Citizenship and identity*, including language policy, cultural development policy, multiculturalism and questions of national symbolic identity;
- *Spatial culture*, including urban and regional culture and planning, cultural heritage management, and cultural tourism, leisure and recreation.

Within the 'concentric circles' model, it would be the first category – that of the 'core arts' – which constitutes the heartland of cultural policy, with the other policy areas radiating outwards from it. An example of such a framework being applied was found with the Australian government's 2011 National Cultural Policy Discussion Paper, which distinguished between the 'core arts' and the **creative industries**, associating the former with aesthetics and cultural identity, and the latter with business skills, commercial production and the application of digital technologies (Department of the Prime Minister and Cabinet (DPMC) 2011).

The focus on the 'core arts' as being at the centre of cultural policy is linked to the common focus of cultural economics on market failure in the arts and culture. Such arguments propose that there is an endemic oversupply of cultural goods and services, and the creative talent that produces it, relative to demand. As the arts and culture have various forms of intrinsic value, ranging from **aesthetic** value to existence and educational value, and their value for future generations, it is incumbent upon government to subsidise the arts to ensure their continued existence, through policy measures that can range from subsidised ticket prices to arts education in order to increase public demand for the arts. The result is a form of cultural policy that is very much tied to both the interests and the funding priorities of the nation-state. A *de facto* alignment of culture with the subsidised arts means that the definition of the core arts becomes, almost by default, synonymous with those fields already in receipt of public funding. Needless to say, this rests upon a somewhat narrow definition of **culture**, aligning it to **art and aesthetics** rather than culture as a way of life. It also bifurcates particular art forms into those which are deemed to be 'cultural' and those which merely provide **entertainment**. In music, for example, a rock band such as AC/DC is clearly a part of the Australian national culture, but not of its cultural policy. The problems in determining which parts of film and television are deemed to be part of a national cultural policy are endemic: does it include cinema targeted at the multiplexes, or only independent cinema? Are the commercial broadcasters relevant, or only the public broadcasters? Intellectually, such distinctions recall arguments from the earlier **culture industry** traditions, where 'real' art with aesthetic value is counterposed to mass-produced culture that takes the form of commodities and has only entertainment or novelty value.

The creative industries paradigm identifies wider economic trends such as technological change, market dynamics and globalisation as presenting opportunities and not simply threats to culture. Drawing upon the growing academic and policy literature about the rise of a **creative economy**, such work has associated the diffusion of creativity into sectors of the economy not typically considered to be 'cultural' with trends in **innovation** and the **information economy**. The creative industries paradigm also repositions the cultural **consumer** from being someone in need of re-education in order to appreciate the arts, to becoming an active driver of cultural change. It challenges the gloomy prognosis that culture in its most valued forms is simply being overrun by commodification and marketisation. It is relevant in this context to note the work of the nineteenth-century German economist Ernst Engel, who argued that cultural consumption in all of its forms – including audiences for the arts – was positively correlated to economic growth and development, as barriers to participation arising from economic subsistence were gradually lifted. In other words, there is a positive relationship between cultural development and economic development, and between cultural consumption and rising material standards of living.

The rise of creative industries policy discourses, and greater interest in the economic contribution of cultural activities, has also acted as a catalyst to more 'whole-of-government' approaches to cultural policy, that include other departments such as those associated with economics, trade, education, health, tourism and services. There has also been a growing interest in urban cultural policies as **globalisation** generates new forms of competition among cities; the vibrancy of a city's culture is taken in the **creative cities** literature to be a driver of success in the global **creative economy**. This has generated renewed interest in the 'soft infrastructure' of producers and consumers that underpin the cultural dynamism of a place, and the roles that policy can play in maintaining and renewing such associational networks (Evans 2009). Finally, the global revolution in transport and communication has created new opportunities for artists and cultural workers to meet, network and collaborate, and these international networks are in turn providing infrastructural support for new forms of cultural activism. Given that one of the historic uncertainties of cultural policy has been the extent to which a state can appropriately represent a nation's culture, cultural globalisation opens up new opportunities for forms of *de facto* cultural policy that are driven by non-state actors.

Culture (History of Concept)

'Culture' is a much-used term in the study of the creative industries (see Introduction). But as a concept it is chaotic, contested and contingent; often deployed to win an argument, as in various 'culture wars'. Perhaps this is why an entire genre of 'key concepts' books (such as this one) has been spawned to unravel the tangle. The first of these was by Raymond Williams (1976). He famously dubbed culture 'one of the two or three most complicated words in the English language' – although the *Oxford English Dictionary*'s longest entry is not for 'culture' but for 'set', which shows that there's a difference between intellectual and linguistic complexity. Williams categorised culture according to its usage in different disciplinary contexts: in philosophy (e.g. Herder), the cultivation of an individual's capabilities; in anthropology, the 'way of life' of a community; and in literary criticism, where it signified artistic expression. The literary usage is the most controversial for Williams, because it is associated with community values, specifically the claimed 'higher' value of **aesthetic** as opposed to commercial culture.

The concept of culture as artistic expression emerged from various **aesthetic** theories of the nineteenth century; most notably, in English at least, the writings of John Ruskin in relation to the visual arts, and Matthew Arnold in relation to literature. Successive generations of influential writers and critics took up the Arnoldian baton to establish a partisan 'definition' of culture as 'high' culture. This proved influential internationally, eventually becoming the default setting of educated common sense, not least because it has dominated the school and university curriculum, especially in 'English' (Mulhern 1979). Matthew Arnold's 1869 book *Culture and Anarchy* sought to understand culture in terms of 'firm intelligible laws of things' – as a science not a set of subjective impressions. But Arnold was a rhetorical rather than a logical thinker, and glossed these laws as the *Hellenic* 'love of light, of seeing things as they are'; as opposed to *Hebraistic* or Puritan 'fire and strength', based on a strict moralistic conscience (1869: 170–3). Culture's laws could only be attained by 'reading, observing or thinking' (1869: 196), but the pursuit of perfection, where aesthetic beauty revealed natural truth, would lead, thought Arnold, to 'spontaneity of consciousness' (1869: 173) – something just as welcome in the sciences as in the arts; and open to surprises and flux rather than fixed by ideology or power.

The man who gave us the notorious 'definition' of culture as the 'pursuit of our total perfection by means of getting to know, on all the matters which most concern us, *the best which has been thought and said in the world*' (viii), was actually trying to found a *science* of culture, one that was motivated by the 'impulse to see things as they really are' (Arnold 1869: 171). He was looking for a 'basis for a less confused action and a more complete perfection than we have at present' (1869: 196).His followers, however, deleted that 'basis' in favour of 'bias' – the 'culture wars' of the past decades have been conducted almost entirely at the level of moralistic ideology and what the BBC's founder John Reith called the 'brute force of monopoly',[1] which was used to impose a partisan definition of culture on everyone. The reason why any of this mattered then, and still matters now, is because the 'we' that Arnold addressed was, in the 1870s, a world empire based on coal, industry and trade. Arnold saw culture as the antidote to the 'anarchy' that he thought was being brought about by market forces (the economy) and democratisation (politics). His argument *against* materialistic power was of interest because his country wielded plenty of it. His version of culture was pedagogic and aspirational, not based on folk customs or even elite pursuits (which he dismissed as 'Philistine'). It should be advanced through education, formal and informal, as a conservative antidote to liberalism.[2] This then

---

[1]See: www.bbc.co.uk/historyofthebbc/resources/in-depth/reith_5.shtml
[2]Matthew Arnold was the son of the most famous headmaster of Rugby School, Thomas Arnold, and was himself an Inspector of Schools.

was the founding rationale for valuing 'high' culture *as opposed to* 'civilisation', where the latter meant modern urban economic life.

The Arnoldian rationale, periodically updated by critics, senior bureaucrats and arts advocates, still motivates public support for the creative arts, whose continuation, especially the 'high' forms of 'serious' music', 'fine' art or 'literary' writing, depends on subsidy and philanthropy. These are justified in the name of educating public taste and preserving the quest for 'perfection' of expression. The Arnoldian model was thoroughly critiqued, not least by Williams (1958), but it has become so embedded that it still forms part of the commonsense and almost the constitution of contemporary nations, not just the UK. It underpins a 'felt' distinction between culture and capitalism, art and the **market**, public good and private gain, perfection and profanity, with attendant evaluative discrimination between – it seems to follow – high-status **public culture** and unworthy private **entertainment**. Such distinctions are not only discursive or ideological; you can walk into them. They are given material form in multifarious cultural **institutions** that are partly or exclusively maintained by public funding, including endowments for the arts, orchestras and opera houses, public broadcasters, arts-funding agencies, galleries, museums and libraries, and educational provision in the creative arts and humanities. None of these was supported by taxation before Arnold. But now, despite disputes about the level of such funding, no modern country can do without them, to such an extent that you can't play on the world stage without such a regime. Emerging economies such as China, Brazil, Turkey or Mexico signal their own global aspirations by *setting up* a subsidised culture. Their capital cities bristle with opera houses and galleries; they want Nobel Laureates for Literature; they spend up big on training classical musicians and artists; they support literary and artistic education.

Meanwhile, beneath the radar, plenty of culture goes unvalued, unsubsidised and unnoticed. Despite its prestige, the institutional apparatus of public support for culture routinely misses what it most values, 'the best which has been thought and said'. It is left to subsequent ages to promote previously neglected, despised or invisible works to the status of high art, and to demote others. The trouble with Arnoldian culture is that it cannot predict such convulsions in taste, and has a terrible track record of undervaluing novelties that arise in the popular as opposed to the subsidised domain. In the process of 'saving' culture, it reduces it to an already-known heritage, to a minority-elite leisure pursuit, and to welfare economics. It distracts policymakers from developing an 'entrepreneurial' model of *culture as innovation*, and it fails to notice or promote those who are engaged in such endeavours. This illustrates how some discursive traditions *don't* change quickly. Once selected and adopted, they can be retained over a long run as seemingly timeless **institutions**, guaranteed by habit, marble porticos and educated opinion. When that happens, the generations who inherit these institutional forms may at some point notice that the values embedded in them are out of kilter with their own times, and reject the underlying concepts … at which point another bout of '**creative destruction**' may be in order.

Certainly Raymond Williams (1976) was up for a bit of disruptive renewal when he contrasted Arnold's 'high' culture with a definition derived from cultural anthropology that designated culture as a 'whole way of life'. This simple formula opened a space for Williams' progressive politics. He was for the democratisation of the concept, having famously argued that 'culture is ordinary' (Williams 1989), and therefore that the study of culture should focus on everyday life. However, Williams was no more a folklorist than Arnold. His vision of everyday life was not nostalgic but modernist – critical, Marxist, urban, avant-garde, with a sympathetic eye for working-class community life (*Border Country* 1960). Here, then, is another twist in the twentieth-century *politics* of culture, which became the prize in a long-running tussle between elitists and democratisers, conservatives and radicals; a tussle that took place in literature, journalism, in the media and in education – the 'culture wars'. At the same time, possibly influenced by these controversies, the term began to be taken up in disciplines well beyond the arts, especially sociology. There was talk of a 'cultural turn' in the social sciences more generally, following the work of prominent thinkers such as Bourdieu, Foucault, Hayden White, Clifford Geertz, Stuart Hall, and authors from the 'new social movements' of the 1960s and 1970s, who were associated with identity politics, especially those connected with gender (e.g. Donna Haraway), race and ethnicity (e.g. Henry Louis Gates), and sexual orientation (e.g. Harding 1986; LeVay 1997). The 'cultural turn' had an impact in the natural sciences too, provoking a resurgence of histories of science and studies of 'science and technology in society' (Collins and Evans 2007).

Both sides of the 'high versus popular' cultural divide have been assimilated into the **creative economy**. The polarising rhetoric began to abate in the search for sustainable business models for artists, arts organisations, cultural institutions and education in the arts. The climb-down from 'high' culture was hastened by increasing social and political acceptance of difference, diversity, multiculturalism and the right of individuals to choose their own mode of culture. The emergence of the creative industries has, to some extent, depoliticised the very concept of culture (but see Carey 1992), or at least it shifted the political debate from **aesthetic** sectarianism to pragmatic decision-making about trade, industry support, tourism and the like (the very things Arnold had counterposed to culture). Culture's meanings and practice have proliferated, dispersed and diffused across a much more varied palette than would have been possible when 'culture' was confined to ethno-territorial descent and aspirational art. In short, culture abandoned marble and entered the **market**. With the post-1960s generation, it began to take on a more important role with the rise of affluent consumption and the **attention** economy. The cultural marketplace supports most of the popular pursuits of the age, which are 'commodified' in various ways, so that you can now *buy* what pre-modern families used to *do*: cooking, sewing, gardening (cultivating), singing, dancing. People's relationships, identities and meanings are all immersed in and shaped through media to an extent that was once available only to the aristocracy. Culture is marketised, but the market has distributed culture universally, and cultural 'consumption' is now more participatory and productive than ever.

The marketplace itself has also changed, along with **technology**, to favour the entry of technologically equipped small-scale and entrepreneurial **creative industries**, including those based on 'micro-production' (see **productivity**) by amateurs, community groups and sole traders, who may access a global online market from their residence, dramatically lowering the cost of entry into the market. Here, at least in some sections and without denying a trend toward corporatisation in online services, we can observe a *culturally progressive marketplace*; one that is often more tolerant, innovative, experimental and even radical than the public culture of subsidised arts that is stoutly defended by ostensibly progressive political parties, who turn out not to be progressive at all in relation to the arts and cultural pluralism. Despite inclusive and egalitarian rhetoric, the lion's share of public funding still goes to the orchestras. Meanwhile, to complete this reversal of the politics of culture, the long-reviled world of commercial entertainment and leisure consumption turns out to be the seedbed of novelty, **innovation** and cultural renewal. This is where the history of the culture concept pays off in relation to our understanding of the emergent creative industries. It teaches us that some inherited attitudes, amounting to 'eternal verities' in progressive thinking, are now directly at odds with the facts of cultural participation. This is not a victory for one side or another in these historic debates, for it is not a simple matter of 'the market' prevailing over culture. Instead, we can observe an **evolutionary** process in big ideas like 'culture', where the process of selection, adoption and retention of the Arnoldian model has effectively run its course. But as the semiotician Yuri Lotman (1990: 123) has pointed out, cultural evolution differs from biological because cultural objects do not become extinct. So, despite its unfitness for contemporary purposes, the 'high' culture model survives in hard-to-change institutional investments, bureaucratic routines, and path-dependent practices, without necessarily commanding the intellectual assent even of those agents who manage the system.

Culture Industry / Cultural Industries

The concept of 'cultural industries' has been used both descriptively and as a theoretical concept, in the singular ('culture industry') as well as the plural form. Where the term is used in **cultural policy** documents, it is typically used in the plural: 'cultural industries'. This also tends to be the preferred terminology of political economists such as Hesmondhalgh (2007) and Miège (1989, 2011). By contrast, the term 'culture industry' is associated with neo-Marxist philosophy and cultural theory; including in the official policy discourse of countries like China where a distinction between the 'culture industries' (media, publishing – propaganda) and the 'creative industries' (small to medium enterprises (SMEs)) is maintained.

In cultural theory, the origins of the term arise from the ideological critique of art and culture under industrial capitalism associated with the neo-Marxist theorists of the 'Frankfurt School', such as Theodor Adorno, Max Horkheimer, Erich Fromm, Walter Benjamin, Herbert Marcuse and Hans-Magnus Enzensberger. Adorno and Horkheimer developed the term 'culture industry' in 1947 (Adorno and Horkheimer 1979). Adorno and Horkheimer's diagnosis was that the once autonomous sphere of culture – art, aesthetics, music, literature, etc. – had become fully integrated into the dynamics of capitalist domination in the form of the culture industry. Drawing an analogy between the European fascism they had escaped and the capitalist democracy of the USA, where they emigrated, Adorno and Horkheimer argued that cultural production under 'monopoly capitalism' had become industrialised and commodified, leading to a growing uniformity of all forms of art and culture. Adorno and Horkheimer referred to this as 'the achievement of standardisation and mass production, sacrificing whatever involved a distinction between the logic of the work and that of the social system' (1979: 350). What appears as greater consumer choice and cultural freedom for the masses, through the generation of minor differences in cultural products, was in fact their complete integration into the machinery of mass culture, where 'something is provided for all so that none may escape' (Adorno and Horkheimer 1979: 351). For these authors, the culture industry functioned as a powerful ideological and propaganda instrument, utilising the new technologies of mass communication and the techniques of mass production to impose ideological control on the mass population as cultural consumers:

> Under monopoly all mass culture is identical, and the lines of its artificial framework begin to show through … Movies and radio no longer pretend to be art. The truth that they are just business is made into an ideology in order to justify the rubbish that they deliberately produce. (Adorno and Horkheimer 1979: 349)

Adorno and Horkheimer presented culture in advanced capitalist societies in terms of 'the overall standardised character of cultural production, and the way in which the culture industry seek to incorporate producer and consumer, artist and audience, into this process' (Negus 2006: 198–9).

The culture industry concept was further developed by Herbert Marcuse (1964), who argued that capitalist industrial society integrated individuals into the economic system of production and consumption by promoting false needs and redirecting intellectual and libidinal energies away from critique and the consideration of social alternatives, thereby creating a 'one-dimensional' universe of thought and behaviour. Such ideas were highly influential in the 1960s, with Marcuse referred to in some circles as the 'Father of the New Left' (Kellner 1984), and they remain influential in contemporary critical philosophy, particularly in relation to theories of **power**. At the same time, other writers in the Frankfurt School tradition, such as Hans-Magnus Enzensberger, questioned the one-sided focus of such accounts on mass media as instruments of domination. Enzensberger (1973) noted that the development of what he referred to as the 'consciousness industry' could only occur at certain levels of political development (the proclamation of universal human rights) and economic development (industrialisation and the development of broadcast and computing technologies), so the call to abolish the consciousness industry runs the risk of being akin to calling for the abolition of industrial society itself. Moreover, as such industries rely upon the input of intellectuals – broadly defined – it is intellectuals who play a more pivotal role in proposing social alternatives. Enzensberger argued that critics of capitalism needed to engage less in critique of the mass media and the cultural industries, and be more willing to identify alternative uses of the new technologies, thereby 'releasing the emancipatory potential which is inherent in the new productive forces' (1973: 96). Frankfurt School critiques of commercial culture under monopoly capitalism continue to have appeal to some activists and critical scholars, who view the popular masses as subject to the hold of dominant ideologies. The anti-capitalist standpoint of the culture industry critique is unambiguous, and that also holds appeal for the advocates of radical political change.

While the names of Adorno and Horkheimer were not known to most arts and culture agencies, the underlying kernel of their thesis – that commercial markets produced a debased form of culture – was certainly an underlying influence on the development of **cultural policy** in the twentieth century. Their continuing influence can be seen in the distinctions made in cultural policy documents between the 'core arts', which require policy settings that are based upon direct public subsidy and the pursuit of excellence, and the 'industrial' strategies associated with the more market-driven **creative industries**.

At the same time, it has been argued that Adorno and Horkheimer presented a one-sided understanding of the cultural commodity, focusing on the role played by advertising and marketing in creating 'false needs', and neglecting the degree to which the demand for commodities, including the demand for **entertainment**, was indicative of cultural producers addressing needs that were widely felt among the population (Dyer 1992). Moreover, the claim that cultural commodities produced under capitalism promoted dominant ideologies has been widely contested. Garnham (2011) has observed that capitalism as an economic system can co-exist with a very wide range of both cultural forms and ideas, and that the market process by its nature is likely to lead to growing diversity of cultural products available for the **consumer**. Culture that is simply a one-dimensional propaganda machine is unlikely to remain commercially profitable. The complexities of cultural production and distribution also mean that there is not a singular logic to the 'culture industry', but rather complex and distinctive dynamics associated with different cultural industries (Miège 1989, 2011; Hesmondhalgh 2007). It is claimed that their critique of **aesthetics** under monopoly capitalism is underpinned by a distrust of the mass media and **technology**, thereby creating a historically misleading picture of a once heroic era of artistic autonomy that has now turned into the contemporary enslavement of cultural producers. The era of *market professional* and *corporate professional* cultural production (Williams 1981) has instead coincided with different degrees of autonomy afforded to cultural producers, so there is no simple process of the once independent artist being inexorably sucked into the maw of the 'culture factory'.

The term cultural industries became more common from the 1970s onwards, as policymakers began to identify culture as a site for economic development strategies. In his work for the Greater London Council in the 1980s, Nicholas Garnham challenged the focus of public policy on a narrowly defined arts sector, instead proposing that the cultural industries were 'institutions in our society which employ the characteristic modes of production and organisation of industrial corporations to produce and disseminate symbols in the form of cultural goods and services generally' (1987: 25). From this perspective, the challenge of a cultural industries strategy was to use public policy to promote local cultural sectors and producers *in* the market, rather than trying to insulate them *from* the market.

In some respects, the **creative industries** sector has built upon these cultural industries strategies, although there remains contention as to whether 'cultural industries' or 'creative industries' provides the appropriate nomenclature. In policy discourses, the two terms are sometimes used interchangeably. For instance, in a 2010 Green Paper, the European Union sought to 'clarify what constitutes the European vision of culture, creativity and innovation and to elaborate political measures … in order to develop European creative industries, incorporating these in a genuine European strategy for culture' (European Commission (EC) 2010: 4). The debate about terminology is less intense in some academic disciplines than in others. In economics, for instance, the debate is not so important, since the boundaries of an industry and what it uniquely does are inherently fuzzy. Throsby observed that 'the concept of industry can be delineated according to groupings of producers, product classifications, factors of production, types of consumers, location, etc.' (2001: 112), In the humanities and cultural studies, by contrast, the choice of name has been considered very important. Hesmondhalgh (2007) preferred the term cultural industries, arguing that it best captured the dynamics of what he considers to be the 'core' sectors of film, broadcasting, music and digital content industries. Interestingly, Hesmondhalgh, like the Chinese Communist Party, places *the media* at the core of the *cultural* industries, while other **cultural policy** documents place *the arts* at the core, and see the media as *creative* industries that are closer to commercial (rather than cultural) sectors such as advertising and fashion (e.g. Department of the Prime Minister and Cabinet (DPMC) 2011). Other critics, such as T. Miller (2009) and Turner (2011), have preferred the term cultural industries for political reasons, arguing that the shift from cultural to creative industries entails 'a retreat from a commitment to the public good and its replacement by a belief in the social utility of a market outcome' (Turner 2011: 693).

In this connection, the assessment of Nicholas Garnham, one of the pioneers of cultural industries research, is instructive. Garnham has argued that the field of 'political economy' of communication 'has become associated, by both its practitioners and defenders and by its critics, with a tired and narrow orthodoxy,' and that '*this general position is both empirically questionable and theoretically and politically dubious*' (2011: 42). Garnham has asked some hard questions of the traditions of cultural industries research. He asks whether the media and cultural policy environment is in fact far more complex than simple market/state dichotomies would suggest, particularly as **convergence** blurs policy distinctions based on the type of media or cultural product, service or sector. He also questions whether general claims about the ideological content of commercial media can be made, given that the rise of capitalist modernity sees societies becoming more internally complex and heterogeneous, and that cultural producers seeking to make a profit have an interest in producing for more diverse cultural markets. Garnham argues that rather than simply engaging in ideological critique and assuming that culture is being aesthetically debased through industrialised forms of production and distribution, cultural industries researchers need to engage more directly with questions of the **information economy**.

Design

Like 'art' and 'media,' design is a creative sector or, better, a rapidly growing series of sub-sectors. The Design Institute of Australia divides the field into three primary discipline clusters: *industrial*, *interior*, and *graphic* design (DIA 2010). Grouped within these broad categories are twenty or more sub-sectors, embracing major fields such as architecture, denoting a steady and impressive proliferation and segmentation of the design field overall. This indicates a rapid growth through divisions of labour as new purposes for design are developed and applied. But it should be kept in mind that some of the greatest examples of contemporary design success mesh industrial and product design with interaction and communication design. For instance, a significant part of Apple's success is attributed to its design leadership, combining simplicity, functionality and style. The design process applies principles of aesthetic quality and inventiveness for functional purposes. While no consensual definition of design exists, there is repeated emphasis on the constrained, purposive process of design, which is contrasted with art: it is 'intended to accomplish goals, in a particular environment, using a set of primitive components, satisfying a set of requirements, subject to constraints' (Wikipedia: 'Design'). The process of designing will most often require aesthetic consideration married with functional, economic, social and political factors. The distinction between 'art' and design' is deeply institutionalised; for instance, in education, where CalArts teaches art but design is taught at Caltech.

There is some controversy over whether the stress on the intangible value of creativity in design has unbalanced our understanding of the creative industries. James Dyson, the design entrepreneur who invented the Dyson vacuum cleaner and bladeless fan, distances himself from the creative industries. Instead, he sees design as part of industrial science and engineering:

> Terms like 'post-industrial' and 'creative industries' only serve to reinforce misconceptions. In two words, they render invisible the significant contribution of science and engineering to the economy. They must go. As long as we continue to invent and make things (no matter if they're assembled in the UK or elsewhere) we're industrial. Less chat about what songs are on the PM's iPod, more about the British brains who actually developed MP3 player technology (no, it wasn't Apple). (Dyson 2010: 12)

design

The outputs of creative industries, however, have always been a mix of high value-added services and manufactured goods. It's a false dichotomy to drive a wedge between intangibles and tangibles, functionality and pure **aesthetics**, as Dyson does. But Dyson's invective does remind us that many analysts of the creative industries concern themselves with the arts, the cultural industries and contemporary digital screen-based media, neglecting design and architecture and their particular industrial manifestations.

Grand claims for design are not new. Herbert Simon considered it to be a master discipline for all the main professions:

> Engineers are not the only professional designers. Everyone designs who devises courses of action aimed at changing existing situations into preferred ones ... Design, so construed, is the core of all professional training; it is the principal mark that distinguishes the professions from the sciences. Schools of engineering, as well as schools of architecture, business, education, law, and medicine, are all centrally concerned with the process of design. (1969: 111)

Simon proposed a *rational or problem-solving model* for understanding design. It has been argued that this influential model does not accord with the empirical reality of how designers go about their work. The process is much more intuitive, improvised and iterative than the rational model would suggest – whether this would make it a more creative process is also subject to debate. An alternative model is *action-centric*, in which analysis, design and implementation are seen as coeval, where designers alternate among 'framing', 'making moves' and 'evaluating moves' (Schön 1983). As with all models, and particularly with a contingent concept like design, we must take care not to mistake the map for the territory. Understanding design is a matter of taking elements from both approaches and testing their currency on a case basis.

Underlining the chameleon nature of design, there is the difference between a supply- and a demand-driven approach to contemporary design. It is posed by Roberto Verganti as a third way between radical innovation pushed by technology and incremental innovation pulled by the market: 'Design-driven innovations do not come from the market: they create new markets. They don't push new technologies, they push new meanings' (2009: 3–5). He sets this explicitly against the current emphasis on user-centred design or the even stronger notion of user-driven design (e.g. European Commission 2009; see **co-creation**). In this very Milanese approach to design, using an explicitly **expert** paradigm, the designer comes closest to the concept of the artist. On the other hand, ambitious claims are made for a user-driven design approach by Cope and Kalantzis (2010: 592), who align traditional architecture with an exhausted modernist command style fixated on auteurist personalities, and contrast it with contemporary participatory-democratic design cultures.

What is not at issue is the degree to which design has come to centre stage in much creative industries industry, workforce and policy thinking. It operates conceptually in many ways as a bridging platform. George Cox (2006) positioned design, when it is thought of as a distinct sector, as a bridge between the arts and engineering sciences – between aesthetic-expressive and technical-rational modes of knowing – and a link between research and enterprise in the innovation chain, where design is thought of as method or mindset that links research into new ideas on the one hand, and the development of practical applications on the other. Design also enters innovation thinking and policy in two main ways. First, it has been inserted into the *science-engineering-technology model of innovation* as the bridging sector between scientific research and consumer technology. This occurred initially in industrial design (as we have seen with Dyson), notably in Finland, home of Nokia. In the mid-1990s, the Helsinki University of Art and Design, with the Finnish government, identified design as a critical sub-system within the national innovation system. The 'Design 2005 strategy' (TEKES 2000) focused on industrial design (Korvenmaa 2009), but over time all design fields have come to be included.

Design was also inserted into the *business model of innovation* as the bridging process between business ideas and the successful roll out of innovations. Here the key concept is *design integration*, which means bringing designers into the business processes of firms, as well as bringing design thinking to bear on all of a firm's activities. Sources such as the World Economic Forum's *Global Competitiveness Report* and the UK Design Council have demonstrated that there is a distinct correlation between design-intensity in enterprise activity and product development, and broad economic competitiveness at the firm and national level (Department of Trade and Industry (DTI) 2005; Swann and Birke 2005; Tether 2005). As one regional report claimed: 'Design can add value across all aspects of a business, including production processes, branding and communications, leadership, and company culture' (State of Victoria 2010: 6). Indeed, the 'input value' of design has spilled over even further, into cutting-edge research and educational practice in business studies. 'Design thinking' is the idea that the mindset, habitus (Bourdieu 1984), or skill-sets of designers are valuable inputs into contemporary business thinking.

Practical, policy-relevant adaptations of the notion of the broad value of design across the economy are exemplified in New Zealand's 'Better by Design' programme. Here, the key strategy was to stimulate growth on the demand side, not at final consumption level but as a business-to-business input, as a priority that may then stimulate growth on the supply side. If design is broadly and increasingly applicable in an 'experience' economy, then companies in any field can identify how it can address their business needs with embedded designers or b2b services. Companies using design inputs displayed a higher level of understanding of customers and their needs and desires, an increased awareness of the role of design in strategic and operational processes, and product and service changes including improved look and feel, particularly for products from engineering organisations. There were observable improvements including more integrated product development, branding, increased investment in design and proportion of turnover from exports and overall turnover growth.

Design is also a major instance of the notion of the 'embedded' creative workforce (see **creative economy**) – that is, creatives working outside the creative industries. Much policy research is gravitating to design as an increasingly vital input economy-wide. Hitherto, design activity has been underestimated in official national statistics and employed designers are so broadly embedded throughout industry sectors that their contributions are significantly undercounted. For example, Higgs et al. (2005) show that designers are embedded in a wider range of other industries than any other occupation. While some design occupations such as architecture and landscape architecture are highly specialised – architects are primarily (85%) employed within the field of architectural services – most other design occupations are highly dispersed across a wide number of industries. For example, designers and illustrators are employed across as many as 84 different industries before 90 per cent of their total employment is accounted for. In total, designers and illustrators are employed across 129 industries. This is reinforced by later findings from a 2008 study (State of Victoria 2010), which demonstrated that over 75 per cent of design employment was in in-house teams, predominantly in the property and business services, manufacturing, construction and retail sectors.

Digital Literacy

Digital literacy is not just the ability to manipulate computer operating systems or mobile apps. It signifies the use of digital (computer-enabled) technologies and systems to *access, understand, to produce and to communicate to others* (i.e. to publish) textual, audio-visual and narrative materials as an autonomous means of communication, along with the social technologies (hardware, software, codes, networks, learning-system) to make this communication possible. Digital literacy is important to the creative industries because it extends the social base of creative **productivity**, and the cultural and economic impact of creative ideas. It is the key capability for social learning (creative emulation) that allows for **innovation** (the growth of knowledge) in networked societies. Digital literacy is not simply an individual skill but also a feature of digital *systems* that allow a communicative relationship to be established in the first place. Thus, digital literacy is impossible without *both* 'producers' (authors, writers, senders) and 'consumers' (audiences, readers, receivers) – who can *both* 'read' and 'write' (or publish) digitally generated and conveyed materials. Thus digital literacy is a feature of large-scale, computer-enabled social **networks**.

Academic interest in the question of popular literacy began with the rise of mass education in and following the nineteenth century. Early studies focused on the *propagation* of literacy, and on the claimed benefits of a literate population for civic, economic and cultural advancement in the context of modern, democratising, trade-dependent nation-states. Ever since compulsory schooling began to be introduced (in 1870 in the UK), considerable resources, both public (schooling) and private (publishing), have been invested in maximising both the number of people who can read and the amount that each person reads. But for most people this level of print literacy was 'read only'. Reading was not seen as a productive act (unless one was reading literature); instead, reading was subsumed into social theory as part of mass consumption. Writing, on the other hand, was regarded as a professional or craft skill; not part of mass literacy at all. 'Getting into print' (i.e. writing for publication) was an **expert** accomplishment. Thus, the relationship between readers and writers in print literacy was organised along strongly *asymmetrical* lines: many readers (of print); few writers (in print).

By the middle of the twentieth century, when print literacy (print-reading; hand-writing) was widely established, along with compulsory schooling (at least in developed nations), critical attention turned to the question of what the populace *did* with their ability to read – especially their *uses* of literacy in the 'consumption' of the products of mass publishing, including newspapers, magazines, popular fiction, advertising and the like. Richard Hoggart's pioneering *The Uses of Literacy* (1957) set the agenda for a generation's educational and disciplinary reform. Hoggart was broadly critical of commercial culture, and while he clearly enjoyed measuring pop culture, pulp fiction and tabloid news against the yardstick of his own sense of working-class communitarian values, he did not seem optimistic that the popular **audience** would be able to pull of the same feat for themselves. Hoggart started an influential tradition of 'critical readings' of *popular* media, where the purpose of literacy education was to equip students with the skills to criticise their own sources of entertainment. This has remained a strong element of 'media literacy' education to this day.

The asymmetry between few writers and masses of readers has changed radically in the shift from print to digital literacy, where, in principle, *everyone* is an author, designer, publisher, journalist and media producer. It is no longer enough to 'inoculate' students *against* such media, even where these are owned and controlled by commercial firms, or used for time-wasting, daydreaming, teenage mischief, or even for straightforward exploitation. The point is that large sections of the population – including children – are using them anyway as both readers and writers, in a process of uptake and impact that is dynamic, energetic, unpredictable, innovative ... and not easily controlled by 'critique'. Schools and formal education providers have not been tasked by government to propagate digital media across the whole population in the same way that elementary schools were used to promote universal print literacy in the industrial era. Instead, digital literacy has propagated itself across new media platforms chaotically: its form, growth, purpose and evaluation is unplanned, unmanaged and demand-led, albeit at vast scale. It was both taught and learned through informal means, using commercial tutorials (or 'watch-me' entertainment formats), peer-to-peer copying, or trial and error.

Faced with the burgeoning growth of 'mass' media, early **media** theorists compared broadcasting to the pulpit or the soap-box, where a single message was shouted from the perspective of some vested interest. The role of the populace was to sit around and passively soak it up. They were the *object* of media messages, not the *subject*. However, in the last few years and at gathering pace, non-professionals have taken up these media as an autonomous means of communication for themselves. 'Writing' is catching up with 'reading'. Now, commentators are remarking on the extent to which consumer **co-creation** is leading the way in finding innovative uses for interactive media. Increasingly, technology is migrating out of organisations and even homes; now we are using mobile devices to 'read and write'. These activities are not only a boost to consumption and entertainment, they are also at the forefront of **innovation**. Even if such activities are pursued by a tiny minority of the estimated total of two billion users, that is still millions more than all of the professional experts put together. The point of such massively extended digital capabilities is that it is no longer necessary to 'pick winners' in advance – novelty, innovation and creativity emerge from the system, not from elite training programmes. Thus, the long-cherished divide between **expert** and amateur is blurring. Non-professionals can have a bigger public impact than corporate producers. Examples include the *political* effect of amateur photos (e.g. Abu Ghraib prison); the *newsworthiness* of mobile-phone pictures (e.g. the 7/7 London Underground bombings); or the *commercial* success of self-made media (especially music and dance) on YouTube. Institutions are learning from individuals (not only the other way around); the economy is augmented by and dependent on cultural activities. 'Serious games' techniques are used to train medical and military personnel, deploying insights, techniques and formats gained from consumers. Social networks are rapidly evolving into major global markets, in which fans, players and consumers themselves can become the next wave of innovative entrepreneurs.

How should we understand such developments? The history of print literacy is again instructive. It teaches us that the eventual 'uses' of new communications technologies cannot be predicted by reference to the intentions of their inventors or even the activities of early adopters. It takes time to build a system of interacting agents who can both send and receive messages autonomously for their own purposes. Two cumulative developments were needed to unleash the full potential of print literacy. First, it took time to build a 'reading public' of imagined co-subjects (what we now call a social **network**) who would be available to read new publications as they appeared. Second, the system only matured once this reading public began to accrue their own, non-purposeful or non-directed *uses* of literacy. Thence, it was only after a literarily connected reading public began to write, on a peer-to-peer basis and not under licence of authority, that Western society produced the Enlightenment (rational philosophy and scientific method), the Industrial Revolution ('useful' knowledge), and democracy ('knowledge is power'), not to mention the realist imagination (the novel). Print literacy thus enabled the entirely unplanned **evolution** of the three great realist textual systems of modernity: science, journalism and the novel. These unforeseen 'consequences of literacy' were profound for the growth of knowledge.

Even though print literacy had escaped the bounds of ecclesiastical and administrative instrumentality, the social reach of these textual systems remained restricted. It was only when the popular classes were politically enfranchised during the nineteenth century that social reformers realised what a friend they had in print literacy, and so began the long haul to invest in it sufficiently for everyone to be a participant (whether they liked it or not). Extending the vote to wage labourers (in 1867 in the UK) hastened universal (compulsory) schooling, free libraries, the 'pauper press', popular literature and eventually mass higher education. What was the return on this investment? Hoggart's pessimistic conclusion can be guessed from the fact that he originally planned to call his book 'The *Abuses* of Literacy'. That pessimism about what people do with media was not auspicious for the era of television that was just beginning in the 1950s. Few thought that a new kind of 'literacy' needed to be taught to exploit the potential of electronic **media**. For most observers, watching TV was thought to be a form of behaviour, learnt unselfconsciously as part of the formation of the self. Experts worried about what sort of behaviour was being encouraged. Where 'media literacy' was taught in schools, it was often justified as an antidote to the power of the media; the idea was to beat them, not join them. So there was no widespread demand for institutional and public investment in teaching 'media literacy' on the scale of what had been needed to render the industrial workforce print literate in the century before the 1950s. Even less attention was paid to the question of how to propagate the skills needed to produce as well as consume using media technologies. The 'educated classes' thought that the knowledge they valued was dependent on print, and threatened by audiovisual media.

This attitude hardly changed when computer-based media came along. As a result, *digital literacy* is developing in the marketplace, not in formal education. The 'Hoggart' question has become relevant again: what are people doing with the media and digital literacy they are learning as part of leisure entertainment? To this we might add a further question that Hoggart never asked: what do ordinary people need to learn in order to attain a level of literacy appropriate for *producing* and *publishing* as well as consuming digital content? On this topic, we need to think carefully about what model of *learning* we take into the digital age (Thomas and Seeley Brown 2011). Will it be an interventionist and state-supported *provider* model (based on supply-side control, standardisation and print); or a *laissez-faire* market-driven model (based on appeal, use and **entertainment**); or something new – a 'demand' model perhaps, where people *learn* because they *like*, where literacy is an attractant, not monopolised by professional experts and controlled by institutional providers?

'Demand' literacy is already developing in the context of 'vernacular' creativity, where processes, technical and production skills are developed on the run; sometimes using online tutorials but more often simply by peer-to-peer assistance. They are learnt in order to complete a job in hand, via just-in-time demand, play techniques, learning by doing, in the workplace, social venue, or at home. A 'vernacular pedagogy' is already diffusing across the net to extend the range of the social networks that are the emergent source of both cultural and economic values. It is this that results in crowd-sourcing (often used among computer geeks to solve technical problems), 'cloud computing' (bringing different domain-knowledge to bear on the solution to a complex problem) and peer-to-peer tuition (check out music tutorials on YouTube). Plain copying should also not be discounted. All of these developments are consequences and uses of digital literacy.

As was the case for print literacy in previous centuries, users are influencing and disrupting former patterns of production and distribution even as they try out new ideas. As Henry Jenkins puts it, 'consumers may gain power through the assertion of new kinds of economic and legal relations and not simply through making meanings' (2004: 36). That 'power' is to use what masquerades as an entertainment format to produce entirely new knowledge, across the scientific, imaginative and journalistic spectrum, just as print literacy itself did, once it was emancipated from official authority. Richard Hoggart was ahead of his time in seeking to understand the role of media usage in ordinary life, but the educational climate of the day – still influential now – sought to counter the media's supposed effects by imposing institutional control (prohibition) and intellectual critique (pessimism). Now that we can see more clearly how the 'uses of literacy' include creation as well as consumption, the challenge for education is to encourage general 'access, understanding and creation',[1] enabling emergent uses, so that everyone can benefit from digital literacy, and by their uses of it contribute to the growth of **knowledge**.

Entertainment

Entertainment is at the core of creative industries, although it is not a well-defined concept, tending to have a 'know it when you see it' quality to many observers (but see McKee et al. 2011). Sayre and King (2010: 4) offer a definition of entertainment as 'a constructed product designed to stimulate a mass audience in an agreeable way in exchange for money'. Among the features that Sayre and King associated with entertainment are:

- It is provided by experienced professionals;
- It is typically the result of team-based forms of production;
- It may be live or mediated, but the experience of it is frequently time-bound;
- Audiences will have cues as to how to experience it from how it has been marketed and promoted;

It is provided on a commercial basis. The global media and 'entertainment industries' are among the world's largest industry sectors. Industry analysts Pricewaterhouse-Coopers estimates their value at $US2 trillion by 2015, or 3.2 per cent of global gross domestic product (PwC 2011). As many entertainment industries are service-related, they are also often large employers: Walt Disney World Resort in Florida is the world's largest single-site service-industry employer, with 66,000 people employed over 3,700 job classifications. The entertainment industries also cater to the cultural needs of many people – about 50 million people, or 1 in 6

88

[1]This is the definition of media literacy adopted by the UK communications regulator Ofcom. See www.ofcom.org.uk/advice/media_literacy/

Americans, visit a Disney theme park over the course of a year. Entertainment is also highly tradeable internationally, and the circulation of entertainment products is a major feature of **globalisation**. Curtin (2007) observes that it is far easier for international media companies to offer packages of movies, sport and children's programming into Asia than news, particularly in China, which is both Asia's largest television market and the most difficult to enter.

Entertainment occupies an uncertain status in academic analysis. In defining what constitutes television entertainment, Jonathan Gray (2008) differentiates entertainment programming from news, information and educational programming on the one hand, and advertising on the other. At the same time, he notes that these distinctions are always at risk of collapsing in on one another: advertisements can definitely entertain and indeed inform; entertainment programming can be informative, as seen, for example, with news satire programmes such as *The Daily Show* and *The Colbert Report* in the USA; and informational programming commonly pursues entertainment values, as seen with the documentaries of social critics such as Michael Moore from one angle, and the plethora of celebrity gossip stories in news programmes from another (Jones et al. 2009). Moreover, Gray observes that 'it is hard to offer a value-neutral definition of entertainment, since it is one of the most automatically moralised concepts. Entertainment can be a compliment or a profanity, and it can represent transcendence or corruption, salvation or sin, depending on the speaker' (2008: 4).

Two quotations can illustrate some of the difficulties. The first is from cultural theorist Andrew Edgar, arguing for the continuing relevance of the Frankfurt School's critique of the **cultural industries**:

> Even within the culture industry, not all of its products are homogeneous. Orson Welles (and later Michelangelo Antonioni) demonstrate that cinema has the critical and self-referential potential that Adorno attributes to all autonomous art; Bette Davis keeps alive the tradition of great acting; and, if the nuances of the text are to be believed, Warner Brothers' cartoons do not share the simple minded capitulation of authority that is the hallmark of Disney. (2008: 84)

Edgar does not propose that *all* entertainment is rubbish – a small section of it is art – but most of it is, and the parts that are not art are definitely rubbish (see **aesthetics**). Such critiques of entertainment frequently present it as the antithesis of **culture**; as it is produced in an industrial context, and realises its value as a commodity in the commercial marketplace, it is therefore frequently accused of being culturally homogeneous, in contrast to 'autonomous art'. For example, Alan Bryman's (2004) critical account of the 'Disneyization of society' presents the branded entertainment of the Disney theme parks as being the antithesis of more authentic forms of local culture. The second quotation comes from the economist Richard Caves, justifying his decision to write a book about the economics of the creative industries:

> Economists have studied a number of industrial sectors for their special and distinctive features … Indeed, few sectors have escaped notice that display some distinctive form of competitive behaviour or pose distinctive problems for public policy. One has

been largely missed, however – the 'creative' industries supplying goods and services that we broadly associate with cultural, artistic, or *simply* entertainment value. (Caves 2000: 1, emphasis added)

In this case, Caves' proposition that some cultural products *simply* have entertainment value is not in fact borne out by his account of how they are produced. He observes that books, plays, recorded music, television programmes and feature films are all among the most complex of creative goods in terms of the coordination activities involved in their production. The economists Andersson and Andersson (2006) similarly observe that, as experience goods, entertainment products have some of the most complex market characteristics. This is particularly the case with live performance, where 'there is no way of knowing the impact of the experience in advance, as the composition of the crowd and their reactions and responses as well as the quality of the performance at the specific location are all inherently uncertain' (Andersson and Andersson 2006: 84). Rather, the assignation of the term 'simple' to entertainment value would appear to refer to the idea that their economic value is simple – people pay to consume them and they do or do not return a profit – as compared to cultural value, defined as 'complex, multifaceted, unstable and lacking an agreed unit of account' (Throsby 2010: 18).

At the height of Marxist-inspired film criticism, Richard Dyer (1992) observed that at the core of entertainment was pleasure. By increasing the leisure options and opportunities for large proportions of the population, at least in the industrial capitalist world, entertainment in its current form is very much a creation of the twentieth century, characterised by growing cultural plenitude (Hartley 2003). Dyer observed that discussions of entertainment are frequently over-determined by its relationship to art on the one hand, and ideology on the other:

> The discourses of both art and ideology tend to take the idea of entertainment for granted, and therefore not to scrutinise it. The former ... either seeks to denigrate entertainment because it is not art ... Discussion of ideology on the other hand tends to treat entertainment as a sugar on the pill of ideological messages ... Once again, though, what entertainment is is not addressed. (Dyer 1992: 1)

Dyer proposed that underlying entertainment is the desire for a *utopian* feeling; 'the sense that things could be better, that something other than what is can be imagined and maybe realised' (1992: 20). Dyer identified five core elements of entertainment products: *abundance*; *energy*; *intensity*; *transparency*; and *community*. The specifically utopian element of entertainment, and the genuine needs and desires it caters to, arises from how it can provide a counterpoint to negative experiences of modern industrial capitalist societies: it promises plenitude rather than scarcity; energy and commitment rather than exhaustion and alienation; and adventure rather than predictability (Dyer 1992: 26).

Jonathan Gray (2010b) has observed that one implication of analysing entertainment is that it 'encourages multimedia and transmedia analysis' rather than platform-specific studies (2010b: 813). Gray is drawing upon Henry Jenkins' analysis of the current phase of media **convergence** as one where *transmedia storytelling* has become more central:

key concepts in creative industries

We now live at a moment where every story, image, brand, relationship plays itself out across the maximum number of media platforms, shaped top-down by decisions made in corporate boardrooms and bottom-up by decisions made in teenagers' bedrooms. The concentrated ownership of media conglomerates increases the desirability of properties that can exploit 'synergies' between different parts of the medium system and 'maximise touch-points' with different niches of consumers. The result has been the push towards franchise-building in general and transmedia entertainment in particular. (Jenkins 2010: 948)

The implications of digital media for entertainment are ambiguous. On the one hand, the digital domain is increasingly the future of entertainment, even if it is often more difficult to monetise entertainment products in digital formats. PwC observe that digital products accounted for 26 per cent of global media and entertainment revenues in 2011, and expected that figure to grow to 33.9 per cent in 2015. At the same time, digital media and entertainment products accounted for 58.7 per cent of the growth in spending over the 2011–2015 period, meaning that non-digital media and entertainment products and services were still accounting for almost two-thirds of revenues, even though the proportionate investment in them is much less than that for digital media and entertainment (PwC 2011). The crisis of value of digital entertainment products – seen most clearly in the 2000s in the music industry – is partly the result of content piracy, as control over **intellectual property** is challenged with the proliferation of digital **technology**. It is also reflective of content proliferation: as more and more content is available, and can be accessed from multiple digital devices, the scarcity value of individual entertainment products diminishes accordingly.

While there is much discussion of the disruptive impact of digitisation on traditional media and entertainment platforms, notably book publishing, music, newspapers and magazines, there has been less discussion of the boom in various non-digital forms of entertainment. Writers' festivals have become an important part of contemporary **public culture** and the branding of cities, and the experience of buying the book seems to be enhanced considerably by the opportunity to hear the author discuss the work in person. Music festivals have similarly boomed through the 2000s, as noted by Charles Leadbeater, who makes the point that one of the most important cultural events in the UK has come to be the Glastonbury music festival, showing how 'entrepreneurship and the market can play a vital role in creating a mass, participatory and self-organising cultural experience' (2005). While the price of individual items of music may have fallen dramatically in recent years, the opposite trend has been apparent in the willingness of consumers to pay for live concert performances, increasingly making the release of songs and records a promotional device for lavishly staged global concert tours.

As the internet and digital technologies make more and more cultural content available to us through various screens and digital platforms, there would seem to be a new valuation taking place of 'liveness', and the association of entertainment events with tangible and lived forms of community experience. Moreover, entertainment as a cultural activity inevitably runs over into the 'experience economy', and major sporting events (the Olympics, World Cup football etc.), as well as tourism, meaning that the boundaries between media, live entertainment and other forms of experience are somewhat fuzzy. The vibrancy of 'street-level' culture has been taken to be an important marker of **creative cities**, and the density of cultural networks is increasingly important to urban cultural policy. In these various ways, creative industries points towards a broader inter-meshing of culture and entertainment

Entrepreneur/ship

Entrepreneurs are key **agents** in the creative industries. The *entrepreneur* (the agent) or *entrepreneurship* (the process) is the action of doing new things in the **market** context of uncertainty with respect to existing value-seeking to create and realise new value. The entrepreneur seeks to discover new sources of value by uncovering contradictions (i.e. opportunities) in extant value structures or by proposing new value structures (i.e. innovations). The entrepreneur's incentive is to claim some fraction of that value created.

Entrepreneurs are like scientists in this respect: formulating hypothesises of what will create value, then testing that on the market. The value created is not equal. Some will create much more value than others and these successful entrepreneurs will disproportionately shape the creative industries. Entrepreneurial success, like scientific and artistic, is a power law phenomenon (see **complex systems**). Entrepreneurship, like science, also works best in well-developed institutional environments, given its reliance on contractual agreements and securitised assets (including reputations and trust) to underpin 'claims'. However, also like science, entrepreneurship creates value by imagining new ideas and opportunities and endeavouring to make them real. Entrepreneurship is both a creative and a destructive process (see **creative destruction**) as an evolutionary process that plays out in complex systems (see **evolution** and **complex systems**). This is especially so in the creative industries because they are a highly entrepreneurial sector, and also because they are a key driver of the innovation process (see **innovation**). Entrepreneurship is a human behaviour that drives progress in economic, sociocultural and political orders alike. The creative industries are central and instrumental to this process, both as sources of entrepreneurial action (Cowen 1998), and also as pathways through which it can work (Potts 2009a).

Two reasons illuminate why entrepreneurship is a key concept for the creative industries. First, there is a curiously innate similarity between the *artist* and the *entrepreneur*. Both are engaged in the creation of novelty in the face of fundamental uncertainty about conjectures of value (Swedberg 2006; Karpik 2010). Both are agents that introduce change into respectively cultural and economic systems. Both are subject to differential success and the prospect of failure, and therefore both are often highly self-motivated and risk-tolerant. All of these aspects sometimes combine in one person, for example in the creative and entrepreneurial vision of the late CEO of Apple, Steve Jobs. Artists and entrepreneurs often proceed by seeing an opportunity or source of value or quality, or indeed make connections that others do not see (Earl 2003). And both are often motivated by complex desires (recognition, status, self-actualisation, lifestyle, as well as material rewards). Moreover, there is substantial overlap in the personality traits and socio-demographic profiles of artists and entrepreneurs (often 'outsiders', highly 'independent', above average intelligence and imagination, high tolerance for ambiguity, risk-lovers, unusual degree of persistence, etc). Entrepreneurs present a useful lens through which to study artistic behaviour, and vice versa.

Second, the industrial structure of the cultural and creative industries tends to have a very large number of micro-businesses (0–2 employees) as well as being substantially composed of small- and medium-sized enterprises (SMEs) (Leadbeater and Oakley 1999). Large businesses constitute less than 1 per cent of all creative industries businesses (although accounting for about 40 per cent of creative industries output). Smaller business tend to depend far more on entrepreneurial endeavour than larger businesses simply because they are less able to compete on advantages of scale and scope. So the quality of entrepreneurship in the creative industries matters for the viability and dynamics of the sector. This is a further reason that innovation policy can often be more important to the vitality of the creative industries than traditional arts and cultural policy, which tends to crowd-out entrepreneurship with patronage.

Both observations have received considerable attention since the re-conception of the creative industries by the UK Department of Culture, Media and Sport (DCMS) that sought to shift policy focus of the arts, cultural and creative industry from a broadly market-failure and welfare-based model of public subsidy toward a policy model centred around innovation and growth (Potts 2011). A central realisation has been the importance of entrepreneurial skills and competence as a critical input into creative industries development. Numerous subsequent reports have worried about relative deficits of entrepreneurial competence, as well as underdeveloped entrepreneurial supports in relation to access to finance, intellectual property protection, the costs of starting small businesses, and the barriers to market entry (e.g. Utrecht 2011).

There are several definitions of entrepreneurship. The classic definition is as the role of *organisation* (the 'fourth factor of production' in Alfred Marshall's phrase) in the value creation process. Entrepreneurs start and run businesses; their income is the share of profit from the value they create (for consumers) in so doing. But this definition mixes entrepreneurship with management (or creative and routine organisation). This is the business school definition of entrepreneurship as a skill. An example is the artist as a small business owner, or a producer/director in a media company.

A second definition is *alertness to opportunities*, such as an arbitrage trade (buying cheap in one market and selling dear in another), or spotting unexploited opportunities to match supply and demand. In this definition, entrepreneurs are the agents in the market economy who, in effect, make the system competitive (see **competition**): they equilibrate markets, bringing order and efficiency. An example is a promoter, who 'sees' the opportunity to bring an exhibition to a city, or sees a demand from creative goods in one market that can be met by supply from a different market. They profit from this activity, but consumers also benefit from lower prices and the competing away of rents. This is the neoclassical economics definition of entrepreneurship as applied rationality.

But perhaps the most well-known is Joseph Schumpeter's (1912) definition of the entrepreneur as the economic agent who introduces *new ideas* into the *economic order*, in the face of uncertainty, and in pursuit of *profit*. The Schumpeterian (i.e. evolutionary economics) entrepreneur is an agent who disturbs the existing economic order with a new idea that may become an innovation. Entrepreneurship is the process of imagining, creating and realising economic opportunities for profit in the face of uncertainty and in carrying the risk for this uncertainty themselves. Examples include visual artists such as Andy Warhol (USA) or Damien Hirst (UK), who created not just new art, but a new art market and business model. The entrepreneur is thus the progenitor agent of evolutionary economic growth and development that seeks to discover new sources of value. The economic order evolves because of the disruptive actions of entrepreneurs.

Schumpeter emphasised entrepreneurship as a two-part process: (1) the entrepreneur as the creative, active agent, proposing and developing the new idea, often integral to management and development; and (2) the carrying of that risk, by the *financier*. Sometimes this dual function meets in a single person, but in practice is often separated because finance is best done through portfolio risk-pooling, whereas active entrepreneurship usually requires deep focus on local knowledge. This aspect in part reflects why many mature creative industries are often built about large holding companies (such as movie studios or publishing houses) that act as the risk-pooling financiers. The creative industries have long had difficulties with finance, in part due to the historical preponderance of the patronage model (whether by royalty or government) and the relative underdevelopment of venture capital markets and other market sources of finance in this sector. Part of the difficulty lies in capitalising assets (which is a requirement for finance), especially in relation to intellectual property. Better finance models thus contribute to improved opportunities for entrepreneurship.

Another model has been developed by sociologist David Stark who argues that this discovery process can also arise in the function of an organisational form itself where 'entrepreneurship is the ability to keep multiple principles of evaluation in play and benefit from that productive friction' (2009: 6). In this way market and organisational spaces can be entrepreneurial when they can join together different senses of worth to create a dissonance that is generative of new conjectures of value.

These four models of entrepreneurship – the organisational model, the arbitrage model, the evolutionary model, and the dissonance model – are useful analytic distinctions, but in practice entrepreneurship usually involves all four. Policy considerations should be similarly constituted to recognise entrepreneurship operating across all four dimensions: (1) as a useful skill, creating jobs and output; (2) as an action that makes markets work better, creating efficiency gains; (3) as a disruptive action, driving growth and evolution; and (4) as a generative form of organisation.

A further general consideration concerns entrepreneurial rewards. Entrepreneurs don't earn a wage; rather they earn *profit*. In accounting terms, this is the residual claimed from revenue minus expenses in proportion to ownership of the enterprise. Of course, entrepreneurs assume the losses when that accounting goes into the red (financiers generally carry most of this risk). Successful entrepreneurs – and the creative industries contains a disproportionate number of extremely wealthy entrepreneurs – can amass large fortunes. But where does that profit actually come from? The technical answer is from *consumer surplus*. The profit entrepreneurs make is a share of the value they create, and it is important to understand that this didn't previously exist (Andersson and Andersson 2006). They create it; they don't 'take it' from someone. Many entrepreneurs will fail in this process of ongoing (artistic) conjecture and (market) refutation (Ormerod 2005), but when they succeed it is because consumers have decided that the outputs are worth more to them than the market price, else they would not choose to pay to consume them. Some of this value goes to the entrepreneurs (as profit) and the remainder accrues as consumer surplus. Observe too that the more **competition** in the **market**, i.e. the less it tends to monopoly or is protected, the greater the value captured by consumers.

The study of entrepreneurship in creative industries is still new and developing. Much of the current work focuses on seeking to apply general studies of entrepreneurship in small businesses, or in relation to general accounts of innovation-driven economies, and seeking to develop targeted sectoral policies to harness and develop entrepreneurial potential in the cultural and creative industries, particularly in relation to skills and capabilities deficits in entrepreneurship, and barriers and regulatory burdens in the creative industries. Entrepreneurship seeks to perceive opportunities and bring them to reality, aiming to capture a share of the value created. While this conventionally plays out in markets, there are four other domains beside producer entrepreneurship: consumer, cultural, social and political. Each intersects with the creative industries.

Consumer entrepreneurship occurs when consumers engage with market choices to use systems of goods and services to solve existing and new problems, often then sharing that with others (e.g., in consumer-co-creation and open-source models of production). With the concept of fashion (Chai et al. 2007; Hartley and Montgomery 2009), this shades into *cultural entrepreneurship* about ideas leadership and media and attention-gathering (Lanham 2006). Consumer entrepreneurship pays off directly through the payoff to the newly artistically/entrepreneurially crafted consumption set. Cultural benefits follow (relying on reputation) if others also subsequently adopt the same idea. Social and political entrepreneurship are the institutionalised forms of these base mechanisms, when subject to specific norms and rules. A *social entrepreneur* is someone who proposes and seeks to develop new ideas in relation to social organisation. A *political entrepreneur* does this in the political domain. In both, the rewards are not usually directly utilitarian or material but accrue to structures of influence, connection and perhaps power as the reward to entrepreneurship.

Evolution is perhaps a curious keyword in creative industries, redolent of 'survival of the fittest' notions and other such *laissez-faire* ruthlessness. But despite that overt politicisation, which can be traced back to 'social' rather than scientific Darwinism, evolution is actually a practical analytic model for thinking about dynamical processes in which variety drives adaptation to change in a system. The contrast is with revolution, which is a type of change foisted from without and implying some kind of political over-turning of an existing order. Evolution, however, is a process of change that occurs gradually from within as new and 'better fitting' variants or ideas gradually replace those less well adapted to a changed environment. The creative industries are constantly evolving, in the sense of changing from within by the differential success of some variants gradually leading to completely new market and industry structures. From a sufficient distance this can even look like revolution – i.e. the digital revolution etc. – but these are all really evolutionary processes.

Evolutionary theory is central to the study of the creative industries as a model of how creative industries *grow and change* through the processes of entrepreneurship, innovation and creative destruction. The creative industries themselves evolve as an industrial dynamic, and they are also part of the broader process of economic and socio-cultural evolution. This is why students of creative industries need to understand the concept of evolution. It is the main dynamic affecting their economic and socio-cultural environment. It also explains why creative industries policy is best centred about innovation policy. The generalised Darwinian theory of evolution (Hodgson and Knudsen 2010) is constructed in terms of three mutually constitutive mechanisms: (1) a process of *variation*; (2) a process of *selection*; and (3) a process of *replication*. These three processes (VSR) constitute the mechanisms of an evolutionary process; anything subject to all three is said to evolve. The creative industries evolve through these mechanisms. But the creative industries are also part of the process by which these mechanisms play out in the wider economic and socio-cultural domain.

First, evolution is a theory of *origins of order* that explains why something is the way it is, or has the structure and form that it does, in consequence of mechanisms of variation, selection and replication. Evolution is a theory of order and form where that order or form is explained as the outcome of a 'blind' or un-guided process with no teleological imperative. The opposite of evolution in this sense is design, planning or top-down guidance as the source of order. Many of the highly coordinated and structured industrial, technological and market outcomes in the creative industries can be explained as the consequence of evolutionary processes of mutual adaptation differential selection. Second, evolution is a theory about *populations*, where evolution is a process predicated on a population of some unit of variation, a unit of selection, and a unit of replication. Logically, this unit must be the same or closely related across the three mechanisms. In biology the unit of VSR is the gene. In economics it is the *technology* (Arthur 2009), or the *rule* (Dopfer and Potts 2008), or the *idea* (Beinhocker 2006). There have been many proposals for what this key 'unit' is and this remains an ongoing problem of debate, with different schools of thought branching from different proposals. But, in all cases, evolution is defined as a *population dynamic* (Hodgson and Knudsen 2010). Evolution is observed not as change in an individual unit, but as change in the structure of the population of types of that unit. Only populations evolve, not individuals. Evolution is ultimately a theory of population dynamics.

All evolutionary models begin by assuming the existence of some population of units (genes, ideas, technologies, etc.) that are candidate solutions to some problem. These might be genes for avoiding predators, for example, or technologies for storing food, or business models for making movies. Variation in these competing units means that some will be more successful than others in solving the problem (e.g. avoiding predators, reducing spoilage, providing entertainment profitably). This is what is meant by 'fitness' and selection, i.e. how well a gene or idea 'fits with' its selection environment. Those variants that are 'selected against' are removed from the population, while those 'selected for' are replicated in the population. The population changes through time as *differential variation* is translated into *differential replication*. An evolutionary process causes the average fitness of a population to increase through time.[1]

The mechanism of *variation* is whatever introduces variety into the population. In biology this is due to mutation and sexual recombination. In economics and culture it is due to creativity and entrepreneurship, which is also largely a recombinatorial process. But variety can also be introduced through mistakes or adaptations made in copying or imitation (Bentley et al. 2007). In creative industries, the 'mechanism of variation' consists of a great many possible processes, including luck, but the main argument made in evolutionary theory applied to creative industries is that new ideas are the result of recombinations of old ideas. This is why restrictions or barriers placed on reuse of ideas, such as with strong **intellectual property** rights for example, can be viewed as barriers to novelty and creativity.

The mechanism of *selection* is the process by which variants are evaluated with respect to the selection environment. In biology there is natural and sexual selection. In economic evolution, the main selection mechanism is the market, which means both institutional rules and consumers select over the offerings of firms and other producers of culture and creative content. In culture, selection is due to differential attention and adoption by consumers. In competitive markets, selection is something done by consumers to producers. In planned economic orders, selection is something done by experts and bureaucracies to producers. Creative industries selection processes involve both.

The *replication* mechanism is the process by which the selected variants are carried forward in time. In biology this is the sequence of generations where the genotype 'information' (the genes) is copied into a new phenotype (the individual organism). In economic and cultural evolution, the replication mechanism is due to investment and learning, often as a process of imitation (Bentley et al. 2011).

evolution

97

---

[1]Technical note: this is called the 'fundamental theorem of selection' or the 'Fisher equation' of covariance.

The VSR model of Darwinian evolution has many further refinements and developments. *Co-evolution* occurs when another species, technology or market is the reciprocal selection environment, resulting in evolutionary processes that can exhibit strong feedback (e.g. predator–prey relations, complementary technologies, or institutions and technology). Another is analysis of *niches*, which are localised selection environments and contexts of variation. Niche theory serves as a theory of market segmentation in the study of economic evolution, including the theory of **clusters**.

Several specific applications of evolution theory bear upon the creative industries: evolutionary economics; evolutionary psychology; technological evolution and the growth of knowledge; and theories of cultural evolution. *Evolutionary economics* is a substantial underpinning of the theory and analysis of creative industries (Potts 2009b, 2011). Evolutionary economics is based on the works of Joseph Schumpeter (1883–1954) and Friedrich Hayek (1901–1991), who presented theories of market dynamics and economic development as an evolutionary process. Modern versions include Nelson and Winter (1982) and Dopfer (2005). In the evolutionary theory of economic growth, the economic order is continually disrupted from within by new ideas that are introduced by entrepreneurs and drive innovation trajectories, at all scales, which result in the never ending endogenous transformation of the economic order: a self-organising structural process of change that Schumpeter called '**creative destruction**', resulting in what Hayek called 'the emergent order'. This process is one of ongoing entry and exit from **markets**, resulting in differential success and failure on the part of producers, and accompanied by job creation and destruction, as well as the **entrepreneurial** creation of new markets and the contraction of some existing markets.

A broader analysis seeks to explain the *growth of knowledge* (Popper 1968; Loasby 1999) and also *technology* (Mokyr 2004; Beinhocker 2006; Arthur 2009) as an evolutionary process. Implicit is the notion that knowledge and technology *co-evolve* with the economy. The creative industries, however, are not singled out in these frameworks for any special role. However, it is entirely reasonable to note that the growth of knowledge and technology is in significant part a process of communication and social learning, as well as socio-cultural and institutional adaptation to new ideas, implying that they are part of the mechanisms of variation, selection and retention in the evolutionary growth of knowledge process.

Evolutionary theory also connects with creative industries through other sciences too. Creative industries involve human behaviour, and *evolutionary psychology* proposes a new model of human behaviour. Evolutionary psychology argues that the human mind is as much a product of evolution as other phenotypic traits, and, moreover, that many of our mental features can be understood as adaptations to the ancestral selection environment of the Pleistocene. These theories propose that modern humans in effect have 'stone age minds', thus explaining characteristic mental processes, social behaviour and individual preferences. Evolutionary psychology provides a foundation for the analysis of why humans tend to like the sorts of art, music and stories that we do, and why there is variation in this. Dutton (2009) has examined what he calls the 'art instinct', and Brian Boyd (2009) has applied evolutionary psychology to the study of stories and literature. G. Miller

(2009) examines how evolved preferences shape consumption patterns. This evolutionary perspective helps us to understand the nature of demand for the product of the creative industries.

Sociological accounts have long skirted the boundaries between developmental and evolutionary accounts of large-scale socio-cultural change and transformation. Explicitly evolutionary accounts of social and cultural change have been developed in the dual inheritance theory of Boyd and Richerson (2004); in the multilevel (cultural and social) evolutionary selection theory of Runciman's (2009) comparative sociology; and by Hodgson and Knudsen (2010), who examine why social science should be built on Darwinian foundations using the concept of complex population systems. Any such evolutionary process between cultural and social evolution will invariably be channelled through the creative industries. This suggests that the creative industries should be understood not only as ends in themselves (providing media and entertainment, etc.), but as part of the process of socio-cultural evolution. They give rise to *positive externalities* that manifest in the ability of a socio-cultural order to adapt and change (Herrmann-Pillath 2010). The creative industries are part of the processes of economic and socio-cultural evolution. This argument was hinted at in the original UK Department of Culture, Media and Sport (DCMS) (1998) conception of the creative industries, and has been further developed by Potts and Cunningham (2008) and Potts (2009a, 2011). All processes of economic and socio-cultural evolution can be represented as a four-phase trajectory of:

1 The origination of the novel idea;
2 The subsequent adoption and adaptation of that idea into the population of agents;
3 The retention and embedding of that idea into habits, routines and new institutions;
4 The **creative destruction** or 'extinction' of the idea and the emergence of others.

The creative industries play important roles in each of these phases of each trajectory of economic and socio-cultural evolution. From this perspective, they are not 'just another industry', but part of the **innovation** system of an economy, society and culture. The creative industries are both sites of evolution, as well as mechanisms of evolution.

Expert

expert

Expertise – the status and role of knowledgeable professionals – is becoming a topic of some contention in the creative industries and across the wider creative economy.

TIME Magazine celebrated 'You' as the person of the year in 2006, recognising the rise of user-created content (see **co-creation**). The magazine noted that these consumers weren't only making content, they were also 'working for nothing and beating the pros at their own game'. This re-engineering of producer-consumer relations is at the core of the creative industries, and it unsettles the paradigm of professional expertise that has dominated the processes of media production throughout the industrial era (Hartley 2009: 131–5). However, not all scholars or commentators are celebrating the changing conditions confronting cultural experts. Andrew Keen warned that the 'cult of the amateur' may undermine and threaten standards of cultural value (2008). He worried that professionally produced newspapers, magazines and music were under threat from a wave of amateur and free content. David Weinberger (2008), on the other hand, saw a potential democratising of cultural knowledge production in which forms of 'social knowing' disrupt the centralised power, authority and control of incumbent media industries.

That leaves us with an opposition between 'the experts' and various versions of 'everybody' – those who are collaboratively creating and sharing (Shirky 2008). In this context, how is expertise being changed or transformed? Are we seeing a different model of distributed and co-creative expertise emerging in the creative industries, one that undermines a certain traditional understanding of experts and their others? What alternative models of expertise might be forming in the belly of the creative industries? A careful reading of Lanier (2011) offers an insight into what is at stake in these concerns about expertise. A celebrated computer scientist and pioneer of virtual reality, Lanier criticises 'Web 2.0' rhetoric that seeks to elevate the wisdom of crowds and associated technologies over the intelligence and creativity of individuals. He worries that celebrated Web 2.0 collaborative platforms such as Facebook do not express and amplify individual creativity, but rather that they level it to the lowest common denominator of cultural expression. Lanier is no anti-technology Luddite. His concern is not with the technologies themselves but with an emerging view of expertise that he thinks underpins Web 2.0 rhetoric: namely, the idea that the collective of users (a crowd identity) can be better at solving problems and creative expression than can individuals. Lanier argues that collectives can be useful for optimisation but not for the more elevated varieties of creativity and imagination that we should cherish.

This view is echoed in Nicholas Carr (2011). Drawing on the neurosciences, Carr argues that the information technology revolution is reconfiguring our brains by fostering habits of mind that may undermine our capacity for individually sustained immersion and concentration. Carr is asking important questions: how technologies change the ways we think and create and know. Although we may want to question the assumption that technologies directly change our brains, he is asking us to consider what it means to be a thinker or an expert in an environment that is increasingly networked and distributed. Carr writes:

> We seem to have arrived, as McLuhan said we would, at an important juncture in our intellectual and cultural history, a moment of transition between two very different modes of thinking. What we're trading away in return for the riches of the Net – and only a curmudgeon would refuse to see the riches – is what Karp calls 'our old linear

thought process'. Calm, focused, undistracted, the linear mind is being pushed aside by a new kind of mind that wants and needs to take in and dole out information in short, disjointed, often overlapping bursts – the faster, the better (19).

But at stake in these discussions is not just thinking or expertise in the abstract. It is the viability of a certain kind of thinker, or the job of thinking. Lanier argues that de-emphasising personhood and individual creativity hurts the middle class:

> As technology gets better and better, and civilisation becomes more and more digital, one of the major questions we will have to address is: Will a sufficiently large middle class of people be able to make a living from what they do with their hearts and heads? Or will they be left behind, distracted by empty gusts of ego-boosting puffery? (x).

Critics such as Lanier and Carr raise important questions about the changing value and status of certain kinds of thinking work often associated with expertise and professionals. Should we therefore assume that the technological and media trends characterising the creative industries are simply replacing the jobs of experts and professional media producers (see **creative labour**)? And even if they are, should we then assume this necessarily threatens the role of valued forms of expert knowledge? Not necessarily, though it may be necessary to consider how expertise and expert forms of knowledge are now organised and distributed.

Certain cultural commentators and experts may sense that their cultural and economic capital and status are undermined by digital and network technologies. David Gauntlett identifies a 'tendency to festishise "experts", whose readings of popular culture are seen as more significant than those of other audience members …'. He also notes a 'preference for conventional research methods where most people are treated as non-expert audience "receivers", or, if they are part of formal media industries, as expert "producers"'. Gauntlett proposes an alternative to such festishisation of expertise: to 'focus on the everyday meanings produced by a diverse array of audience members, accompanied by an interest in new qualitative research techniques'. He suggests that such new methods would recognise people's own creativity by brushing aside 'outmoded notions of "receiver" audiences and elite producers' (2011b: Chapter 2). Gauntlett identifies important shifts in producer/consumer relationships and the related unsettling of professional identity and expertise.

But again, we need to keep in mind that this analysis is offered by an expert in debate with other experts in the context of an academic discipline, in this case media studies. There is a risk here of categories such as 'non-experts' functioning in what John Frow (1995: 60–9) describes as a 'substitution of voices'. Categories such as 'the people', 'the popular' or 'non-experts' become textual delegates for the position and interests of the analyst. The point here is not to decide whether Gauntlett is correct as opposed to Lanier and Carr. All of them ask important questions about profound changes in the conditions of knowledge-production and their implications for the identities and social status of experts. But these various experts are simultaneously engaging in an all too familiar contest and debate about the authority to determine who and what counts as knowledgeable. They are not neutral observers above the fray; and neither party speaks *on behalf of* 'the people' in their new guise as 'non-experts'.

The challenge, especially in the context of the creative industries, is to consider how we might develop models of expertise that situate and coordinate the expertise of citizen consumers alongside professional creative expertise. This problem is hinted at in the work of Gauntlett (2011a). It is helpfully characterised by Collins and Evans (2002, 2007) as a problem of 'expertise extension', which they describe as the need to extend the domain of technical decision-making beyond the confines of a professional qualified elite, to include, for example, the 'experience-based expertise' of people who are not recognised by certification or professional standing. Collins and Evans (2002: 237) do not suppose that this is easy to achieve; they acknowledge the difficulties of *extending recognition* of diverse forms of expertise, and also of establishing grounds for *limiting the extension* of decision-making rights. They are interested in how we can 'begin to think about how different kinds of expertise combine in social life, and how they combine in technical decision making' (2002: 251; Collins and Evans 2007). They develop an idea of 'interactional expertise' in the context of forming 'trading zones' that permit exchanges and transactions across various disciplines and knowledge practices. Interactional expertise is the skill set and competencies that enable communication and exchange across expertise divides. In this approach, expertise becomes a *coordination problem* rather than simply an opposition between individual professional experts and an ill-defined mass 'wisdom of the crowds'. As Axel Bruns suggests, the challenge is to reconcile 'traditional expertise and emergent community knowledge structures' (2008: 214–19). We need to consider what kinds of skills and knowledge are needed to make such distributed expertise networks work effectively and fairly.

This emerging *co-creative expertise* (Banks 2009) should be about so much more than simply using the mass 'wisdom of the crowd' to optimise datasets. At stake here are also quite fundamental categories and identities, including the jobs and working conditions of professionals. What and who are now counted as knowledgeable? Thinking and expertise are increasingly *distributed and externalised* through networks of technologies, interfaces, professionals and amateurs. For instance, Steven Levy (2011) describes how Google – as an organization – can be understood to 'think'. Such thinking is constituted by an elaborate network of servers and algorithms, the expertise of professional engineers and designers, and by harnessing the behaviour of searching users to generate innovative machine learning. Levy describes Google as a 'practical large scale machine learning system' that processes and harnesses the feedback from users (2011: 65). But at the very heart of Google are the many talented designers and engineers – Levy calls them 'Googlers' – who:

> all grew up with the Internet and considered its principles to be as natural as the laws of gravity. They were among the brightest and most ambitious of a generation that was better equipped to handle the disruptive technology wave than their elders were. Their minds hummed like tuning forks in resonance with the company's values of speed, flexibility, and a deep respect for data. (2011: 5)

John Hartley (2009) suggests that tackling problems of expertise coordination (i.e. *co-creative expertise*) requires a *dialogic* approach between professional experts and amateur users. In reference to digital storytelling workshops, Hartley comments that:

> the *problem* of the expertise of the facilitator … would not be solved by simply firing all the filmmakers and letting consumers get by on their own. It is important not to fall for an 'either/or' model of digital storytelling: either *expert* or *everyone*. (2009: 133)

Honing expertise skills to undertake this task is a pressing challenge for the creative industries. It is also a looming challenge for higher educational institutions seeking to educate and train the professionals and consumers who will engage in such dialogue. But these are challenges that are well suited to the creative industries. In videogames companies, and throughout many other creative industries organisations, we are seeing the adaptive experimentation and organisational innovations that combine and coordinate various different types and sources of expertise, both professional and amateur, to generate new and compelling forms of creative expression (Banks 2009, 2012). Distributed, co-creative expertise, and how it may contribute to growth of knowledge, are among the most exciting prospects for the creative industries over the coming decades. How might the skills being refined and practised by creative players of games such as *Minecraft*, for example, help us to understand better the kinds of **digital literacy** needed to engage whole populations in growing knowledge? Michael Nielsen (2011) gives us insight into what this co-creative expertise might look like with his accounts of how new cognitive tools that harness the internet may be accelerating scientific discovery. He describes how 250,000 amateur astronomers working on the Galaxy Zoo project are contributing to new discoveries. But Nielsen's point is not so much that these online collaborations are solving particular problems. The value here is that by increasing the 'cognitive diversity' of the participants, co-creative expertise networks may well be in process of reinventing scientific method. Asking how the creative industries can contribute to such an endeavour – this is a question well worth considering.

Globalisation

Expanding international trade, particularly in services, including cultural services. Globalisation and the development of the creative industries have tended to occur as parallel processes. This is due in part to the weakening of traditional ties between cultural experience and geographical territory that the global circulation of cultural commodities entails, particularly as they take an increasingly digital form and thus can be moved swiftly between places through technological networks (Tomlinson 2007). A series of mutually reinforcing relationships has promoted both globalisation and the creative industries including:

- Deregulation of national cultural and media policy frameworks, which promotes cultural trade, particularly in the audiovisual sectors;
- Rising consumer affluence, particularly in developing countries, which promotes creative industries in terms of demand (growth in demand for discretionary goods and services with high cultural content) and supply (younger people in particular identifying the creative industries as attractive places to work and to develop their skills, motivated by both monetary and non-monetary factors);
- Digital technologies and the global internet, which has transformed production and distribution platforms for media and cultural content, leading in particular to more globalised value chains for many creative industries, such as films and computer games (T. Miller et al. 2005);
- The rise of services in the global economy, which generates new demand for creative industries outputs such as design, advertising and marketing, as well as generating greater returns for intangible investments in human capital;

Globalisation became a key concept in social theory in the 1990s and 2000s. In a large literature, globalisation has been defined by Anthony Giddens as 'the intensification of worldwide social relations which link distant localities in such a way that local happenings are shaped by events occurring many miles away and vice versa' (1990: 64); and by David Held and Anthony McGrew as denoting 'the expanding scale, growing magnitude, speeding up and deepening impact of transcontinental flows and patterns of social interaction' (2002: 1). A core question in globalisation theories is whether they are describing something fundamentally new. After all, Christopher Columbus's journey to the Americas in 1492 was experienced as globalisation by the indigenous populations affected by that journey, as was Captain James Cook's travels to the South Pacific in the 1770s and numerous other colonial ventures. Put differently, the question is whether a *scalar shift* has occurred in social, economic, cultural and other relations.

Some writers have seen the key driver of change as being globalisation of economic activity. Manuel Castells (1996) associated the rise of the *network society* with the rise of multinational corporations (MNCs), the rapid globalisation of financial markets (where annual turnover is now over 30 times that of world gross domestic product), and the development of global production networks and outsourcing, all of which he has seen as fundamentally shifting the balance of economic relations from a national to an international scale. Advocates of free trade and open markets, such as Thomas Friedman, have equated globalisation with the 'inexorable integration of markets, nation-states and technologies' (2005: 9). Critics have often viewed economic globalisation as a process that has shifted the balance of **power** away from nation-states and towards global corporations. Hardt and Negri propose that global capitalism had now reached a phase where 'large transnational corporations have effectively surpassed the jurisdiction and authority of nation-states', to the point where 'government and politics come to be completely integrated into the system of transnational command' (2000: 306–7). Others have drawn attention to the significance of cultural globalisation, particularly where it intersects with information technologies and digital networks (Giddens 2003). At the end of 2011, over two billion people were on the internet, or 30.2 per cent of the world's population. There was a 480 per cent growth in the number of internet users worldwide between 2000 and 2011, with the fastest rates of growth in developing countries in Africa, Middle East, Asia and Latin America (Internet World Stats 2011). An important part of cultural globalisation is **media** globalisation, and indicators of the globalisation of **entertainment** media abound. The number of television viewers worldwide was about four billion in 2008; Hollywood film and television products provide internationally recognised signifiers of 'global culture'; and global media events and global media spectacles, such as the Olympics and World Cup football, continue to attract huge **audiences** (Hartley 2008a).

While it is impossible to deny that globalisation is occurring across multiple dimensions, there is an important debate in the literature between proponents of what can be called the *strong globalisation* thesis, and its critics (Flew and McElhinney 2006). 'Strong globalisation' arguments are derived from the observation that there have been important *quantitative* shifts in the global economy, society and culture, to make the stronger proposition that globalisation marks a *qualitative* shift in the pattern of economic, social, political and cultural relations within and between states and societies that is without historical precedent. This can be in terms of creating a global culture, weakening the power of nation-states, or bringing forth a fully integrated global economy. Critics point out that capitalism as a world system has been marked by successive waves of global expansion and contraction: much of the world today was brought into the world system through successive waves of European colonial expansion. Hirst et al. (2009) have made the point that the growth of foreign trade, foreign investment and cross-border migration all have clear historical parallels, most notably in the period from the 1850s to 1914. The economic geographer Peter Dicken (2007) has argued that changes in the extent to which the world's largest corporations operate on a global rather than a national scale are incremental, and that the bulk of the world's largest corporations remain national corporations with international operations rather than truly globally integrated firms. Multinational corporations themselves seek to balance the benefits of being a global brand on the one hand, with immediate recognition throughout the world, with the risks that can arise from failing to be attuned to local cultural differences and to political, religious and other sensitivities that exist in different nations and regions.

In the content of the creative industries, cultural and media globalisation has sometimes been seen as synonymous with *cultural imperialism* (but see McNair 2006). Political economists argued that the period since the 1980s saw the rising **power** and dominance of a small number of global media corporations over the world's media and creative industries, enabled by the global spread of deregulatory neo-liberal ideologies. These were promoted by – among others – the global news and entertainment media (Schiller 1999; McChesney and Schiller 2003). Miller et al. argued that the globalisation of media production promoted a new international division of cultural labour (NICL), through which 'global Hollywood' dispersed production activities worldwide to take advantage of lower costs and capture new markets, while centralising control over **intellectual property** in order to maximise profits, cultural power and control over global media markets (T. Miller et al. 2005). John Tomlinson (2007) has cautioned against seeing the imposition of a neo-liberal global culture as the inevitable by-product of economic globalisation. He argues that such approaches underestimate the capacity of the users of cultural products – audiences or consumers – to reshape apparently global phenomena towards their own 'local' purposes. There is also a need for caution about conflating 'media' with 'culture': while global media corporations take advantage of satellite and information communication and technology (ICT) distribution **networks** to acquire global reach for their cultural commodities, the take-up of media retains distinctive national and regional patterns. Jeremy Tunstall (2008) has argued that we are in fact now in the twilight of US mass media dominance, as the rising powers of the world, such as China, India, Brazil, Russia and Korea, have strong national media infrastructures, and are themselves significant exporters of media content, particularly in geo-linguistic markets such as East Asia, South Asia or Latin America. Tunstall further argues that audience preferences for national media content continue to be strong: he estimates that about 80 per cent of the world television content is produced and consumed on a national basis (Tunstall 2008).

If culture is one of the key variables that sets limits to globalisation, another is public policy. Indeed, a feature of the **internationalisation** of creative industries policies in the 2000s, particularly as they developed outside the UK and Europe, was the extent to which they emerged as a response to limitations that had arisen in policy discourses around the **information economy** that had prevailed in the 1990s. For a number of the countries that had been early adopters of strategies to build an internet-driven information policy, such as Singapore, South Korea and Malaysia, the 'dot.com' crash of 2001 drew attention to the limits of focusing too strongly upon developing digital media infrastructure, and the need to pay more attention to development of their digital content industries. This focus upon the distinctive enabling dimensions of creative industries policies, as drivers of competitive advantage, has most recently been drawn upon by the United Nations Conference on Trade and Development (UNCTAD 2008/2010). UNCTAD has identified opportunities for developing countries to better distribute their cultural products online to capture niche market opportunities at comparatively low cost, as the global demand for cultural goods and services continues to rise with higher average incomes and access to new technologies, and as the creativity of their people and communities can be more effectively harnessed as intangible assets in a global **creative economy**.

While many focus upon 'globalisation from above', as it has been approached by established institutions such as large corporations, nation-states and public policymakers, new ICTs have also enabled a massive 'globalisation from below', as a multitude of individuals, communities, organisations and activists identify new ways to network, collaborate, distribute information and challenge power through utilisation of global digital platforms. The 'Arab Spring' of 2011 demonstrated quite dramatically how oppositional movements in countries such as Tunisia, Egypt, Libya and Syria could make use of Twitter, Facebook and YouTube to get their messages out to the world, after decades of suppression of information in these countries by state-run media acting in the service of authoritarian government power (Lotan et al. 2011). There is also the tale of two Wikis – Wikipedia and WikiLeaks – that draws attention to the potential for disruptive **innovation** that can arise through the new global networks of information:

- Wikipedia has become the world's largest online encyclopaedia, with over 20 million entries in November 2011, created or modified by over 14 million individual registered users – including 90,000 regular contributors – from around the world, since the site was first established in 2001. Almost 80 per cent of Wikipedia entries are in languages other than English, and there are 279 different language editions of Wikipedia (see also Liao and Petzold 2010);
- In December 2010, the WikiLeaks organisation released over 400,000 diplomatic cables from US embassies and consulates around the world. Headed by the peripatetic Australian-born Julian Assange, WikiLeaks was an effectively 'stateless' operation, notionally headquartered in Iceland, owing to that country's extensive protections for 'whistleblowers'. The question of what jurisdictional powers that governments may have over an entity such as WikiLeaks continues to challenge lawyers and policymakers, in ways that are profoundly different from those of more territorially based print and broadcast media organisations.

While being profoundly different entities that have arisen for very different reasons, both Wikipedia and WikiLeaks draw attention to the scope that now exists for open global **networks** to provide opportunities to challenge institutional structures and forms of authority as well as traditional value chains of media production and distribution. If globalisation is read from one perspective as 'the incorporation of societies globally into a capitalist modernity' (Dirlik 2003: 275), and hence as the geographical extension of long-established power relations to a global scale, it can also be seen as being profoundly disruptive of established institutional orders built around national cultures and political territory. The creative industries sit on both sides of this: they are both about the extension of reach of global media and entertainment brands, and the enablers of disruptive innovation and more open systems for knowledge and creative practice.

Information Economy

The concept of the information economy emerged (before the internet, and before the concept of creative industries) at the confluence of two sets of debates about the role of knowledge in technologically advanced countries. First, there is the extensive literature on the *economics* of information and knowledge, the ways in which information as an economic good differs from other commodities, and how incorporating information into economic analysis challenges established models. Second, there are debates concerning the information *society*, a term popularised by sociologist Daniel Bell (1973) with his related concept of postindustrial society. Studies from the perspectives of *futures research* have attempted to map the growth of information-based industries and their implications, and to make forecasts for governments on the basis of these findings. Creative industries have been linked to the information economy by authors such as Charles Leadbeater, who identified sectors such as music, entertainment and fashion as generating high value-added services, but differing from law and accounting on the basis that 'the knowledge base of these creative industries is less formalised than in [the] professions ... where training is tightly controlled' (1999: 49).

While it has long been apparent that information was important to how economies operated, it was not until the 1960s that major contributions were made to the field now known as the economics of information. The economist Kenneth Arrow observed that while information can be a commodity – it can be bought and sold in the market – it is not simply a commodity like others for three reasons: (1) the value of information is indivisible from how it is used; (2) information is not lost when it is consumed, and is therefore easily shared; and (3) information has public good characteristics, which creates a dilemma of how to balance the interests of its creators in acquiring income from its distribution in the form of **intellectual property**, and the public interest in distributing and freely sharing new information. Arrow's analysis of the unique economic properties of information was highly influential in supporting public investment in science and technology, and continues to influence arguments that there is a role for government in investing in the digital infrastructure on which new platforms and services can be developed for media **convergence**. A second major figure in information economics was Fritz Machlup. In his voluminous studies of the role of information and knowledge, he estimated that information and knowledge-based industries already accounted for 29 per cent of the US gross domestic product by the late 1950s. Machlup also drew attention to the distinction between information and knowledge, arguing that the 'value' of information was not a question that could be addressed independently of its use. In other words, you could not measure the value of information simply through the process by which it was transmitted; there needed to be consideration of the value of the informational content, and this would vary among its users in unpredictable ways (Machlup 1993). In this way, Machlup's work draws attention to the point made by Lamberton that 'a market system with information elements cannot lead to the traditional efficient allocation of resources' (2006: 368).

Machlup's empirical work on the US information economy was followed up in a later study by Marc Porat, which estimated that information-based industries in the US economy accounted for 46 per cent of jobs by the mid-1970s (quoted in Kumar 1995). There were comparable analyses of industry and employment trends developed in the 1970s by Yoneji Masuda (1990) for the Japanese government, and

Simon Nora and Alain Minc (1980) for the French government. All pointed in the direction of a decline in traditional industrial employment, and the rise of information-based industries and occupations. A study of the largest industrial economies undertaken by Castells and Aoyama (1994) found that, in 1990, 48.3 per cent of jobs in the USA and 45.8 per cent of jobs in Britain were engaged with handling information as distinct from handling goods, with information-related employment growing sharply in these countries from 1970 onwards.

Daniel Bell identified the rise of the services economy and the growing use of computer-driven knowledge technologies as central to what he described as both a 'postindustrial' and an *information society*. He drew upon occupational data coming out of futures studies in an influential book (Bell 1973), proposing that a 'Third Industrial Revolution' was occurring, where:

> Knowledge and information are becoming the strategic resource and transforming agent of the post-industrial society … just as the combination of energy, resources and machine technology were the transforming agents of industrial society. (Bell 1980: 531, 545)

Bell's thesis was developed in explicit opposition to Marxist theory, which he argued was a theory of industrial society. Bell proposed that the socialist movement was tied to the fortunes of an industrial proletariat, and that it was now in decline, both numerically and in terms of its ability to control the forces of production. In an information society, he argued, the central contradictions would no longer be between capital and labour, but between an emergent 'knowledge class' and a rising group of potentially alienated white-collar workers. One manifestation of this would be between, on the one hand, the values of technocracy and professionalism and, on the other hand, campaigns against bureaucracy and elitism with demands for greater participation in the provision of public services. Bell would later describe this as one of the cultural contradictions of capitalism, between the hedonistic impulses he saw as promoted by both modernist **aesthetics** and consumer society, and the culture of savings and self-restraint that had been central to what Max Weber termed the 'Protestant ethic' that promoted early industrial capitalism and bourgeois society (Bell 1976). At the same time, however, there were more critical analyses of postindustrial society developed by sociologists such as Andre Gorz and Alain Touraine, who saw the 'new class struggle' as being about control over one's work, with intellectuals and knowledge workers being particularly pivotal in such struggles (Mattelart 2003).

It is important to note that the information economy concept precedes the development of the internet, but the internet has acted as a catalyst for social analysis that has echoes in the information society debates, such as Manuel Castells' (1996) theory of a **network** society and Charles Leadbeater's (1999) concept of a **knowledge** society. There were also a stream of national policy statements on the information economy in the 1990s, following the Clinton–Gore administration's calls for the development of a national information infrastructure for the USA in 1993, and a global information infrastructure in 1994 (Flew and McElhinney 2006). Among the leading policy statements were the European Union's Bangemann Report, the Singapore government's 'Intelligent Island' policies, and the ambitious strategy of the Malaysian government to develop a multimedia super corridor (MSC) in the newly developed 'Cyberjaya' region.

The information economy has raised some recurring questions. One relates to the evidence that is drawn on to underpin claims about a fundamental shift in the nature of society. Kumar (1995) and Webster (2006) have disputed the claim that the various statistical measures used to demonstrate a *quantitative* shift in contemporary economies, such as the greater use of information technologies and the rise of service employment, constitute evidence of a *qualitative* shift in modern capitalist societies. Another issue relates to the manner in which the concepts of 'information' and 'knowledge' are used interchangeably. With the rise of the internet, there is a global proliferation of information in the form of digital data; over one trillion URLs were in existence in 2011. The circumstances under which such information becomes knowledge, and the role played by knowledge communities in such developments, becomes critical. While authors such as Leadbeater (1999) have seen the rise of creative industries and the information economy as being interconnected, there have been others who have seen the rise of the creative industries, and the concept of a **creative economy**, as an alternative pathway to that of an information economy and information society. For instance, John Howkins distinguishes between an information society 'characterised by people spending most of their time and making most of their money by handling information, usually by means of technology', and a creative society, where 'we also need to be active, clever, and persistent in challenging this information' (2005: 117–18). Kieran Healy (2002) has also drawn attention to the ways in which authors such as Richard Florida have presented creativity as a new 'axial principle', in a manner akin to how Daniel Bell used information and knowledge as alternative axial principles to that of labour.

In practice, the proliferation of digital technologies and the phenomena of media convergence have made it difficult to make sharp distinctions between the categories of creative industries and the information economy. For instance, a critical element of making information more useful involves the design of the digital sources from which it is being accessed. This is the 'creative' side of developing both information devices and user interfaces, where a company such as Apple under Steve Jobs' leadership retained its ascendancy through the design qualities of its products, even as other comparable products were made available to consumers and businesses at lower prices.

Four elements of the economics of information can be identified that draw attention to the extent to which information questions are comparable with those that arise in the creative industries more generally:

1   Information goods are typically costly to produce and cheap to reproduce, i.e. they have high fixed costs and low marginal costs. This generates uncertainty about what is the suitable rate at which to price them, as prices bear a highly variable relationship to original costs. In a globalised economy, it can also act as an incentive to illegal copying, as prices are not seen as 'fair', particularly in developing nations;

2 The management of information as **intellectual property** remains an endemic concern. While content owners seek to be able to extract rents over time from both information and creative content, information has the characteristics not only of a public good, but of what Michael Perelman (2002) refers to as a *meta-public* good, as it generates positive benefits to a community in ways that cannot be calculated in terms of current value, as they feed into future innovation;

3 Both information goods and those of the creative industries tend to be *experience goods*, whose qualities are hard to know in advance of consumption (Shapiro and Varian 1999);

4 The proliferation of the amount and sources of information means that the scarce resource is no longer the information itself, but the time available to its prospective consumers. This means that the economics of **attention**, the ability of individuals and organisations to build profile, status and reputation, becomes critical (Lanham 2006).

It is notable that interest in the creative industries in Asia picked up considerably after the economic downturn of 1997–98 and the 'dot.com' stock market crash of 2001 exposed significant problems with state-led approaches to developing a national ICT sector in industries that are inherently globally mobile. With their focus on building linkages between the arts, media, intellectual property and ICT industries, creative industries strategies may present a more inclusive and holistic approach to policy development, in a context where core activities related to information technologies themselves, such as programming, are increasingly exportable. Creative industries policy strategies have instead been built upon the premise that, in an age of globalisation, it is the 'cultural' or 'software' side of ICTs that can generate distinctive forms of intellectual property and sustainable competitive advantage, and that the 'hardware' of the information economy is a necessary but not sufficient condition for their development.

Innovation

The word innovation has become somewhat clichéd in the burgeoning creative industries context, mostly through unspecific over-application. The creative industries promote innovation, they say – and the creative industries are highly innovative too. But whatever weariness has accrued to meet such generalisation, the underlying observation of a deep connection between creative industries and innovation remains a key concept to understand in respect of both the value creative industries adds (innovation economics), and the appropriate policy models (innovation policy).

Innovation is the primary mechanism that drives long-run economic growth and development. An innovation process is normally modelled as a three-phase trajectory.

This begins with (1) the invention or *origination* of a novel idea (von Hippel 2005); then (2) the *adoption* or diffusion of that idea through the economic system (Rogers 1995); and then (3) the *retention*, normalisation or embedding of that idea in the economic system. Such an innovation trajectory results in structural change in the economic system, because of the effect of the novel idea and the consequences of its adoption and retention. This is the 'growth of **knowledge**' process that describes economic growth as an evolutionary process (see **evolution**). Innovation is the process of economic change through the origination, adoption, and retention of new ideas into the economic order.

Note that innovation is therefore not synonymous with invention, or the creation of a new idea per se. That is simply a necessary precondition for innovation, which refers to the process by which that new idea leads to a changed economic order through the subsequent adoption, diffusion and retention process. Creative industries matter to innovation through their role in this entire process, and not simply in the initial creativity or invention. This is an important point, for it highlights that the value proposition and policy significance of the **creative industries** are at least as much about innovation (both within the creative industries and across the broader economy) as about *creativity* or about a sectoral set of *industries*. The predominant meaning of innovation refers to a process of economic change that is coordinated by market processes (see **markets** for discussion of why this is so) and results in the endogenous transformation of industrial structure due to the effect of new ideas or technologies, broadly understood. Innovation, in other words, is the process by which an economic and socio-cultural order transforms from within as an ongoing evolutionary process that is without overarching design or planning. This notion of innovation as the central process driving economic growth was developed by Joseph Schumpeter (1942; see McCraw 2007) and is associated with his theory of economic evolution (see **evolution**) and his notion of **creative destruction**.

The theory of innovation is built about two overarching analytic concepts, both of which have strategic and policy significance: (1) the notion of an *innovation process* or innovation trajectory, as above; and (2) the concept of an *innovation system*, as the set of interconnected **institutions** that support the innovation process An innovation system consists of the set of institutions, organisations and policies that function to facilitate the innovation process at various levels, including regional, sectoral or national (Nelson 1993), or in relation to technologies or markets. The innovation system is the focus of *innovation policy*, which is also the policy framework that is increasingly central to the creative industries. Innovation is a central concept in the creative industries for two overarching reasons: (1) because the creative industries can themselves be highly innovative (Handke 2006b; Müller et al. 2009); and (2) because the creative industries are key drivers of the innovation process (Potts 2009a) as well as contributors to the innovation system (Bakhshi et al. 2008). It is important to appreciate that each of these factors is in itself significant: the creative industries are an innovative sector not just because they are 'creative' and engaged in the novelty generation business of entertainment and meaning-making, but for a more subtle and arguably more powerful reason, namely that they are highly competitive (see **competition**), and often compete on a global scale. They are highly innovative because high rates of innovation are an effective competitive strategy. This can be seen, for example, in the games industry, which is a heavy user of experimental new digital technologies, as are the new media and social media industries. This sets up a symbiotic relationship between creative industries and information communication and technology (ICT) or digital technologies. That is one reason connecting creative industries and innovation, but a second reason is equally important, namely that because the creative industries are involved in social communication and meaning-making, they are also significant contributors to the broader innovation system, and in particular on the consumer or demand side in shaping preferences and facilitating adoption and ongoing retention of new ideas and technologies from the rest of the economy (i.e. from the 95 per cent or so that isn't the creative industries). This is what Potts et al. (2008a) meant when they defined the creative industries as 'social network markets'.

Let us elaborate. First, what is innovation, and what role do the creative industries play in this evolutionary process? As indicated, innovation is a process that begins with the invention or *origination* of a novel idea. The original inception might be from an artist, or an inventor, or any other creative **agent**, but the key agent here is the **entrepreneur** who is the person who recognises the potential economic value of that idea and seeks to develop it by taking it to market. This process often proceeds through the creation of value by recombining existing ideas in new ways. This is the first phase of the innovation process. It takes us from **creativity** to the entrepreneurial creation of a **market** opportunity. The second phase of innovation occurs as the process of *adoption* (or diffusion) plays out, usually in a market context, as other agents choose to adopt the novel idea. This involves learning or imitation, or experimentation, and results in a growth in the *population* (see entry on **evolution**) of the novel idea as it is differentially adopted and adapted by other agents, whether other businesses or consumers. This phase of an innovation trajectory is the most dynamic, and is often characterised by intense competition, by the growth of some businesses and the decline of others (i.e. **creative destruction**), by entry and exit dynamics in markets (see **markets**, and **evolution**), and by industrial transformation as resources are reallocated between firms and as new market niches are carved out. This is innovation as a process of the growth of knowledge, as new ideas enter and displace other ideas, often leading to a changed space of relative prices, constraints and opportunities. Contemporary examples of this process can be observed in the music industry, the videogames industry, and the newspaper industry. This phase of an innovation trajectory is often characterised by high levels of uncertainty, significant changes in market share, and thus profits and losses, and usually in mergers and market entry and exit. Consumers are often equally troubled about which formats or platforms to adopt or how to structure the purchase of complementary assets.

By the third phase of an innovation trajectory, the value of the novel idea has been realised and there will be, often, a new market structure and a new industrial structure that reflects the effect of the new technology, idea or business model.

innovation

Consumers will have adapted to the new opportunities the novel idea offers and will normalise their behaviour and expectations accordingly. This is the phase of a new mature industry or a new market order. Radio in the 1950s or television in the 1970s or the music industry in the 1980s looked like this (even through all were to be subsequently shaken up by new innovations). This three-phase process is the dynamic of economic growth as a novel idea is originated, adopted and retained into a new economic order. The result is the growth of knowledge and the evolution of the economic order. As an illustrative aside note that the fashion industry (which is perhaps the most free-market of all the creative industries sectors) also has the highest level of innovation (Raustiala and Sprigman 2006; Hartley and Montgomery 2009). Indeed, one can think of the fashion industry as having completely endogenised the innovation trajectories such that they occur several times a year, and according to institutionally defined timetables (associated with 'seasons' and 'collections').

The creative industries are involved in all three stages – origination, adoption and retention – of an innovation trajectory. In the first phase, they contribute to the generation of new ideas. This is the standard inference about the creative aspect of the creative industries. But it is also perhaps the smallest contribution the creative industries make, compared with, for example, that of science and technology. Empirically considered, it is in the second and third phases of adoption and retention that the creative industries can claim to make their most significant contributions to the innovation process, and therefore to economic growth and development, by facilitating the adoption of new ideas and their embedding into both a socio-cultural and a new market order (Potts 2011). This occurs in many ways. For example, the advertising industry is obviously involved in developing consumer demand for new goods, and the media and publishing industries are plainly involved in normalising these new ways of being. Design sectors, broadly conceived, are central to the adoption and retention of new ideas, and so on. The point is that while science and technology may be attributed with developing new ideas and possibilities, for this to translate into economic growth it needs to be widely adopted, and this is the function that the creative industries serve from the evolutionary growth perspective. An innovation is only an innovation if it is widely adopted into a social order, such that it changes the underlying market and even industrial order. Unless people change what they do, and how they think about the world of opportunities and prospects, then it is not an innovation. This is why creative industries are integral to the innovation process on the demand side.

From the policy perspective, the creative industries are presently involved in a shift of focus from cultural and industry policy, which is based about welfare-theoretic arguments from a cultural economics perspective, toward competition and innovation policy, which is based about evolutionary growth-theoretic arguments. This shift in the classification of creative industries policy (from industry policy to innovation policy) proceeds from recent recognition of the significant contribution that creative industries make to the innovation process. Note that this also seeks to justify public intervention into creative industries (i.e. policy) as based less on a market-failure or welfare-theoretic argument, as was implicit in the old cultural industries model, and instead to base the logic of intervention as proceeding from a 'public investment in innovation' approach (Potts and Cunningham 2008).

What of innovation policy in the creative industries? The results are somewhat mixed in the various countries that have endeavoured to develop creative industries policy in this way (e.g. UK, Australia, Singapore, New Zealand, Canada). This is in part due to the difficulty in transitioning from a model of industrial support largely dependent on subsidy to preserve existing cultural production (based on the market failure model) to one that is driven by very different objectives. Some of this difficulty arises with the necessity of engagement with an entrepreneurial and market-focused conception of policy support that is often at odds with dominant folkways and cultural norms in arts and cultural policy. So there has been no small amount of culture shock and resistance from cultural and creative industries lobby groups (Garnham 2005). But the process of engagement is also hard because it is new and still partially experimental. A number of research and policy institutes (such as NESTA in the UK) have sought to add structure to this *policy experiment* by funding and analysing experiments in innovation policy in creative industries. Whether innovation policy continues to develop as the lodestone of creative industries policy will thus depend on the outcomes of policy experiments and the results of policy learning and subsequent diffusion and eventually retention.

Institution

The common English usage definition of an institution has two meanings. One pivots off an organisation as 'an organisation founded for a religious, educational, professional, or social purpose'; hence the Catholic Church, Oxford University and the Eastern State Penitentiary are all institutions. The second turns on a social custom or 'an established law or practice' (*Oxford English Dictionary*); hence the institution of marriage, the institution of ad-breaks on free-to-air television but not on publically funded television, or the institution of public education or central banking. In the creative and media field, there is the institution of public broadcasting, or the institution of public arts funding, the institution of turn-taking in conversation and the institution of the television or radio talk show. Institutions are thus what society is made of, and much of culture and the economy too. Institutions are the furniture upon which we arrange our social lives and the building-blocks with which we assemble economic and political orders. They form the social givens upon which much of the creative industries, as with many other industries, build value propositions.

In philosophy, according to John Searle 'an institution is any collectively accepted system of *rules* that enable us to create institutional facts [which are] the collective assignment of status function' (2005: 21–2). An institution thus becomes what we collectively agree something is. That's interesting, because it signals that institutional analysis is ultimately an inquiry into *social ontology*: or the rules of what exists from the perspective of shared human being. Two points matter: one, institutions are social constructions in this sense; but two, and arguably more interesting, they are subject to socio-cultural and economic evolution. Institutions underpin the social functioning and possibilities of collective action upon which cultures and economies are built, and institutions evolve. The creative industries, like all industries, are built upon the *social technologies* of institutions. But unlike other industries, they are also key, nay central, producers of those same institutions. The creative industries are thus institutionally complex. They are built upon institutions, they shape and exploit existing institutions, but they are also producers and shaping forces of new institutions. This is not unlike the role of 'silicon valley' with respect to computation, technology and society. It is built within it, but it also creates it.

In economic theory, as well as in sociology – and particularly in relation to the study of the structure of economies and societies and the processes by which they change – institutions also have a technical meaning that defines them as the building-blocks of social and economic life. For example, Thorstein Veblen defined institutions as 'settled habits and thoughts common to the generality of men' (1919: 239). Fellow economic sociologist or institutional economist John Commons defined them as 'collective action in restraint, liberation, and expansion of individual action' (1931: 2). For Walton Hamilton, in a classic 1932 definition, institutions were 'a way of thought or action of some prevalence or permanence which is embedded in the habits of a group or the customs of a people' (cited in Hodgson 1999: 143). Economist Geoffrey Hodgson explains institutions as the 'systems of established and embedded social rules that structure social interactions' (2006: 18). For economists and sociologists alike, institutions are widely shared behaviour that facilitated large-scale social and economic coordination. This was the proto-view of institutions as *social technology*, a concept that did not fully arrive until the late twentieth century with the combination of game theory and historical analysis. Game theorist Andrew Schotter defined institutions as 'a regularity in social behaviour that is agreed to by all members of society, specifies behaviour in specific recurrent situations' (1981: 11). Economic historian Douglass North explains: 'Institutions are the *rules of the game* of a society or more formally are the humanly-devised constraints that structure human interaction. They are composed of formal rules (statute law, common law, regulations), informal constraints (conventions, norms of behavior, and self imposed codes of conduct), and the enforcement characteristics of both' (1990: 3).

This 'rules of the game' concept has become the underpinning of the modern analytic formulation of institutions. The elegance of this concept is that these *rules* are thus subject to evolutionary analysis, in the sense of variation in rules, selection of rules and differential replication of rules as characterising different societies and economies (see **evolution**). This provides a way of *naturalising* institutions as the equivalent of 'the selection environment' and of allowing that different outcomes in economies and societies, such as entrepreneur-led economic growth or politically induced stagnation can be explained in terms of different institutional environments or the incentive effects that different institutions set up. For economic historians (see also the work of Robert Fogel, Joel Mokyr, Angus Maddison, Deirdre McCloskey, and Gregory Clark, among others) the central meaning of this idea is to show how, in the long run, it is 'good institutions' that are the single most important factor in explaining the rise or success of nations, economies or societies, and that all other factors, such as technology, natural resources, political leadership, and so on are ultimately less significant than effective 'rules of the game' within which economic action and interaction take place. A further line of this has been developed by Elinor Ostrom (1990), who has examined how communities can develop their own institutions for the governance of common pool resources. Ostrom initially looked at natural resources such as fisheries, but modern work on 'the commons' has begun to emphasise knowledge commons, including the internet. This line of thinking about 'good institutions' and economic growth is now mainstream in modern growth and development policy, and this insight has also bled over into creative industries analysis. It is why getting the right institutions is a key part of economic growth and development policy, and also part of effective creative industries policy design. A key lesson relates to creating institutions appropriate to market-led coordination and capable of evolutionary development.

Creative industries are involved in the creation of the institutions that construct the socio-cultural and economic order, as well as being industries with their own interests in themselves. This is why creative industries have inevitable political purchase, and why they are invariably caught up in public funding debates, namely because they are effective in shaping the social technologies that underpin other parts of the economic and socio-cultural order. This also connects to the entries on **innovation** and **evolution** that explained how the creative industries are a part of the national innovation system by their role in shaping demand and preferences for new or novel goods and services. To the extent that economic growth depends on innovation, and that innovation depends on consumers adopting new ideas and doing new things, then a constraint on economic growth can accrue from barriers to adoption and change by consumers. The creative industries, like science and technology for example, form part of the institutions of national innovation systems.

Creative industries institutions, like arts and cultural institutions, are subject to evolutionary processes. They are not necessarily permanent but are subject to entry and exit as new institutions develop and displace existing institutions (see **evolution**). Institutional entrepreneurship can be a driving force in creative industries when organisations or agencies actively set out to lead institutional change by nudging behaviour in particular directions. For example, network television devoted considerable resources to inculcating institutions associated with scheduling (e.g. the six o'clock news hour, the Sunday matinee, etc). New business models often require significant change in those same institutions (as, for example, in the switch to view-on-demand scheduling). Because much of the creative industries involves social consumption, it also involves solving significant coordination problems or collective action problems in delivery. This is why entrepreneurship and

institution

117

innovation in creative industries is much more bound up with institutional change than in many other industries.

It is also important to recognise the flip-side of this, namely that institutions are a consequence of what economists call 'bounded rationality', recognising that **consumers** often use simple 'rules of thumb' to navigate their consumption environment, and that these can become locked in, difficult to displace, and thus subject to historical or *path dependency*. While institutions reduce costs of actions by relegating much behaviour to auto-pilot, they can also produce substantial inertia and conservatism, in the sense of seeking to conserve what already exists because change requires not only effort and enthusiasm, but also involves un-learning and then re-learning new institutions. This can explain why many institutions continue to live on well beyond the point at which they are functionally or rationally justified, something that can be readily observed in the resilience of many arts and cultural institutions. Examples here will always be contentious, but public funding of high arts and **culture** such as opera and ballet can fall into this category, as can national public broadcasting. In these instances institutions can become what Veblen (1899) called 'ceremonial', existing because they exist, tied to identity and the like and having long since lost rational justification, a point also developed by Marshall Sahlins in *Culture and Practical Reason*. Still, just as these can accumulate in the cultural and creative industries, so too can the creative industries themselves be key agents in removing largely ceremonial or otherwise dysfunctional institutions and facilitating the origination and adoption of new institutions.

Modern institutional economic theory and the study of economic history suggest that the creative industries will develop to the extent that they can develop good institutions to facilitate trade, coordination and investment (Cowen 2002). This means developing effective **intellectual property** rights institutions to encourage investment and effective institutions for trust and governance, to encourage trade and contracting. It is a point of serious debate at present about the extent to which the creative industries require special new institutions, or whether good institutions for these industries are essentially the same as those for other industries. Either way, there remains considerable scope for creative industries policy to learn from the differential success and failures of other notions of ongoing and experimental institutions.

Intellectual Property

Intellectual property (IP) is conventionally divided into industrial property rights (patents, designs, and trademarks) and rights in artistic and literary works (copyright). By definition, intellectual property is a product of the mind (or intellect) that has a commercial value. Use often involves royalty payment or permission; however, this is not always the case as many countries don't have a concept of or laws regulating intellectual property. Where there is no law, or very weak laws, moreover, there may well be more innovation (Montgomery 2010), a position that goes against the grain of arguments historically put forward for intellectual property protection. Indeed, whereas the issue of innovation has come into the spotlight in the digital age, solutions to ensuring an equitable modern system remain perplexing for governments, stakeholders and users. A continuum of positions exists in relation to intellectual property law and its implementation. The commercial end of the spectrum is represented by international treaties such as the Trade Related Aspects of Intellectual Property Rights (TRIPS). These were primarily designed, negotiated and implemented to protect the interests of large copyright holders and their representatives, for instance the Hollywood majors and the Motion Pictures Association of America. TRIPS came into force in 1995 under the regulatory umbrella of the World Trade Organization (WTO). It has attempted to implement a global standard for protection of 'rights' associated with 'the creations of people's minds'.[1] The WTO argues that adhering to the global regime will aid development and attract investment from developed countries. While the rhetoric is positive, the reality is that many people in developing countries are unwilling or can't afford to pay for such rights. Infringement, for instance piracy of software and CDs or downloading of music from file sharing sites, is deemed to be a criminal activity by many copyright owners. However, it has been shown that piracy 'clearly makes a contribution to economic growth' in developing countries (Rajan 2006: 38; see also Karaganis 2011). At the other end of the spectrum are subversive anti-capitalist groupings including advocates of piracy and culture jamming, organisations such as Copyleft and the Pirate Party. In reality there are a number of positions depending on the nature of creative endeavour and the beneficiaries of intellectual property 'rents'. Occupying middle ground is a range of actors and interests.

Intellectual property is historically wedded to **innovation**, despite the news media's focus on enforcement and acts of violation. This is not altogether surprising when one considers that international media companies are significant intellectual property rights holders. But are institutions that have come to serve the interests of big companies actually working for all participants in the digital age? Laws designed three centuries ago in the time of the printing press could not have anticipated the World Wide Web. Do these laws create economic incentives for innovation or do they obstruct innovation and economic growth? According to the UK Hargreaves Review (*Digital Opportunity*), existing laws need to adapt if the creative industries are to fulfil their potential. While the report is responding to the interests of the UK government, the key message is clear for all nations: 'Government should firmly resist over regulation of activities which do not prejudice the central objective of copyright, namely the provision of incentives to creators'. (Hargreaves 2011: 8).

---

[1]www.wto.org/english/tratop_e/trips_e/intel1_e.htm

Critics of intellectual property invariably point to the tension between incentives to innovate and monopoly. They maintain that new ideas produce social benefits. The failure of the market to produce an adequate supply of new ideas is generally tackled in one of two ways: first, through public funding (see **public culture**) and second, through the creation of artificial imperfect competition – a temporary monopoly that enables the producer to recoup the fixed costs of production through monopoly rents. Proponents argue that significant transaction costs are imposed on the creator – the costs of search, administration and in the case of infringement, enforcement. However, commentators including Lawrence Lessig (2001) and Yochai Benkler (2006) have been vocal in pointing out the adverse effects of such exclusivity to the development of a commons, a metaphor to describe collective intelligence. With much digital content copyright protected, new ways are required to manage copyright in order to harness the potential of Web 2.0. One of these is open content licensing. Creative Commons (CC) is the best recognised licence. As the default rule is that one cannot use copyright material without permission, the key issue is how you could – if you wished – share your copyright over the internet. Creative Commons licensing provides a generic and automated process of 'permissioning' in advance through labelling content with a badge. This is linked to a flexible set of licensing conditions. Using these as you create content allows a downstream re-user to work with the material without fear of being sued. Today Creative Commons is a global cultural and economic force, harnessing the value of social networking and internet technologies through greater access to knowledge and culture (Fitzgerald et al. 2011).

While trademarks are utilised in the creative industries, for instance in the fashion and design sectors, the most widespread form of creative intellectual property is copyright. Copyright has been associated with creative endeavour since Gutenberg's invention of the moveable type printing press in 1450 in Germany and its introduction into England later in the same century by William Caxton. The printing press enabled production of multiple copies of books. It increased literacy, in turn facilitating the dissemination of ideas and the expansion of literary genres. It wasn't until 1710, however, that British authors received recognition for their creative 'work' (Samuels 2000 Chapter 1). The Statute of Anne attempted to balance interests between publishers and authors. The latter were given a period of time to exploit their exclusive rights as long as the 'work' was registered, a process that entailed delivering nine copies of the book to a repository. Such physical 'registration' signified a key feature of copyright. The work required fixation; it required a material support with some degree of permanence. With the exception of sound and television broadcasts, copyright does not exist unless the work takes a material form; for instance it does not apply to spoken words, an impromptu musical performance or the idea of writing a story on a particular topic. However the act of 'registration' does not apply today in countries that are signatories to the Berne Convention.

Prior to the advent of the printing press and the photographic plate, imitation was regarded as a creative act: for a novice it was a means of acquiring an individual style; it paid homage to a tradition as well as to a master. In many non-Western cultures, the concept of intellectual property, and the attendant notion of an individual creator, are filtered though collectivist values. According to the United Nations

Declaration on the Rights of Indigenous People (2007),[2] where traditions have been passed down through generations, often in oral form, they may constitute traditional knowledge or traditional cultural expressions. However, this convention has not been adopted universally. Moreover, in many societies creativity is expressed as acquired technique, essentially emulation, which some dismiss as copying. Elsewhere copying entailed a definite creative function: for instance, the French Situationists of the mid-1900s would hijack images and messages, placing them in a new context, a precursor to what is now widely celebrated as 'remix culture'.

The important point to note about copyright is that the definition of originality is contingent on the application of some skill, judgement, selection, ingenuity, labour and expertise (Fitzgerald et al. 2011). For this reason some creative ideas, such as slogans, short phrases and headings, do not qualify for copyright protection; the question of what constitutes triviality or author's skill is often left to copyright lawyers. Another important concept underwriting copyright is that it does not protect ideas, information or fact but the form in which those ideas, information or facts are expressed. Interestingly, copyright does not pertain to television formats such as reality game shows. The *Castaway Television Production Ltd v Endemol Entertainment International* judgement in 2000 adjudicated that there was not enough 'substantial similarity' between *Survive*, the original reality game show television format (later known as *Survivor*), and Endemol's *Big Brother* to warrant damages (Malbon 2003). The originator of *Survive*, Charlie Parsons, had claimed that his idea – a group of people living in a restricted environment filmed by ever-present cameras – was initially offered to Endemol as a format. Interestingly, claims and counter-claims of copying have dogged reality television producers since then.

Law pertaining to intellectual property has followed developments in technology. The history of technological change demonstrates that new technologies inevitably lead to new types of creative works and innovations, in turn allowing ideas to be disseminated more easily. On the other hand, the author's right to control public release, reproduction and dissemination – the right to copy – is challenged by new technology (Rajan 2006). Copyright has become more utilitarian in nature over time as information and communication technologies have become more sophisticated. The concept of 'the work' has been displaced by information, forms have dematerialised, the criterion of originality pertaining to copyright has been lowered and the author's role has been redefined. Nevertheless, copyright is unquestionably a foundational element of the creative industries. The UK Department of Culture, Media and Sport manifesto enjoins 'individual creativity, skill and talent' and *'the generation and exploitation of intellectual property'* (DCMS 2001: 4). The question of what constitutes 'a copy' divides opinion and makes much intellectual property law uncertain. In a study of cinema, Laikwan Pang (2006) notes that copying pertains to idea copying, which includes copying of themes styles, characters and plots, sometimes referred to negatively as plagiarism and appropriation or positively as homage and tribute. Similar terms are used in studies of art, literature and architecture. Importantly copyright law does not protect a genre, type and style as the scope

[2]United Nations, Declaration on the rights of Indigenous peoples 2007: www.un.org/esa/socdev/unpfii/en/declaration.html.

intellectual property

121

is too broad; that is, the provision of such protection would excessively hamper creativity.

A second form of copying in cinema is 'direct product copying' or piracy. The term applies as well to the music industry. When it comes to tackling piracy and protecting their intellectual property, content owners are often faced with three options:

1 Do nothing;
2 Fight to enforce the current copy protection laws in order to protect their content;
3 Use technology to protect and monetise content.

Industry experts claim that the use of the third method has put the power back in the hands of the content owners (Van Tassel 2006). This third option is now widely referred to as digital rights management (DRM), which is simply a range of technologies that assigns controls and rules to manage, end to end, the various processes associated with content creation and distribution – starting from content creation to packaging to content presentation to distribution and delivery. Amazon.com was able remotely to delete purchased copies of George Orwell's *1984* and *Animal Farm* from customers' Amazon Kindles after providing them a refund for the purchased products. This, critics say, is just one more example of the excessive power in the hands of corporations such as Amazon to censor remotely what people read through its software (Free Software Foundation 2009).

Intellectual property, and in particular copyright, remains a contentious issue in the creative industries. While the means of production are passing to the 'multitudes' as the internet delivers greater prospects for **digital literacy**, moves to strengthen copyright and enforcement of intellectual property rights remain strong. In many developing countries the costs of enforcing intellectual property infringements are high. Advocates of stronger protection in such countries (for instance China and India) maintain that creative industries need to be sustainable and pressure is brought to bear on lawmakers. Meanwhile other critics argue that better business models, such as cheaper product, need to be found to monetise creativity. Populations have come to expect free content. Globally, culture jamming, the emergence of the DIY society, the Creative Commons movement, and 'cut and paste' culture represent a collective groundswell against strong intellectual property laws.

Internationalisation (of Creative Industries)

The origin of the creative industries moment is a contentious topic. Likewise its global diffusion, together with its sibling concept, the 'creative economy', has taken unpredicted turns and expedient interpretations. Initially nurtured in the womb of liberal democracy, creative industries is sometimes associated in a negative sense with aspects of neo-liberalism. Others see the creative industries more pragmatically, as a mechanism to effect positive social change. Significantly, policymakers in highly regulated cultural markets have warmed to its renovating potential, celebrating the transformational capacities of the new 'international discourse'. In the main creative industries discourse has found favour in large cities, particularly those with world city aspirations.

Noting the diffusion and adaptation of the creative economy 'script' throughout Asia during the first decade of this century, Chris Gibson and Lily Kong write: 'The script may be characterised as follows: to compete in the new creative economy, cities should seek to implement particular initiatives: encourage creative industry clusters, incubate learning and knowledge economies, maximise networks with other successful places and companies, value and reward innovation and aggressively campaign to attract the "creative class" as residents' (2005: 550). At the level of the nation-state, the master-script generally advocates a combination of exports and national branding: in turn regions, cities and districts have utilised the discourse to promote cultural quarters, creative incubators (**clusters**) and urban regeneration projects.

Are the creative industries transformational? Are they global? Are they largely confined to large cities? Critics rightfully contend that cultural and creative product markets have existed for centuries in some countries. The creative industries are therefore not new, rather a contemporary instance of cultural policy, mostly concerned with regional development. In many instances, particularly in developing economies, the creative industries encompass activities that can also be counted as manufacturing: the high degree of outsourced production of fashion, animation and software is testimony to this. While the term 'industries' implies a certain degree of scale, data collected under the name of creative industries and creative economy seeks to collate the outputs of small and medium enterprises as well as large cultural institutions or transnational media companies. Creative industry activities occur with different degrees of dynamism in open market economies such as the USA, the UK, Germany and Japan, compared with nations such as Singapore, China and Indonesia, where cultural policy operates at a shorter arm's length. While creative industries can be found anywhere, the locus of activity is generally concentrated in large cities, close to related creative service sectors, where there are large numbers of affluent consumers to drive the generation of fashions and prototypes. As urbanisation continues to gather pace, however, the differential between large cities and second-tier cities is likely to change with the latter experiencing more evidence of creative lifestyles and occupations (see **creative cities** and **creative class**).

Globally the creative industries idea functions as a link between cultural production and commerce (see Caves 2000); it does so in different ways across different regions and jurisdictions according to the balance placed on the key terms: culture, creativity and industry. In most instances the term 'industry' is unproblematic whereas ideological divisions have occurred in relation to culture and creativity: these terms are thus given different considerations in regional policymaking.

In order to explain the ascendency of creative industries in different geographical regions it is useful to reflect on its immediate predecessor in the UK, the cultural industries. While the term **cultural industries** was invoked by scholars prior to the 1990s, its association with heavily controlled state culture in some countries has led to the rise of the more modern creative industries; for instance in China. In short, weariness with state-directed forms of cultural planning in China, epitomised by protectionist national pronouncements by the Ministry of Culture, opened the door for the creative industries, which were seen to be at greater arm's length from government as well as being more international. For this reason they are attractive to young people entering into university: all of China's top-tier universities now offer cultural and creative industries courses. The values of entrepreneurship, self-reliance, and competition have been welcomed as a means to reshape China's future (Keane 2012). This is best illustrated by the publication of *How Creativity is Changing China* by Li Wuwei (2011), a key national policy adviser. The concept is believed to have originated in Australian national cultural policy in the 1990s before being taken up in the UK by the Department of Culture, Media and Sport (DCMS). However, 'creative industries' was used in economic development policy documents in Singapore as early as 1990 (Kong et al. 2006). Likewise 'creative economies' was found in regional reports authored by economic geographers in Europe in the early 1990s (Bianchini 1993). The link between cultural quarters, cultural industries and urban regeneration policy found expression in the UK city of Sheffield (see **cluster**). Contestations over origin, however, have little direct relevance to the actual content of creative industries policy and its global diffusion, which occurred following a formal 'national launch' in the late 1990s.

The birth of the creative industries policy idea occurred in a national context. While the DCMS's thinktank articulated what would become the standard creative industries definition, this has undergone considerable adaptation globally, as well as encountering rejection in some regions and countries. Creative industries policy is currently based on a few generative studies, the core ideas of which have been taken up by city and district officials. District, city, regional and national governments throughout the world have accepted the prescription that the creative industries are fast-growing, value-adding, and essential to economic development, and that creative classes need special environments to flourish and therefore special policy assistance. As Kong et al. (2006) note, diffusion has been made possible by the movements of experts, often from the UK: these scholar-consultants have engaged in advocacy of the creative industries idea in new territories. While the DCMS model underpins the migration of the creative industries idea, its uptake in many developing and emerging economies is underpinned by faith in its transformational capacities: that is, creative industries are a means to 'upgrade', to change the structure of industry and the mentalities of populations. In examining the global diffusion of the creative industries idea from its UK home base, we notice initial reception among the former British colonies of Singapore and Hong Kong, together with a positive reception in New Zealand and partial uptake in

Australia and Taiwan. Singapore had begun to engage with the challenge of cultural renovation by the 1990s with the establishment of a Creative Services Strategic Business Unit in order 'to develop Singapore into a centre of excellence for the various creative industries' (EDB 1992: 2). By 2002, creative industries had become a key element of Singapore's 'renaissance', even to the extent of branding initiatives as Renaissance City 2.0, Design Singapore and Media 21. In the following year the *Hong Kong Baseline Study of Creative Industries* was launched. This report, produced by a team at the Hong Kong University Cultural Policy Unit led by Desmond Hui, showed how Hong Kong intended to adapt the DCMS model to promote strategic sectors, particularly film, television, design and interactive media. By the end of the first decade a new wave of creative industries advocacy had begun to occur in Hong Kong and Taiwan. In 2009, an agency called Create Hong Kong was established by the Commerce and Economic Development Bureau (CEDB) with a mandate to develop initiatives. Similarly, the launch of the 'Creative Taiwan' campaign in 2009 and the formalisation of the Cultural and Creative Industries Development Act the following year showed that Taiwan was beginning to reassess the value of its economic development model, which had previously been tied to technology industries. Similar processes occurred in Indonesia, Malaysia and Brazil. In 2011 the Brazilian 'creative economy' was launched in Sao Paulo. The difference in emphasis from the DCMS 'parent' in this iteration is quite significant: the instigator of Brazil's initiation was the United Nations Conference on Trade and Development (UNCTAD) (see below), which has campaigned since 2004 for an alternative to the United Nations Educational Social and Cultural Organisation (UNESCO) model of cultural development, typified by the latter's focus on protecting diversity and traditional culture. The Brazilian creative economy embraces entrepreneurship, intellectual property reform, creative clusters, districts and regions, skills training and networking of creative professionals.[1]

In many of the policy documents emanating from these countries we find references to successful projects in developed countries, often concluding that innovation can be engendered by focusing attention on creative clusters. The heavy focus on clusters, however, is indicative of a mindset that looks for fast transformation: the cluster model is preferred as it appears to operationalise resources and human capital. While East Asia has taken a lead in accepting the idea of the creative industries, South Korea, Japan and India stand out as exceptions: the creative industries 'idea' has made minimal impact in these countries and this might be explained by the strength of media and communications industries there: that is, these countries already have significant cultural 'soft power', a term referring to potent media and communications sectors with evidence of export capabilities. In Japan the term 'gross national cool' has captured attention while in nearby Korea the term 'Korean Wave' exemplifies regional soft power. Likewise, the creative industries mother

125

---

[1]www.cultura.gov.br/site/wp-content/uploads/2011/09/Plano-da-Secretaria-da-Economia-Criativa.pdf

discourse has not settled easily in the USA, where a somewhat different trajectory of creative renovation has occurred following the work of Richard Florida (2002) and others. In the USA a community-based focus is often found combined with place-based, regional and municipal development strategies (see, for example, Michigan Department of History, Arts and Libraries 2005). Accordingly, the term 'creative industries' is employed sparingly. Despite some variations (Caves 2000; Mitchell et al. 2003), the sectoral categories nominated by the UK definition devolve into arts and culture on the one hand and the entertainment/copyright industries on the other (Cunningham 2009).

Creative industries policy has made inevitable inroads into Europe, following initial resistance and a perception that it was too UK-styled to succeed in Europe. However, the emphasis that creative industries policy places on design industries was inevitably a strong factor in its diffusion. Cities such as Amsterdam began to enact creative strategies associated with urban renewal programmes. One influential report emerging from Amsterdam took up the categorisation of creative industries into arts, media and design, echoing the earlier Singaporean designation of creative clusters (*Our Creative Potential* 2009). Much of the stimulus has come from city and regional governments, keen to use the idea to engender growth. A significant contribution to the globalisation of creative industries has come from UNCTAD in the form of *The Creative Economy Report* (UNCTAD 2008/2010). The definition espoused by UNCTAD is pragmatic, encompassing 'heritage, arts, media and functional creation'. Compared with the DCMS, there is less emphasis on information, knowledge and communication sectors (Garnham 2005) and more on knowledge-based activities, allowing the inclusion of traditional arts and crafts, as well as attendant tourism services. UNCTAD notes creative industries are at the crossroads among the artisan, services and industrial sectors. By virtue of this pragmatic definition, UNCTAD's 'trade data' allow categories such as wildlife preservation park services and toy manufacturing. A criticism of the UNCTAD classification system is that mundane industrial activities and products get bundled in with creative goods, so, for example, the manufacture of *empty* CDs was counted, not just the creative content encoded on them. This over-inclusive approach allows China to be ranked first as creative exporter, followed by Italy. The UNCTAD Creative Economy discourse has seen the creative industries move to other developing countries, notably in Africa, where its contribution to economic growth and welfare is demonstrated by the Nigerian film industry, known as Nollywood (Lobato 2010). In South Africa, the creative industries have been reshaped to fit according to the following definition from the South African Department of Industry:

> those areas of social and economic activity that are premised on or closely allied with: individual or collective intellectual or artistic creativity, innovation and originality; or the preservation, teaching and celebration of cultural heritage including language. (Govender 2008)

This seems to be the contemporary global form of creative industries, a wide-ranging umbrella concept that can stretch to fit the aspirations of policymakers, developers and academics.

The importance of knowledge to creative industries is on the surface uncontroversial. The creative industries originate and coordinate change in the knowledge base of the economy. Creative industries' value therefore lies in the development and adoption of new knowledge (Potts and Cunningham 2008). Most people readily accept the proposition that the creative industries are knowledge-based; this in turn reflects a view that certain environments attract knowledge professionals – for instance Florida's **creative class** – and that these kinds of people are potentially powerful change agents particularly in the renewal of cities. While this proposition is often exploited in the interest of stimulating investment in cultural and technological infrastructure in order to attract knowledge workers, a more salient point is that 'increasing returns' come with investment in knowledge (Romer 1990). The original exposition of increasing returns concerned the production of technology and its cumulative payoffs in the stock of knowledge (Beinhocker 2006: 42). Creative industries policy has been quick to exploit the view that creative processes add value to existing stocks of knowledge. A key concern of creative industries policy therefore is to facilitate **innovation** by nurturing human capital, either individually or collectively. But questions remain: what do we mean by the stock of knowledge? How do networks and communities of practice distribute knowledge? How is knowledge shared to generate 'new knowledge'?

Essentially knowledge is the codification or the transmission of ideas. More often ideas are discoveries – 'the accurate recognition of something that already existed but was concealed' – rather than invention (Foray 2000: 14). As often noted, there is a common sense motive to the dissemination of knowledge: that is, if you give a person a fish you may feed him or her for a day, but if you teach the same person how to fish then much more is accomplished; skills can be copied, passed on, modified and improved. However, as Douglas Thomas and John Seeley Brown argue, there is a 'catch': this assumes there will always be an endless supply of fish, or in this case knowledge. In the past people generally believed that there was stock of knowledge that remained unchanged (although some of it may be as-yet undiscovered); this is the basis of much cultural tradition and the inclination to maintain certain ways of seeing the world. To continue the metaphor, the pool of unchanging resources is shrinking and the pond is 'providing us with fewer and fewer things that we can identify as fish' (Thomas and Seeley Brown 2011). The issue is that rather than seeing a world where relatively few elements of knowledge change, punctuated by new paradigms, or new ways of seeing, it is more likely a case of constant change which is both cumulative and complementary. Simple ideas and **technologies** are becoming more complex; these can spillover into or add value to both public and private goods. Knowledge is therefore continuously forming: the 'growth of knowledge' is essential to **innovation**. While it is the application of information that generates new knowledge, the ways that information is distributed and reassembled into new knowledge are increasingly reliant on social **networks**.

Throughout history, individuals who bring forward ideas (and knowledge) have been located in typical social patterns: intellectual groups, networks and rivalries (Collins 1998: 3). In many instances ideas that regenerate societies come from outside national and cultural boundaries. Ideas from outside have contributed to economic growth; nations and societies have engaged in trade, exchanging skills and knowledge; at other times cultural values have been imposed though invasion and colonisation (Bernstein 2008). The impact of some of these forces has been generative; at other times it has been destructive to cultural values. During the late twentieth century, thanks to the rapid spread of information technologies, particularly the internet, the international flow of ideas accelerated, challenging tradition, changing worldviews and confronting authoritarian regimes. Knowledge production and dissemination occurs in communities. The term 'community of practice' describes how shared understandings are acquired through practice (Brown and Duguid 2000). Within most knowledge communities we find epistemic cultures that create and certify knowledge, producing what is often called 'best practice'. In the past creative professions would lay claim to a codified knowledge base; for example journalism, marketing, and design professionals. In academic research disciplinary knowledge is certified through peer review. Communities of practice represent a specific kind of social network, the latter term referring more directly to situated knowledge: 'in which knowledge resides not only in the minds of individuals and in external codified forms, but also in situational contexts of spaces and places, languages and other media, organisations, networks and other systems of social interaction (Potts et al. 2008b: 460). The intensity of social network activity is unprecedented, as is the rate of formation and types of networks. Networks are peer-to-peer rather than peer reviewed.

The sociology of knowledge generally bifurcates into two approaches: (1) *knowledge is socially determined*; and (2) *knowledge constitutes a social order* (McCarthy 1996). The former approach is best represented in Marxism, particularly the view that human knowledge is determined by productive activities: structures of work, institutions and forms of technology. The argument that knowledge is socially determined also reflects structuralism (Levi-Strauss 1963; Hawkes 1977). Socially determined knowledge reflects an expanded field, broadly conceived and inclusive. Berger and Luckmann (1966) have noted this includes all the possible types of knowledge in past and present societies, whether religion, custom, tradition, magic, science or psychoanalysis. In effect, a marriage of knowledge and culture, the expanded field, is readily accepted by 'creative economy' scholars aligned with developing economics (United Nations Conference on Trade and Development (UNCTAD) 2008). One of the reasons is that the stock of knowledge in many developing countries is heavily reliant on traditional culture. Societies with a strong legacy of Confucianism for instance have accorded great emphasis to canonical knowledge and respect for the past. However, overemphasis on tradition and settled categories of thought can be counter-productive when it comes to creating new knowledge. Tradition and modernity inevitably clash. Hagel and Seeley Brown say that as change accelerates, 'stocks of knowledge' diminish in value: 'the life-time value of knowledge rapidly shrinks as the rate of obsolescence in knowledge increases' (2006: 11). The second variant: *knowledge constitutes a social order* lends itself to multifarious interpretations. A critical perspective argues that social orders are determined by discourses, 'knowledges with institutional moorings' or 'regimes of rationality' (Foucault 1982). This perspective sheds some light on 'the creative economy'. In an account 'Knowledges of the creative economy', Kong et al. (2006) show how a package of discourses (creative industries, creative economy, creative city, and creative clusters) was introduced into the hitherto Confucian knowledge-based societies of Singapore, Hong Kong and Mainland China, opening the way for a steady stream of knowledgeable consultants dispensing solutions to growth.

However , the kind of knowledge that is distilled into creative industries discourse is heterogeneous. In the much disputed initial formulation of the creative industries idea by the UK Department of Culture, Media and Sport (DCMS 1998) value resided in 'wealth and job creation through the generation and exploitation of intellectual property'. Emphasis rested on individual creativity, skill and talent, essentially a very liberal democratic account of the growth of knowledge. Misgivings about this definition evidently stemmed from its emphasis on 'individual' and the subsequent heavy weighting on intellectual property. In comparison to subsequent iterations the DCMS definition pays little attention to tradition, knowledge that has been peer reviewed by history and politics (see UNCTAD 2008). Knowledge societies are therefore not new. Information, however, has changed the way we understand the term 'knowledge-based society'. Knowledge is qualitatively different from information. The information society conjures up an image of unprecedented access to information: prior to the internet age and the use of the term 'information technology', it was believed that limited or imperfect information was a key challenge to growth; for instance lack of information produced what the economist Ronald Coase (1937) called 'transaction costs'.

In creative industries, policymaking information is represented in evidence-based policy; for instance information about population demographics, market characteristics, export opportunities, and clustering of businesses can lead to better policy making. Information, however, is structured and formatted data that remains inert until used by those with the knowledge to interpret and process them. Knowledge is much more than information; knowledge is a cognitive capacity, conventionally understood as expertise. In conventional media and cultural sector value chains professional knowledge (expertise) is generally seen as an input into content generation, delivery and sales (i.e. marketing). Knowledge has become an essential component of innovation policy as more governments look to a sustainable future. Joel Mokyr (2004) claims that 'propositional knowledge' has been a driving engine of technological innovation in the modern 'Western' era. Propositional knowledge is different from 'prescriptive' knowledge, which is codified as techniques (*techne*). Prescriptive, explicit or codified knowledge refers to recipes as well as instruction manuals for constructing complex technical systems. Propositional knowledge is therefore *epistemic*: it observes, classifies, measures and catalogues, as well as establishing regularities, principles and natural laws. Propositional knowledge therefore seeks knowledge about 'what' and 'how'. It is concerned with both process and progress, and in this respect it is transformational and cumulative: it gives rise to new ideas and opens new lines of research (Foray 2000).

Knowledge can be sticky: that is knowledge is often difficult to transmit or export. The term absorptive capacity refers to the ability to absorb knowledge 'spillovers'. Both spillovers and absorptive capacities are due to the fact that an organisation or an individual cannot capture all the benefits resulting from inventive activity. In this sense the role of clustering is important, both geographically and metaphorically. Localised spillovers and cultures of interaction frequently occur when participants are close to the knowledge source; for instance, Silicon Valley and Hollywood. Such clustering allows the exchange of tacit knowledge: in order to become smarter people need to interact with each other. This applies particularly to the creative industries. Creativity, learning, knowledge networks and innovation occur because of skilled labour markets and movement of people. Arts and cultural policy generally support the professions as the privileged site of creativity. In many creative industries learning-by-doing is a major factor: this can take place in the creative generation or production stage, for instance, the craft workshop model or master-apprentice system of acquiring knowledge. However, learning (and learning-by-doing) frequently occurs in the utilisation stage: that is, user-led innovation provides a feedback loop into production. The rapid dissemination of codified knowledge due to intensive adoption of information communication and technologies (ICTs) has shifted the locus of knowledge production. Social network markets facilitate the transmission of knowledge, much of which is integrated into better design and performance.

The term knowledge capital can describe a firm's workforce, its customers' demands or preferences and its systems, products processes and capabilities. Customer demands are monitored by professional agencies; for instance television audience ratings or internet usage. However, knowledge capital is increasingly dispersed and volatile. Finally, in today's society the profusion of transdisciplinary knowledge is significant. Transdisciplinarity reflects the fact that creative industries in particular and the creative process more generally deal with different kinds of knowledge. Helga Nowotny writes: '[Knowledge] seeps through institutions and from academia to and from the outside world. Transdisciplinarity is therefore about transgressing boundaries' (2004: 1).

Knowledge, and the growth of knowledge, is intrinsic to the creative industries. If we accept the position that the creative industries are more than just sectors (disciplines), we can see how knowledge brokered in design seeps into 'non-creative' professions, such as manufacturing. The creative industries in this view are key drivers of the innovation system. The significance of the creative industries is not in terms of their relative contribution to economic value but due to their contribution to the coordination of new ideas or technologies, and thus to the process of change. In this view, the creative industries are mis-specified as 'an industry' (Hartley 2009: 42–6), and better modelled as an evolving **complex system** that derives its economic value from the facilitation of economic **evolution** and the process of innovation.

The standard economic definition of a market is that it is an institution for the purpose of exchange of goods and services. When economists analytically represent a market, they tend to do so with intersecting demand and supply curves, representing the behaviour of buyers and sellers at a schedule of different prices. But what these diagrams do not represent very well is the more important aspect of markets as mechanisms for *price discovery* and as spaces in which opportunities to create value are tested and revealed, and thus mutually beneficial actions between many different people can be coordinated. Markets are thus a powerful kind of *social technology* (see **institutions** and **competition**) to efficiently coordinate human action with respect to scarce resources (including time and attention). Markets are certainly key concepts in creative industries in the specific sense that markets are the main *coordinating institutions* of these industries, and precisely because these are highly dynamic sectors with new ideas constantly being proposed and value propositions tested, and in which many different parts of both resources and knowledge have to come together for production to occur. Market systems are able to process this complexity (see **complex systems**) more effectively than centrally controlled systems because markets are far superior mechanisms of information processing and distributed computation, giving rise to effective adaptation (see **evolution**).

Markets are not perfect institutions (and indeed they continue to adapt and evolve), but they are in most cases far better than alternative mechanisms of coordination (e.g. barter, gift economies, traditional hierarchic orders, central planning, rule of experts/bureaucrats, etc). Put differently, the parts of the creative industries that are most market-based, and where those markets are freest, also tend to be those parts that are the most economically vibrant and growing (Frey and Pommerehne 1989; Peacock 1993; Cowen 1998, 2002; Raustiala and Sprigman 2006). That's an entirely unsurprising result once we understand the theory of markets.

Markets are institutional mechanisms for coordinating economic activity through voluntary and mutually beneficial exchange using price signals. Markets work by coordinating the production or consumption plans of thousands or perhaps millions of individual economic agents through the mechanism of price signals. Price signals carry information about relative and local scarcity or demand. Both buyers and sellers adjust their behaviour (their plans) in response to changes in prices; in this way the economic order is continually re-coordinated in response to changes issuing from anywhere in the system, whether a change in local demand, a change in technology or in supply conditions, or any other change. Moreover, this entire process operates without any central direction or control. As suggested, markets are thus appropriately thought of as an information-processing (i.e. computational) social coordination technology. There are several *classes* of market: commodities markets for final consumer goods and services; intermediate markets (outputs of one firm that are inputs into other firms, or capital goods); factor markets (for labour, resources, etc); and financial markets. There are different *types* of market mechanism: ranging from simple posted-price markets (e.g. a shop) to more complex double-auction markets (e.g. a stock market). Different classes and types of market differ by the institutional rules that compose them. Markets also differ by *degree of competition* (see **competition**), ranging from perfect competition with many buyers and sellers and free entry, to degrees of imperfect competition (fewer buyers or sellers due to barriers to entry), the limit of which is monopoly (one seller) or monopsony (one buyer).

In all cases though, markets function to coordinate the mutual actions of buyers and sellers through the mechanism of price. The class and type of market affects the mechanisms and *transaction costs* (Caves 2000 is a comprehensive account of the effect of transaction costs on creative industries) by which this is achieved and degree of competition affects the *efficiency* of the price mechanism. Prices are bid up or down, immediately in a double-auction market or over weeks or perhaps months in a posted-price market, such that the quantity supplied to the market equals the quantity demanded. This is the 'equilibrium price' that clears the market. Prices are information signals produced by markets. A market is a mechanism that produces a price; they are in this way a 'price discovery' technology, and a way of figuring the value of what is being produced. This information is used to coordinate the respective economic plans of buyers and sellers. Markets are institutions to coordinate dispersed information and fragmented knowledge through the response and adaptation to price signals. Markets, using prices, are thus an alternative to economic coordination by other more hierarchical or centralised means, such as by direction (e.g. in an hierarchical organisation), or by central planning (by a government). Economists favour market mechanisms because they make the best use of distributed local information and focus this into a single 'bit' of information – price. This observation holds in even where creative industries markets involve zero prices for the final goods and services (such as some media models) because the consumers themselves are on-sold to intermediate markets (this time as audience or eyeballs, etc); value is still revealed, even when some prices are zero.

Two further points on the theory of markets. First, markets *create* value, by definition, wherever an exchange is voluntary. Market exchange is a 'positive sum game'. When a consumer exchanges US$4.00 for a muffin,[1] what they are saying is that that muffin is worth more than the $4.00 cash is to them, else they wouldn't offer to buy it. But at the same time, the seller is saying that the $4.00 cash is worth more to them than the muffin, else they wouldn't offer to sell it. At the end of the exchange both parties have gained. All market exchange is like that (the same cannot be said about other forms of economic coordination, such as in a command economy, where one's gain may very well be equal to another's loss). The crucial part of the story is

---

[1] Our hypothetical muffin is the one used for The Economist's famous Big Mac Index, which compares different countries' price parity with the US dollar: see: www.economist.com/blogs/dailychart/2011/07/big-mac-index.

the voluntary nature of market exchange. The corollary of this is the requirement of *free entry* (or the absence of barriers to entry) to a market. This is significant in relation to the creative industries, where various regulations, licensing requirements, public sector competition (e.g. public broadcasters), and other forms of legislative monopoly (such as intellectual property) act to limit entry into markets or raise the cost of entry into markets, thus constraining the value they can create.

Second, an often-cited justification for public intervention in arts and cultural markets (but less so in creative industries) is due to so-called *market failure*. The concept of market failure derives from what is called 'Pigovian welfare economics' and associated with the concept of an *externality*. An externality is a positive or negative effect (pollution, for example, is a commonly cited negative externality) of an 'equilibrium' market outcome. The market is said to 'fail' because the price it produces (and the equilibrium level of output and consumption at that price) is the 'wrong level' once the externality is factored in. Hence public intervention is said to be necessary to correct the externality by artificially changing the price by either tax (e.g. a pollution tax) or a subsidy (in the case of a positive externality, such as directed at public health or education).

It is commonly argued in cultural policy circles that there is widespread market failure in the provision of cultural and creative goods and services due to the unaccounted for but significant *positive externality* associated with its production and consumption. Markets, in other words, by themselves produce price incentives that lead to *too little* arts, cultural and creative goods production from the social welfare perspective. This allegedly justifies public subsidy to correct this 'market failure'. While this is an almost axiomatic position from the perspective of arts and cultural lobby groups, not all economists support this line of reasoning. They argue that many of these positive externalities are not public goods, but are widely captured as private benefits (e.g. Peacock 1993). There remains considerable debate about the extent to which we do observe market failure in creative industries. But a growing body of research finds no market failure in market incentives to produce creative output once the effect of both regulation restricting market entry and business model adaptation is properly accounted for (e.g. Boldrin and Levine 2008).

A perennial question is what determines the extent of the market. Those who seek to control economic activity must invariably seek to increase the scope of planning and to limit the extent of the market. It is well known in economic theory that firms exist because of 'transactions costs' associated with the use of the market (see Shirky 2008 on how the internet lowers transactions costs to form organisations and the implications for creative industries). That is, with sufficiently low transaction costs it can be less costly to coordinate economic activity in firms rather than via the market. The extent of these transaction costs and the scale economies that can be achieved by this means of organisation determines the size of firms. The creative industries are home to some of the biggest firms in the world, especially in relation to large media aggregators and publishing companies. Yet the reason for this size is not so much to achieve scale economies in capital or distribution channels (although that remains considerable), as to create a sufficiently large portfolio of diverse creative content (Caves 2000). This explains the largely monopolistic structure of creative industries markets with a few large (global) aggregators, and many smaller (local) producers. A further observation about creative industries markets concerns the role of marketing. Advertising and marketing are not superfluous or 'wasteful' features of market economies, but are essential to their functioning. Branding, for example, works as an 'information shorthand' for consumers that enables them to make assessments of quality, service and other factors at relatively low search and discovery cost. Brands are part of the information economy that enables markets to function efficiently and at ever-increasing scale. Creative industries play a considerable role in the processes of marketing and in the shaping of consumer demand and in developing the attention economies that increasingly underpin modern economic systems (Lanham 2006).

The creative industries can be understood not so much as a set of (11 or so) industries, but rather as a class of markets: specifically, *social network markets* (Potts et al. 2008a). Markets in creative industries are, by and large, not markets for known generic quantities (such as Texas Light Sweet crude oil, or gold, or Big Macs) but instead for novel products for which it is difficult to judge quality or even to form preference expectations prior to consumption (Karpik 2010). Creative industries markets are typically experience goods in this primary sense (Hutter 2011). A social network market occurs when consumer choice is determined by the choices of others, providing proxy information about quality and the likelihood of utility. Creative industries markets are thus commonly social network markets. In consequence, we should expect such markets to be institutionally characterised by the prevalence of such social network feedback information and intermediation. We should expect to observe significant path-dependencies and winner-take-all effects. And we should expect to see the economic significance of creative industries in proportion to the extent of **innovation** in the economic order. A further prominent line of analytic inquiry concerns the internal institutional working of markets (an economic sociology of markets) that shows how order emerges for consumers and producers through the various component sub-mechanisms of a market (e.g. pricing, scheduling, information flows, etc.). Aspers (2010) for example, develops a comprehensive analysis of the micro-institutional structure of the fashion markets. Finally, markets are also of course *sites of culture*. This typically occurs when a market consists of multiple related markets (e.g. a shopping district such as a medieval bazaar or a modern mall) that combine deliberate search and purchase with attendant browsing behaviour, often in a highly social environment.

Media

The media have been well understood as a concept and as a term in common use, predating by almost a century the term 'creative industries'. It began to be used in the 1920s as conglomerated power and influence crystallised around newspapers, the movies and radio, but has its real origins as far back as the fifteenth century with the invention of the moveable-type printing press (Eisenstein 1979). Since the 1920s, the term 'media' has become synonymous with 'mass media' – large-scale, one-to-many, mainstream information and entertainment industries including print (newspapers, magazines, book publishing), broadcasting (television, radio), film, recorded music and more recently video and computer gaming. These are the media of the industrial age, often using methods of production, distribution and marketing similar to those of other mass-produced industrial products and services.

Owing to their standardisation and reach, the mass media were seen in terms of powerful 'senders' and passive 'receivers,' leading to the widespread adoption of the 'effects paradigm' of media research, predicated on a view of mediated communication as a one-way flow of 'who says what to whom in what channel with what effect', according to the famous dictum of US political scientist Harold Lasswell (1948). Such a framework generated traditions of study in psychology (effects on individuals) and in political economy (effects on society). The latter sought to analyse the influence of monopolistic firms and oligopolistic markets (Lasswell's 'who'); and studied the organisations that have grown up to marshal the production and distribution of media content (Lasswell's 'what'; and 'what channel'). Then there are audience, reader and fan studies, which look into the attitudes, opinions, behaviour, and responses that mass media consumption brings ('to whom', 'with what effect'). Most of the assumptions built into the effects tradition have been challenged by theorists working from a cultural rather than a behavioural perspective (Hartley 1992, 2011), and are challenged further by changes wrought by forces of **globalisation**, **convergence** and digitisation.

Before we look at what 'new' media might look like, we should first consider the place of media in the cultural and creative industries. David Hesmondhalgh sees the media as 'core' **cultural industries** rather than creative industries, 'because they deal primarily with the industrial production and circulation of texts' (2007: 12). He assigns the arts (see **aesthetics**, **culture**) to 'peripheral' status (2007: 13) and makes no mention of **design**. Hesmondhalgh prefers the tradition of thinking about media that starts with the Frankfurt School, which is structured around industrialised modes of production. But a creative industries framework for media would emphasise the increasingly blurred edges amongst various types of cultural and economic activity. By placing media *alongside* arts and design, a creative industries framework points to the fact that much cultural activity occurs or originates outside the market and industrial process, and that much market-based activity is not merely the final consumption of products (e.g. media texts) but productive inputs into other forms of business activity (see **co-creation**, **consumer**, **productivity**). While placing media within the array of creative industries achieves a useful contemporary comparative dimension, we also need to consider the temporal dimension; the dynamics of change. One of the key debates in contemporary media and communication studies is the rate at which established media are being changed, transformed or destroyed (see **creative destruction**). Is there a 'post-industrial' media age, as has been posited for the **information economy**? Has there been a substantive break that makes terms like 'old' and 'new' media meaningful?

The fact is that change is continuous, but it is less clear what we might make of it. Are we contemporary 'witnesses to and participants in the largest, most fundamental transformation in the history of the media since the advent of typeface, the moving image, and terrestrial broadcast transmission' (Levin 2009: 258), or, alternatively, is the evidence for the wholesale supplanting of the old media by new media actually 'sparse and thin' (T. Miller 2010a), ignoring the lessons of history which tell us that it is more likely for the new to be folded into the old, adding to it rather than killing it off?

What then are new media? Almost by definition, it has been a movable feast – new media are whatever is new at the time. An historical perspective on this is important to avoid 'now-ism'. Eisenstein (1979), Ong (2012), Winston (1986), Marvin (2008), Streeter (2011) and others are on hand to help, reminding us that the printing press, newspapers, radio, television, cable television, and so on, were new media in their time, disrupting the old order, in a tradition of thinking going back to Harold Innis (1950) and Marshall McLuhan (1962). Even papyrus was once the new medium, replacing stone tablets! But the key shift we are dealing with now is from industrial to 'social' media or 'Web 2.0', introducing platforms and activities which are, at least initially, of a different order from that of mass media, in that they arise from the 'household' sector, not the commercial or public sectors. It is this fact that leads major writers like Benkler (2006) and Hartley (2009) to posit a qualitative break from *all* 'mass' media.

Overlaid on these disagreements about the depth of change are normative differences of value, taste and politics. The extremes of these differences are seen in, for example, the utopian 'glass half full' approach of Clay Shirky (2008, 2010) and the dystopian dismissals of Andrew Keen (2008) of the democratising, empowering potentials of social media. Always in the frame, as well, are disputations over the empirical evidence for rates and depths of change. There can never be other than complex answers to these questions: while newspapers face closure and television stagnates in many parts of the 'advanced' West, both are coming into their own in the emergent areas of China, India, Brazil, etc. There are also fundamental disagreements about media decline in the West (see T. Miller 2010a). These complexities are the stuff of ongoing research. Students and citizens have a direct stake in this debate and its outcomes, since 'everybody' is both a participant in some form of social media and a consumer of traditional media.

The conceptualisation of contemporary new media is being worked through in research that is enriching our understanding of creative industries *as* industries. There are the changes wrought inside mainstream television 'on the ground', for which John Caldwell has coined the terms 'first and second shift **aesthetics**'. 'First-shift' refers to traditional linear approaches in television to attracting mass audiences – programme schedules, time slots, advertising, etc. But the internet, personal video recorders, and multitasking have made this an 'unrealistic and improbable goal' (Caldwell 2003: 135). Second shift practices are 'an attempt to bring new forms of rationality to unstable media economies'. Programming strategies have shifted from notions of programme 'flows' to tactics of audience/user 'flows' and the way networks are attempting to achieve this are through aggregation, tiering of brands/content and brand equity.

There are the radically blurred boundaries around what constitutes a media text. For Jonathan Gray (2010a), paratexts (including previews, movie trailers, advertisements, interviews with creative personnel, spoilers, internet discussion, entertainment news, reviews, fan creations, posters, games, merchandising, DVDs and spinoffs) are big business and generate more revenue than that generated by texts themselves. An example is the merchandising, licensing and franchising revenue generated by *Lord of the Rings*, Disney, *Star Wars* and *The Simpsons*. However, traditional screen studies focuses predominantly on media texts with little regard to the paratexts they generate. Gray (2010a) advocates a new approach to screen studies, which he terms 'off-screen studies', to move beyond medium-specific analyses to study hype, synergy, promos, and peripherals.

And, most fundamentally, there is the phenomenon of 'transmedia'. Henry Jenkins says it is 'a new aesthetic that has emerged in response to media convergence', where audiences act as 'hunters and gatherers, chasing down bits of the story across media channels' (2006: 20–1). A 'transmedia story, he says, ' unfolds across multiple media platforms, with each text making a distinctive and valuable contribution to the whole … a story might be introduced in a film, expanded through television, novels, and comics; its world might be explored through game play or experienced as an amusement park' (2006: 95–6). A key issue is that each platform 'is a point of entry into the franchise as a whole' and 'each franchise entry needs to be self-contained so you don't need to have seen the film to enjoy the game, and vice versa' (2006: 96). Transmedia stories are most effective when they are built around a deep narrative, or a narrative with a detailed world which can be explored in greater depth in other media (i.e. an online website or electronic game) as 'reading across the media sustains a depth of experience that motivates more consumption' (Jenkins 2003: 3). While not all screen projects have the potential to become transmedia, such storytelling is becoming increasingly desirable for major studios and television networks to maximise profits across the value chain, thereby fuelling demand for such production.

Jenkins' (2010) model of transmedia is fundamentally about storytelling. There are also models that stress transmedia as a business model, responding to the crises of viability for independent film and screen producers, that are tapping into the potential for new market creation through social media **network** effects. A report for the Tribeca Film Institute sums it up: 'What has become clear is that more work needs to be developed in analysing new financing models; new pricing and sales models; new distribution models; and new production models … and to study the music industry, to see how the crisis of that sector can be avoided in this one' (Kaufman and Mohan 2008: 17). There are now many models and examples of filmed entertainment using cutting-edge social media communication strategies and the full affordances of the digital value chain. Beneath all this activity is a strong revaluation of what David Stark calls 'accounts of worth in economic life' (2009). This is a good description of the transmedia space now being carved out of the crisis of screen business. The old defence of professionalism is being overtaken by new modes of value creation through deep engagement with social media affordances, where the rhetoric of community versus commercialism, professional versus amateur, entertainment versus education, information or service doesn't work anymore. This is a space where copyright control regimes are less important than socially networked touchpoints into multiple potential markets; where weak **intellectual property** enforcement (everything can be replicated rapidly by competitors) means rapid exploration of new ways to manage risk. Fundamentally, it means moving out of a filmed entertainment comfort zone, engaging with discontinuous social and cultural fields, and delving deep into the world of social media.

Networks

Networks are extensible systems interconnected by nodes (the 'knots' in the 'net'). The concept of networks can be understood at three levels. First, there are *technical networks*, or the physical infrastructure that connects devices to one another in order to enable the flow of matter between them. Examples include the electricity network, the telephone network and – most significantly for the creative industries – the *computer network*. The computer network is a combination of computers and interconnected devices that facilitate communication and enable the distribution and sharing of information and resources. The internet is a global 'network of (computer) networks' that combines the technical infrastructure of computers and other digital devices that are permanently connected to high-speed telecommunications networks, with forms of content, data, communication and information sharing that occurs across and through these networks.

The second level is that of *social networks*. Platforms such as Facebook and Google+ provide our clearest contemporary images of what a social network is, but the concept has a longer history in social theory. Social network analysis is a methodology used in the social sciences to map interpersonal linkages using statistical and graphical techniques, focusing on the interdependencies that exist among agents, the role played by relational ties in facilitating the flow of resources, and how resulting network structures demonstrate durable relationships (Wasserman and Faust 1994). Social network analysis has a long history in research into **power**, as seen in studies into business elites and the relationships between political and economic power (e.g. Mills 1956; Miliband 1973). In internet research, the relationship between social networking and interconnections established through technology has led to a range of mapping projects to identify relationships among 'online publics' (Wellman 2007). Social networks have also featured in **creative cities** research as part of the *soft infrastructure* that enables individuals and institutions to interact effectively to promote creative industries in particular locations (Landry 2000).

The third level is that of *socio-technical networks*. The internet can be seen as a socio-technical network *par excellence*, as its social implications derive from elements of its technical form, particularly the development of an open architecture network environment, whereby all computers and computing networks can communicate with one another in a common language. The internet thus takes the form of a communication technology that is inherently public, global, non-proprietary at the level of the network, and open to continuous and radical innovation at its 'edges'. Drawing upon media technology theorists such as Harold Innis (1950) and Marshall McLuhan (1962), the internet promotes decentralised, many-to-many forms of communication, in contrast to broadcast media, which promote centralised production (one-to-many communication) and privatised consumption.

Carlota Perez (2010) has identified five 'techno-economic paradigms' over two centuries:

1 The Industrial Revolution (1780s–1830s);
2 The Age of Steam and Railways (1840s–1880s);
3 The Age of Steel, Electricity and Heavy Engineering (1890s–1930s);
4 The Age of Oil, the Automobile and Mass Production (1940s–1980s);
5 The Age of Information and Telecommunications (1990s–present).

A *techno-economic paradigm* is a cluster of technological innovations that not only generate new products, services and industries, but also have a transformative impact throughout the economy and society. This socio-economic transformation occurs in three ways: (1) through effects on the costs of production (including costs of distribution); (2) through new opportunities for innovation and entrepreneurship; and (3) in the manner in which they reshape organisations and infrastructures. The concept of techno-economic paradigms has parallels in the notion of 50-year 'long waves' of technological and economic innovation proposed by Joseph Schumpeter in the 1930s, and drawn upon by John Montgomery (2007) in his analysis of the growth and decline of major cities.

Perez sees the internet historically as the core of the fifth paradigm. If we contrast the fourth and fifth paradigms, we can see how the impact of networked digital media technologies extends well beyond the information communication and technology (ICT) sectors (Perez 2010: 197):

- *Age of Oil, the Automobile and Mass Production:* Mass production/mass markets; Economies of scale: bigger is better; Standardisation of products; Energy intensity (oil based); Synthetic materials (e.g. plastics); Functional specialisation: hierarchies within organisations; Centralisation of urban form: metropolitan centres/suburbanisation; National powers/economies within an international framework;
- *Age of Information and Telecommunications:* Information-intensive: microelectronics-based ICTs; Decentralised integration: network structures; Segmentation of markets/proliferation of niche products and services; Knowledge as capital:

networks

139

intangible value added as key to new wealth creation; Economies of scope, and product/service specialisation combined with scale; Globalisation: interaction between the global and the local; Production/geographical clusters and networks of collaboration/learning; Instantaneous global communication across multiple platforms/devices.

The interest in networks from an economic perspective has been considerable. The concept of *network externalities* refers to the degree to which an individual **agent** (a person, corporation, organisation) derives benefits from being within a larger network, through access to information, new knowledge, contacts and feedback. The result is that there can be *first mover advantage* to facilitating development of a network, on the basis of switching costs that arise from leaving the 'first mover' for a competitor. The underlying principle behind Facebook, for instance, is that there is value for an individual in maintaining a profile in a network with over 500 million other people on it, even if it may be more problematic in how it operates – in relation to privacy to take a commonly cited example – than a network with fewer participants. Theories of economic **institutions** also point to the value of networks in managing transaction costs and pooling capabilities, in order to maximise benefits associated with organising interdependent relations, in a context of market failure, imperfect information, and endemic uncertainty. Williamson (1985) has developed a theory of the corporation as a *nexus of contracts*, in contrast to the industrial-era understanding of corporations as hierarchically organised internally in order to maximise efficiency gains, and this concept has been drawn upon by Caves (2000) in his analysis of the economics of the creative industries.

Two theorists who have addressed the wider socio-economic implications of networks are Manuel Castells and Yochai Benkler. Drawing on the concepts of socio-technical networks and techno-economic paradigms, Castells argued that networks 'constitute the new social morphology of our societies' (1996: 469), to the point where the network society is the dominant social structure associated with a globally networked **information economy**. Networked forms of organisation are seen as being the central drivers of globalisation at the economic, geopolitical and cultural levels, and a link between the creative industries and the network enterprise form is seen in the rise of project-based work. Jeremy Rifkin (2000) has argued that the 'Hollywood model' of project-based work has becomes generalised from the creative industries to many other forms of business organisation. Yochai Benkler (2006) has identified networks as being at the core of a twenty-first-century networked information economy, to the rise of social production – models of information, knowledge and cultural production that are loosely collaborative, not necessarily driven by market criteria, and not directly proprietary in terms of who owns and controls the use by others of the final product. Benkler's work emphasises the importance of non-economic motivations to the development of what he terms *social production*:

> Decentralised individual action – specifically new and improved cooperative and coordinated action carried out through radically distributed, non-market mechanisms that do not depend upon proprietary strategies – plays a much greater role than it did, or could have, in the industrial information economy. (2006: 3)

The classic example of what Benkler describes is Wikipedia, which pioneered a radically decentralised approach to the production of articles, and collaborative editing of its online encyclopaedia, and has grown from about 20,000 articles in 2002 to nearly four million articles by 2012 in English, plus 270 other-language Wikipedias.[1] Wikipedia is a case study in the new nature of collaborative expertise and co-creation in the context of digital networks. Wikipedia would have no entries in the absence of **experts** willing to contribute their knowledge on specialist topics, but their expertise would lack an outlet in the absence of a distributive system able to make their expertise globally spreadable.

The internet is a necessary but not sufficient condition for social production. Benkler identifies three further critical factors: (1) the rise of information, knowledge, and creative industries requires production systems that are more flexible and more reliant on intrinsic motivations than traditional manufacturing industries; (2) the existence of the internet itself has given a major boost to non-market forms of information-production and distribution, as there are network effects that result from a multiplicity of individual actions in a concentrated space (*Google* search, *Wikipedia* entries, *Facebook* status updates, etc.), that exponentially enrich the networked information environment; (3) there is the rise of peer production of information, knowledge, and culture through large-scale cooperative efforts. The conceptual and practical origins of this can be found in the free and open source software movement, but the rise of Web 2.0 and social software has seen its impact diffuse across a range of domains.

Potts et al. (2008a) have argued that the creative industries are best understood through the continuous interaction among agents in complex social networks, which generate their distinctive production and consumption dynamics. The decisions made by individuals are determined by the decisions of others within their social networks, so that they rely upon 'word of mouth, taste, cultures, and popularity, such that individual choices are dominated by information feedback over social networks rather than innate preferences and price signals'. The result is that 'other people's preferences have commodity status over a social network because novelty by definition carries uncertainty and other people's choices, therefore, carry information' (Potts et al. 2008a: 169–70). They argue that the creative industries emerge at 'the liminal zone between the social and the market' (2008a: 179). One consequence of the resulting complex institutional dynamics is that traditional **cultural policy** instruments such as public subsidy for established institutions, or industry policy strategies such as 'picking winners', may prove difficult to apply to the emergent creative industries sectors such as games, design or social media.

Networks are a central element of analytical frameworks such as *actor–network theory* (ANT). Bruno Latour defines a network as a means through which action can be redistributed between agent and system, so that 'an actor is nothing but a network, except that a network is nothing but actors' (2011: 5). For Latour (2004), networks provide ways of conceptualising the relationships among actors around particular issues or what he terms 'matters of concern', without recourse

---

[1] en.wikipedia.org/wiki/Wikipedia:Size_of_Wikipedia

to overarching concepts such as **power**, or reference to society as an abstract entity of which individuals are merely small parts, or parts of wider aggregations such as social classes. Latour argues that the ability to map social networks that digital technologies have enabled, means that a greater capacity now exists to demonstrate the *materiality* of networks and the relationships between actors within them, without recourse to abstractions such as society, the individual or power.

An important feature of Latour's work, and that of other actor-network theorists, is that while they focus on the capacities of **agents** to transform their social environments, rather than being primarily subjected to abstract forms of social power, the concept of agency is extended to non-human actors. If we were to consider the conflicts and tensions around Muslim populations in European countries, for instance, the *hijab* or headscarf worn by many Muslim women is itself an agent in the network of associations that exist around such issues, as the positions of some participants around the issue cannot be understood independently of the existence of this form of dress: many European politicians do not proclaim an objection to Islam *per se*, but rather to the wearing of the *hijab* in public spaces. Such work (see also Hawkins 2009) provides examples of how the concept of networks reaches well beyond the study of digital media into the politics of culture more generally.

Power is the exertion of force by one entity on another. The concept of power has a long history, being at the centre of political theory and philosophy. John Thompson has identified four primary forms of power (1995: 16–17):

1 *Political* – institutions and practices primarily concerned with coordination and regulation; this form of power is primarily held through government and the state;
2 *Economic* – the ability to control processes of production, distribution, prices and markets, and accumulation; such power is most notably held by corporations, but may also be held by other institutional agents, such as trade unions or producers' associations;
3 *Coercive* – the capacity to use actual or potential force against others, particularly in combination with political power, notably associated with the armed forces, the police, etc.;
4 *Symbolic/cultural* – power associated with the ability to control the production, transmission and reception of symbolic forms, or 'the means of information and communication', broadly defined.

From this perspective, questions of power as they relate to media, culture and the creative industries are connected to symbolic/cultural power, or the ability to define

key concepts in creative industries

and shape **representations** of social reality. Historically, the major theories of power to influence the study of media and culture have been *liberal-pluralist* theories in mass communications, and *critical-Marxist* theories in critical political economy. The question of 'media power' was first raised around the question of effects. Drawing on a distinction made in pluralist political theories between *having* and *exercising* power and influence, and making the assumption that political, economic and cultural power were relatively distinct, innumerable empirical studies have investigated the role played by mass media in shaping personal behaviour. Many came to find the power of media over individual behaviour to be limited, as there were too many intervening variables that needed to be considered in such empirical research models.

The political economy of communication approach challenged pluralist theories of power, seeing them as limited by their focus on individual behaviour rather than social relations, and by separating political from economic and cultural power. For critical theorists, power is not only about the capacity to influence the *behaviour* of others, but also concerns the ability to shape the **representation** of *reality* that others rely upon in order to make decisions. In particular, media ownership has been seen as a critical variable in generating the capacity to represent reality is such a way as to further proprietors' own political and economic interests. Critical theories of media and communication typically propose that there exists a *dominant ideology*, that is 'a symbolic system which, by incorporating individuals from all strata into the social order, helps to reproduce a social order which serves the interests of the dominant groups' (Thompson 1990: 91). These come with varying degrees of strength. In the most *instrumentalist* versions, such as the *propaganda model* developed by Chomsky and Herman, the mass media are presented as the instruments of the dominant classes, who are 'able to filter the news …, marginalise dissent, and allow … dominant interests to get their messages across to the public' (1988: 2). Political economists such as Golding and Murdock modify this strong economic determinism, arguing that economic power dominates, but 'owners, advertisers and key political personnel cannot always do as they wish … [but] operate within structures that constrain as well as facilitate' (2005: 63).

Some approaches within the critical tradition identify a greater degree of autonomy for cultural power. Louis Althusser conceptualised 'Ideological State Apparatuses' such as cultural, media and educational **institutions**. These promote dominant ideologies, but contestation is specific to each sphere. How cultural institutions work in practice cannot simply be 'read off' relations of power and dominance in the political and economic spheres. Examples of contestation include competing methodological traditions in academic disciplines, or the politics of 'objectivity' discourses in news journalism (Hall 1985).

Another distinctive direction, which gives a central role to the media and cultural spheres, is the concept of *hegemony*, as developed by Stuart Hall (1985) among others. Work inspired by the concept of hegemony has given more critical consideration to the role played by cultural intermediaries and media professionals engaged in the production and distribution of culture, as well as the role played by **audiences** as active participants in the creation of cultural meaning, meaning that even if media texts are presenting messages consistent with dominant ideologies, there nonetheless exists the capacity for resistance to these dominant ideologies (e.g. Negus 2002). In the early twenty-first century, the dominant critical approach to understanding power and ideology has been through the notion of *neo-liberalism*, defined by David Harvey as:

> A theory of political economic practices that proposes that human well-being can best be advanced by liberating individual entrepreneurial freedoms and skills within an institutional framework characterised by strong private property rights, free market, and free trade. The role of the state is to create and preserve an institutional framework appropriate to such practices. (2005: 2)

From this perspective, the rise of the media and creative industries to greater prominence globally has coincided with the rise of neo-liberalism, generating a policy response described by critics as a 'process by which market exchange increasingly came to permeate the cultural industries and related sectors' (Hesmondhalgh 2007: 110). There have also been those who associate **creative industries** with neo-liberalism (T. Miller 2009; Turner 2011), owing to its greater focus upon entrepreneurship and commercial markets than the traditional focus of arts and **cultural policy** upon public sector cultural institutions and arts subsidy. In considering major theories of power, it is important to note a distinction that Hindess (1996) makes between approaches where power is a capacity to act, which some people have and others do not; and those where power is a capacity grounded in the consent of those subject to it. The first type typically approaches power as an instrument that is used by dominant social groups against others, but which can also be captured through radical political action (Abercrombie and Turner 1978). The second type, which associates the effective exercise of power with the support of self-governing subjects, is found in some ways in hegemony theories, but far more significantly in the later work of French philosopher Michel Foucault (1991) (and see 'Power' in Hartley 2011).

Theories of neo-liberalism generally – but not exclusively – work with the first approach to power. From this perspective, neo-liberalism has been understood as a global political and ideological project, with its roots in the Reagan–Thatcher administrations, which has sought to shift power and resources to corporations and elites. It successfully co-opted notionally left-of-centre political leaders such as Bill Clinton in the USA and Tony Blair in Britain, and spread internationally through the hegemony of institutions promoting **globalisation** such as the World Bank and the International Monetary Fund. But the idea of neo-liberalism was developed in a quite different direction in the later work of Michel Foucault (1991, 2008). For Foucault, what other critical theorists call power is what he describes as domination, where power relations are relatively stable and hierarchical. Foucault defines power more generally, with domination as a sub-set. He sees power as inherently *relational, contingent, unstable and reversible*; resistance is a necessary and inevitable corollary of such power. The important point is that power is largely exercised over free subjects, rather than being something imposed upon people against their will;

this is particularly the case with governmental power as it has evolved in modern liberal democracies.

Foucault's interest in power lay less in questions of who has it and whether it is used properly or improperly, than in the technologies and rationalities of government, how they seek to define a social problem and act upon it, and how they use indirect as well as direct means to influence the behaviour and conduct of free subjects. The challenge for understanding liberal forms of government, according to Foucault, is that power is increasingly *dispersed* rather than concentrated, and 'is exercised over those who are in a position to choose, and it aims to influence what those choices will be' (Hindess 1996: 100). This is what Foucault calls *governmentality*, or the historical emergence of distinctive arts and techniques of government in liberal democracies (Foucault 1991).

Foucault identified both continuities and significant differences between classical liberalism and neo-liberalism. Both are grounded in the notion that power in democratic societies needs to work on free subjects, and that economic freedom, as seen in the operation of markets, is a component of that individual freedom. The difference is that the neo-liberals viewed **markets** not primarily in terms of the setting of prices, but rather as a mechanism that promotes **competition**. But markets and competition are by no means a natural order upon which the state intervenes, which had been the general direction of economic liberalism from Adam Smith to John Maynard Keynes; instead, the neo-liberals proposed that the state must continually act to generate policies that produce competition. This entails a rejection of certain dualities in liberal thought about economic governance, particularly those between the market and the state, and between competition and regulation. Instead, it is argued that the market and competition 'can only appear … if it is produced by an active governmentality … One must govern for the market, rather than because of the market' (Foucault 2008: 121). While this sounds similar to the neo-Marxist critique of neo-liberalism, Foucault was very clear that it is not simply class rule by another name. He argued that this underestimated what was radically new about this form of governmentality: 'neo-liberalism is not Adam Smith; neo-liberalism is not market society; neo-liberalism is not the Gulag on the insidious scale of capitalism' (Foucault 2008: 131). While it points to a historically new form of economic governance, namely governance *through* the market as distinct from governance in order to *control* the market, it can be consistent with a number of different types of government, from the German 'social market economy' to the US 'Tea Party' movement. Mitchell Dean has observed that 'there is more than one type of neo-liberalism … it is necessary to analyse particular forms of political rationality and the ways in which they connect themselves to regimes of government' (1999: 58).

A final question that arises in considering power is the purpose of such an undertaking. In the more instrumentalist approaches, the purpose is to identify who has power, in order to work out who critical scholars should be opposing: what the Occupy Wall Street and other related movements were describing as the 'one per cent' who controlled the major political, economic and cultural institutions. Yet as Stuart Hall observed some years ago, theories of power that emphasise the overt control by a few key people over the media and creative industries, and hence over the circulation of ideas, would point to a situation where 'all that would be required would be to pull out their four or five key controllers and put in a few controllers of our own' (1985: 101). Instrumentalist approaches to power also raise the question that definitions of cultural studies as being primarily *about* power run the risk of subordinating much of what is interesting about popular culture from a research point of view to questions of political and cultural power. Mark Gibson (2007) has proposed that a focus upon power is not the only 'true' vocation of cultural studies research: it could, for instance, be focused on questions of negotiating cultural difference in more diverse, multicultural societies. Gibson also proposes more intellectual modesty in claims about the ability of cultural critics to see through power. A similar point has been made in a different way by Bruno Latour who has asked 'what if explanations resorting automatically to power … had outlived their usefulness and deteriorated to the point of now feeding the most gullible forms of critique?' (2004: 230). Such questions point to the risks that critical theories of power, particularly those which point to an all-powerful dominant ideology, may fall too easily into a version of conspiracy theory

Productivity

Productivity is a term from ordinary language, where it means 'the state of being productive', as in the productivity of the soil, or that of an author. From there it has crossed into several specialist disciplines: chiefly economics, where it refers classically to the productivity of labour, but in the modern sense to multi-factor productivity, a.k.a. 'total factor productivity', meaning the productivity of all input resources, disaggregated and analysed. Productivity is also a concept in bioscience, where it refers to the capability of a given individual, population or area to produce new biomass. In the context of the creative industries productivity continues to carry both ordinary and specialist senses on both sides of the 'creative industries' pairing: for 'industries' it is an important measure of the value-add or efficiency of the creative sector of the economy; while on the 'creative' side, the concept retains an earlier sense of an individual's productivity in creative expression – a talent for new ideas.

Traditionally, economic productivity has been looked for through increased efficiency at the level of the individual firm – getting more output per unit of input. Similarly, creative productivity has been looked for at the level of the individual artist. But in the context of contemporary digital culture, both types can refer to the overall *productivity of a system*. Increases in productivity are often sourced to *technology*, as for instance the early modern increase in textual productivity when printing overtook manuscript copying. But they are also a characteristic of *popula-tions*, when a previously scarce or elite capability is extended to general availability. This happened to visual representation after 1839, when William Henry Fox Talbot and Louis Daguerre both exhibited for the first time what Fox Talbot called his 'photogenic drawing' process. Since then, the previously common occupations of artist, illustrator, engraver, etc. have been transformed (blown to bits by 'gales of **creative destruction**'), and the talent-and-training based scarcity of the skill of visual representation has become ubiquitous through camera phones and Flickr. Such increases in productivity don't emanate from firms (economy) but from *everybody* (culture); and there are both individualist (enterprise) and collectivist (network) modes to productivity (see **agent/agency**). Thus, the creative industries, perhaps uniquely, allow for a simultaneous consideration of economic efficiency (by individual producers or firms) and the *creative productivity of whole systems*, which include technological systems such as digital networks, or cultural ones like language or a particular cultural form, as well as socioeconomic ones such as mar-kets and nations.

As an economic concept, productivity measures the amount of output of a given production process per unit of input: for instance, how many goods do you get for how much labour? Gross domestic product (GDP) is a measure of labour produc-tivity in a country's economy. Productivity matters because economic growth can only occur by one of two means: by increasing the quantity of input factors into production, or by increasing productivity. As US economist Paul Krugman explains: 'Productivity isn't everything, but in the long run it is almost everything' (1992: 9). Productivity also underpins the economic theory of income. This assumes that under competition wages will come to equal a workers' marginal revenue product (the additional output of an additional unit of labour input times the output price). The economic theory of growth in real wages is based on increased productivity due to increase in skills, specialisation, capital or improved technology.

Productivity matters because it explains levels and changes in individual and aggregate income; improvements in productivity lead, under market competition, to higher wages and income. Of course increased productivity can also be 'spent' on a firm's growth in market share via lower prices: this means, in microeconomic theory, that the social benefit of increased productivity is captured directly by consumers via the 'substitution effect' rather than indirectly by workers via the 'income effect'. In practice, and depending on the degree of competition in the respective factor and goods markets, productivity growth is distributed over both higher wages and factor incomes *and* lower prices. Under **competition**, suppliers, producers and consumers all benefit from productivity growth anywhere in the system. Labour productivity, for example, changes when labour inputs increase in skill or experience, or are combined with increasing quantities of capital and/or with improved technologies (Arthur 2009). Total factor productivity (TFP) is the relation between output and all input factors. TFP is thus a way of measuring technological change. Productivity growth thus occurs as more output is produced with the same input, or the same output with less input. Economic growth is thus explained in two parts: increases in inputs, and increases in productivity. In the long run, productivity growth is the primary explanation for economic growth. The older 'economics of arts and culture' perspective, where the main issue concerned 'market failure' and positive externalities, had little to say about productivity. But in the creative industries productivity is a more central issue, and key concept, because of the impact and effects of new digital technologies and their affordances on new types of production and the consequences for existing industries and markets (see **creative destruction, evolution**), as well as the greatly increased productivity now available to consumers, amateurs, user-co-creators, and the like (see **co-creation, digital literacy**). In creative industries, concern with productivity (or sometimes *micro-productivity*, to refer specifically to the effects on individual creativity and capabilities) refers, for the most part, to the effect of new digital computational technologies and internet-based affordances that enable individual 'creatives' to variously: (1) increase their range of output; (2) lower the cost of output (with quality unchanged); or (3) increase the quality of output (with cost unchanged). These productivity improvements are the driving forces behind the growth of the creative industries and the increasing role of amateur, consumer or crowd-sourced creative production and also innovation (Leadbeater 2008; Shirky 2008).

A widely held belief in cultural economics was the notion that productivity growth in the arts and cultural sector will always be less than other sectors because of the inherent difficulty in making labour-capital substitutions in cultural production or in effecting labour-saving technological changes. This is known as Baumol's *cost disease* (Baumol and Bowen 1966). It makes the case for ever-increasing public subsidy of arts and cultural production as productivity growth, and thus under competition wage growth in other sectors, forces ever higher costs on arts and cultural production (for the counter-argument, see Cowen 1996). But this does not necessarily hold in the creative industries where almost the opposite productivity argument can be made by focusing on the dramatic improvements in the technical capabilities afforded (for example in editing, copying, distribution, etc.) and in the equally dramatic reduction in the costs of these technologies that can, for example, bring professional capabilities into the realm of amateur production. The positive impacts of **globalisation** and the increased access to markets and therefore to economies of scale, and also to profitable niche markets, is another potent source of productivity improvements (Cowen 2002, see also the entry on **institutions**).

Productivity is a key concept in creative industries not only because of its impact on efficiency, markets and income, but also for dynamic reasons associated with **innovation** or *dynamic productivity*. **Competition** in creative industries markets is often characterised by high levels of entrepreneurship and innovation in creating new products and services, new markets, new business models and so forth. This process drives economic **evolution** when the micro-productivity of creative agents increases, thus increasing the market reach and significance of those who have relatively higher productivity, whether by improving their cost advantage in the market economy, or increasing their profile in the attention economy (Lanham 2006). Productivity growth thus spreads through the creative economy. Productivity in creative industries can also be considered and evaluated in terms of *organisation*, in the sense of an ordering of inputs, both physical and social, into a **complex system** (Magee 2005; Arthur 2009; Stark 2009). Different forms of organisation will have different effects on productivity, both in the static sense of efficiency, and in the dynamic sense of search, discovery and adaptation. This can play out at the level of organisations (Shirky 2008), at the level of **networks** and **markets**, or the level of **clusters**, cities (Currid 2007) or industries (Scott 2006a).

Unlike productivity growth in mature industries – which is dominated by managerial imperatives to move down cost curves by exploiting scale economies in production and distribution, or by finding ever cheaper sources of supply or manufacture – productivity growth in creative industries often relies on *entrepreneurially dominated imperatives* to develop experimental processes of search or discovery along with *ad hoc* learning and adaptation. Productivity growth in this form requires methods of experimentation and processes of continual adaptation and trial-and-error learning, often needing a high tolerance for failure, along with a willingness to embrace low levels of certainty in respect to forecasting and planning. Productivity growth in creative industries thus tends to be less an outcome of rational planning and more due to experimental learning and adaptation. Productivity growth can also feed on itself. A wider locus of production, caused by productivity growth, implies wider sources of productivity, which then feeds new opportunities for productivity growth and so on. This process accelerates when new ideas for creating value (see **innovation**) are extended beyond in-house research capabilities in firms and outward to consumers, users, producers and citizens, to everyone, in effect. This effect, mediated by **digital literacy** and digital affordances, is appropriately called *digital micro-productivity*.

A general trend towards the exploration of *micro-productivity* is observable across economic, environmental and creative life. For instance, there are experiments in the 'micro-generation' of electricity; in 'microfinance' by such organisations as the Grameen Bank; in intellectual property through the shift of copyright from firms to consumers (where 'micro-payments' are the business model); and micro-manufacturing using three-dimensional (3D)-printing, linking networked code and household fabrication. Micro-productivity occurs wherever productivity can emerge by tapping into local information and seeking then to exploit it on a global scale (Hayek 1945). This occurs everywhere we see a transition from *industrial* to *networked* productivity, bringing together individual and system agency through micro-productivity. But this development remains a little-investigated aspect of *creative* productivity. In the field of creative industries studies, scholars with a media background still tend to see 'productivity' as the outcome of media or textual 'production', which is productive of *meaning*, and therefore belongs to the (supposedly) 'unproductive' realm of the consumer, household or culture. Economists continue to see it in the way that the Productivity Commission does – as a measure of industrial *efficiency*.[1]

---

[1] See: www.pc.gov.au/about-us/principles; www.pc.gov.au/research/productivity/primer; and www.pc.gov.au/research/productivity.

Creative micro-productivity occurs everywhere, all the time. Speech is the 'holo-type': every able member of *Homo sapiens* produces novel creative output every time they open their mouths. The economy comes into the picture when it is possible to combine technology, population-wide capabilities and agency, and various mechanisms for bundling myriad individual performances (via YouTube, Flickr and other social media), and for stimulating improvement (e.g. **digital literacy**), such that a social network of exchange can be established and observed for analysis.

Despite their different histories and uses, both economic and cultural notions of productivity are useful for the future, with overlaps as well as differences (von Hippel 1988). Given the growth of global networks like the internet, micro-productivity has already proven an *efficient distribution system*, in common with other engineered systems like power and electronic data (Barabási 2002), leading to phenomena such as crowd-sourced solutions, open-source innovation, **co-created content**, and cloud-culture sharing (Leadbeater 2011). The investigation of creative micro-productivity in the creative industries, especially audio-visual and digital media, the arts and social networks offers an *experimental field* of great dynamism that may yield principles for understanding how myriad individual agents contribute to the creation of new meanings and values across large-scale, complex systems (Leadbeater 2008; Shirky 2008). The conceptual quarry is the *productivity of innovation and discovery*, not that of production efficiency in existing processes.

Public Culture

The term **public culture** has two interconnected meanings: first, it describes areas of cultural and creative industries activity that are funded by the public purse; in the second sense it refers to cultural activity that is recognised by a particular public or community. The first sense is the most widespread understanding of public culture. Taxation provides resources for a range of cultural programmes, which can be categorised in three levels: publicly supported or publicly funded arts; public facilities (galleries, libraries and museums); and public service broadcasting (e.g. the British Broadcasting Corporation (BBC)). This raises questions of how to make optimal use of public resources and draws attention to long-running debates about the extent of government involvement with cultural production. Should they direct resources, if at all, towards flagship institutions (e.g. opera companies, orchestras, national broadcasters); or use resources to stimulate small creative enterprises and provide resources for communities to self-manage? Should resources be channelled into public art programmes? Should funds be administered according to national cultural identity objectives or economic objectives?

Critics agree that governments have a key role to play in matters of public good and the national interest. National film industries are one sector of the creative industries that draw on public resources either directly in terms of tax offsets or indirectly in the case of film development bureaus. Many cultural facilities are not designed to make profits and are regarded as public assets, for instance galleries, libraries and museums (the GLAM sector). In many cases public intervention may generate outcomes which cannot be captured wholly by private interests. However, while public resources invested in arts and culture are limited in comparison with many other key industry sectors, governments earn significant revenues from creative industries sectors and can bask in the kudos when these achieve international success. Public investment in many cases acts as a catalyst for the development of commercially viable activities. The public investment in the Edinburgh Fringe festival for instance has paid off by launching many successful careers including Rowan Atkinson, Hugh Laurie and Stephen Fry. State investment in public broadcasting provides a testing bed for new programmes and formats that are subsequently utilised by commercial networks. In taking risks that would not be countenanced by advertiser-supported channels this mode of public culture investment provides an important outlet for emerging creative talent.

Subsidy is an instrument of government normally associated with public culture: at times it facilitates business development and entrepreneurship by providing incentives; it may encourage creative risk taking by providing grants or a guarantee of funding; this may in turn facilitate audience development; at times limited resources are channelled into strategic sectors, genres and activities. Potts and Cunningham (2008) refer to the idea of the 'welfare' or 'market failure' model of the cultural and creative industries. In this view, some cultural activities have a net negative impact on the economy, and cannot recoup their costs in the market. In other words, they consume more resources than they produce. The argument is that subsidising creative culture is welfare-positive, owing to the production of commodities of high cultural value but low market value.

Cultural policy, whether national or local, mediates between art and commerce, between public and private interest. Cultural policy has been redefined in many countries and regions owing to the **internationalisation** of the creative industries idea. The creative industries cover a spectrum from the resolutely non-commercial to the high-tech and commercial. This larger clustering of sectors and its focus on economic growth provides new challenges to cultural policy, particularly in regard to the impact of creativity and innovation on public culture(s). In the past cultural policy has recognised how culture generates value in complementary sectors such as tourism. In museums and art galleries public funding is usually required. Galleries may expend public resources on acquisitions to enhance collections or to 'buy' a blockbuster exhibit. This in turn generates more visitors, which enhances the image of the city or district. In summarising the juxtaposition of arts and industries John Holden has drawn attention to how public culture provides a range of benefits. He says: 'Greater numbers of people are engaging with the content and spaces of publicly-funded culture, while the working lives of greater numbers of people are taking on the characteristics and processes of cultural practitioners' (Holden 2007: 8–9). There are two broad ways of defining cultural policy, which have implications for public culture (Craik 2007). First, cultural policy refers to the regulation of the 'marketplace of ideas and creative practice'. From this perspective, government's role is to regulate production and consumption, often with the aim of developing national culture, promoting the macro environment for creative business or in some instances helping to generate export potential. The role of government is at arm's length, enabling and making strategic policies. Second, cultural policy refers to policies that manage cultural resources and institutions, such as performing arts companies. In this model, governments play an active and sometimes interventionist role. The relationship between governments and culture is most likely to be a combination of models depending on what sectors of the cultural sphere are being administered. In the main we see constant interplay between national cultural policy and regulation that is deemed essential for the national interest – both the imagined national community and the multiple publics that constitute a multicultural society.

Craik (2007) sees government as the 'elite nurturer', selecting a small number of elite cultural organisations to receive a one-line budget and/or other generous subsidies. Guaranteed recurrent funding insulates them from having to compete with 'outsider' cultural organisations and from market failure. From a cultural diversity perspective this can be detrimental, if the nurtured organisations consume the cultural budget to the extent that there is little opportunity to fund new or experimental cultural forms, thus risking conservatism, or stasis, of cultural development. Clearly, this model can only support a limited number of cultural producers. In recent years, moreover, debates have turned from **aesthetic** policy approaches towards **innovation** policies. The role of the **creative economy** discourse is crucial. The concept of a *creative* 'innovation system' can help to focus on the changing role for government in an increasingly digitised environment. George Yúdice (2003) has shown how government agencies, non-governmental organisations (NGOs) and consultants have worked together to advocate a role for culture in the regulation of economic development, the alleviation of social inequality, and in lobbying and legislating for cultural diversity. Government funding, often backed by private investment, is increasingly being directed towards projects and programmes rather than to elite institutions. One of the best examples is creative **clusters**, a term used loosely to describe geographical concentrations of practitioners and businesses. While clusters occur spontaneously, in recent years significant public resources have been directed at such projects, especially in China, where government has recognised a need for creative incubation spaces.

A different sense of the term public culture arises from the fact that publics and citizens make and adjudicate meanings. Analogous to the notion of the 'public sphere', an idea associated with informed debate, 'public culture' in this sense represents a meeting-place of communities. Gitlin (1998) coined the term 'public sphericules' to convey his pessimistic view of the fragmentation of modernist public commonality. Sinclair and Cunningham (2000) however see these 'sphericules' in a more optimistic way, citing instances of multicultural sense-making. Communities do indeed interrogate the boundaries of cultural norms in creative ways, but their formations of 'publicness' are not necessarily aligned with national culture (see Papacharissi 2010). The latter is regularly challenged by transnational cultural messages and forces and by indigenous critiques from various sectors that continuously threaten the cultural hegemony of the nation-state (Appadurai and

Breckenridge 1988). Multiple publics are a central feature of pluralism and are essential to civil society. Authoritarian regimes often look suspiciously on such public cultural formations, particularly artists and intellectuals, preferring to maintain the imperative of 'official culture'.

Representation

In the creative sphere, representation refers to the way that any medium, from language to art, uses materials, signs and symbols to stand for something else, in order to communicate its meaning, characteristics or nature. It is a straightforward concept when applied to an artwork that resembles its subject: for example a sheet of copper sculpted in the likeness of a person, say, Anna Maria Augustea Charlotte Beysser Bartholdi. In such a case the sculpture simply *represents* the sitter. It is equally uncontroversial to take a step further and say that this same likeness *represents* an abstract meaning in the form of Libertas, Roman goddess of freedom and personification of a myth, whose attributes in turn *represent* (symbolise) the national identity of the United States of America. We know that Mme Bartholdi's face represents these abstract values because she was the mother of sculptor Frédéric Auguste Bartholdi, who used her likeness to portray the face of the Statue of Liberty (1886). In this case, the most abstract or symbolic level of representation is the immediate one; while the most literal one (the sitter's unique look) may not be known by the casual viewer. Indeed, the literal source of such a representation may distract from its 'real' meaning. For it is said that the Statue of Liberty's torso and arm are modelled not after Bartholdi's mother, but his wife Jeanne-Emilie Baheux de Puysieux, making 'Lady Liberty' a somewhat Oedipal figure (where mother and desire are mixed, albeit unconsciously), representing ideas that would surely have been repudiated by the sculptor, but which nevertheless motivate the form and beauty of the work.

Once a representation becomes public, its career takes it ever further from its maker's intentions. Its symbolism can be *re-presented* (presented again) with completely different meanings. This has certainly been the fate of the Statue of Liberty, which has featured in numerous science-fiction movies, such as *Planet of the Apes* (1968), to signify pessimism about the future. Here it *represents* the exact opposite of its ostensible meaning: the optimistic, democratic and heroic vision of freedom becomes a sign of dystopian despair at humanity's self-destructive folly and aggression. In turn, *Planet of the Apes*' now-famous post-apocalyptic representation of Mme Bartholdi's head emerging from the sands of time is itself available for re-presentation and parody (and auction),[1] in *Futurama*, *The Simpsons*, etc. It

---

[1]See www.originalprop.com/blog/2007/12/12/planet-of-the-apes-statue-of-liberty-prop/

follows that the concept of representation cannot be confined to an original, real or authentic link between a thing and what stands for it. It is part of a dynamic circuit of semiotic **productivity**, involving elements of myth, symbolism, national identity, psychology, copying and parody.

Given the powerful creative possibilities abounding in such semiotic uncertainty and multivalency, and the evident promiscuity of representation across media, it would not be too much of a stretch to designate the **creative industries** as that section of the economy whose special function it is to exploit, extend and elaborate the complexities of representation for technically equipped international culture. It can be argued that *representation* is what the entire sector does; it's the 'output' of **creativity**.

The established or dominant mode of industrial-scale representation in the current era of Western modernity is *realism*, although this is by no means the only one. Realist signs are assumed to be motivated by something *outside* of the sign system (like Mme Bartholdi's own face), even when that sign 'represents' something arbitrary and abstract like freedom (or its opposite). Realism has been incredibly productive since the Enlightenment, if not the Renaissance, generating the three most important 'textual systems' or *institutions of representation* of the modern era:

- Fiction (representation of the psychologically real);
- Journalism (representation of the politically real);
- Science (representation of the naturally real).

But this 'realist regime' is continuously challenged and undermined by the *means* of representation. Linguistic and other signs mean what they do only in contrast to other signs. Also, disturbingly for realism, any medium that can be used to tell the truth must also be able to lie, as Umberto Eco pointed out: 'If something cannot be used to tell a lie, conversely it cannot be used to tell the truth: it cannot in fact be used "to tell" at all' (1976: 7). Even if one wants to represent the world truthfully 'as it is', whether as a scientist, a journalist or an artist, representation is a chief means by which one must do that, and language, together with many adjunct textual systems including audio-visual **media**, will play their own part in the process, sometimes duplicitously and frequently at cross-purposes with the 'will to truth' – which in any case, after Foucault, seems as much a ruse to power as a road to enlightenment (Sheridan 1980; Taylor 1984).

In its institutionalised forms – science, journalism and fiction – realism appears triumphant. But realism's obviousness is an illusion. It is neither universal nor eternal; nor is it 'natural'. In the West it was preceded by medieval arts of memory (Carruthers 2008, Ong 2012). It is arguably under attrition, if not succession, by various postmodern or 'post-realist' modes of representation (Beer and Hariman 1996). It co-exists with oral, abstract, musical and ritual forms of knowing (including play), and with systems of representation from non-Western cultural traditions, for example non-figurative Islamic representation, land/story fusions in Aboriginal 'dreaming', or the elaborate courtly rituals of classical culture in China, Japan or Thailand. It is therefore important to isolate three senses of the term that are of relevance in the creative context:

- *Semiotic representation*: A theory of representation where one thing (word, image, sound, phoneme, or 'sign') is made to stand for another (meaning, referent, signified). Representation of this type has been theorised in philosophy since Aristotle (language *brings something to mind* by describing it mimetically), in linguistics since Pierce and Saussure (language *stands in place of* reality which is represented through sign systems), and in media theory via cinema studies and semiotics (signs *produce* reality within culturally and technologically mediated systems; Chandler 2007);
- *Political representatives*: representative democracy is common in modern states (for the rationale, see Paine 1792, Chapter 3), where citizens do not make legislative decisions directly, but vote for representatives who do. Each member of the legislature is elected by and represents a large number of citizens in a given area or list;
- *Statistical representativeness*: this relates to the idea of the sample, where a few of (x) represent many of (x), often all of them (a 'population'). Here the goal is to find a sample that may be said to be representative of (i.e. to typify) a total population, by making sure that variations within it (e.g. differences in age, class, gender, region, family circumstance, etc.) are proportionately present in the sample.

These three senses of representation are analytically distinct, and are in fact studied in different and increasingly divergent disciplinary contexts:

- Semiotic representation is studied in the *humanities* (fiction);
- Political representation is studied in the *social sciences* (journalism);
- Statistical representation is studied in the *mathematical or exact sciences* (science).

In practice, these three types of representation continuously infect one another in contemporary media systems. Equating semiotic with political representation is so routine that 'representative representation' is a normative expectation in the most popular media. A given movie, TV series, literary work, computer game, artwork or photograph is appreciated, or criticised, for the extent to which it 'stands for' a whole community. Soap opera and sitcoms are especially prone to the habit of associating fictional entertainments with national character. Sometimes this can be an intentional component of the work, as it is for the Statue of Liberty; sometimes it's an unstated representation of a given 'imagined community'. Conversely, some semiotic representations are held *not* to 'represent' the community – thereby defining it negatively. Certain types of reality television, from *Big Brother* (1997–) and *Jerry Springer* (1991–) to *Keeping Up with the Kardashians* (2007–) have been criticised for failing to 'represent' various national values. This negative representativeness is also used to regulate media content directly, most obviously through the test of decency in many jurisdictions, where obscenity is defined by reference to what a 'reasonable adult' – a *representative* normal citizen – would find obscene. Thus, semiotic and political representations coalesce.

Statistics come into the picture when a country's identities and values are 'read back' into a given representation by counting the extent to which the various component groups in a nation are present in it. A *mathematical* question arises: are there enough women in drama or the news; is there enough diversity of ethnicity, sexual orientation and ability in representations of ordinary life; what happened to the children on the news; are the characters 'like us' in *Modern Family* (2009–)? Thus, many studies have analysed how a chosen attribute is 'represented' in the media, from various types of identity, such as race, gender, sexual orientation, age, nation, class, etc., to various socially significant themes, for example representations of alcohol use, welfare, sex, violence, 'bad' language, etc. Statistical under- or over-representation of a significant group or value is widely seen as a form of political disenfranchisement. Here is found the evidential basis for charges of media bias or prejudice in media representation. Television drama, sitcoms, soap operas, and movie rom-coms, routinely *over*-represent heterosexual white people in a certain age range, especially those from favoured countries who show signs of affluence and 'marriageability' (*Friends* (1994–2004)). Conversely, people of colour, blue-collar workers, migrants, children, same-sex couples and people in routine occupations (etc.) are *under*-represented. To make matters worse, when people of colour *are* represented, it is often in connection with crime (Russell-Brown 2009 Chapter 2). In action movies, statistically skewed representation is also routine, but differently organised: men are over-represented; women are victims; children are hostages. News is a representational minefield; almost everyone seems to feel that certain points of view are over-represented, to the exclusion of those held dear by the observer (e.g. see Mody 2010).

In this context, mathematics becomes doubly politicised: first, 'hard numbers' are much easier to 'take account of' than are cultural values – numbers are the currency of policy. Second, and consequently, choices about who is counted and how they are demographically classified can render unequal power relations into statistical facts. An apparently scientific choice about whether and how to count different demographics among overall populations leads directly to a politics of inclusion and exclusion – some people literally *don't count* as members of the modern polity. Section 127 of the Australian Constitution (since repealed) required that: 'in reckoning the numbers of the people of the Commonwealth, or of a State or other part of the Commonwealth, aboriginal natives shall not be counted' (cited in Rowse 2006: 2). Here, statistical discounting is tantamount to political annihilation. From federation in 1901 to the 1967 referendum that changed the constitution, the Australian nation – as a *representative* 'fact' – contained no Aborigines! This use of stats is extreme, but not uncommon in settler and colonial nation-building (Axelsson and Sköld 2011).

The realist system of statistically proportionate 'representative representation' is under increasing attrition in creative media, especially following the rise of interactive, participatory and digital technologies, where direct public *self-representation* can be undertaken by anyone with access to a computer network. The ability of ordinary individuals to represent themselves by publishing creative, political and even statistical materials online, in the blogosphere, on YouTube, via Facebook, Twitter and other social media, has led some commentators to think about how representation can be shifted to a do-it-yourself (DIY) and cooperative mode, where 'representation *by* the people' is more prominent (Green and Jenkins 2011). This is a challenge for the creative industries, to join a shift from representation to action; away from providing 'representative representation' *to* and *for* the population, towards facilitation and sharing *with* and *by* users (Leadbeater 2009) who are learning how to represent themselves. With that shift, semiotic, political and statistical 'liberty' will not be confined to representative symbols and statues; they may be practised directly by the descendants of those 'huddled masses' who were once made welcome by the face of Marie Bartholdi.

Technology

Technology is often used as a synonym for 'tools' – from Palaeolithic chopping tools to the Hubble telescope; but tools cannot exist without systematic knowledge and social organisation, to provide the 'skill, craft or art' (Greek: *techne*) that enables a tool to solve a problem or perform a function. Knowledge, organisation and tools are subject to rapid and dynamic change, which leads Brian Arthur (2009) to argue that technologies *evolve*. Technological change in digital media and information and communication technologies (ICTs) is also central to the economic and cultural dynamics of the creative industries. These technologies are transforming the conditions of cultural production and consumption. Charles Leadbeater (1999) notes that the 'new economy' is driven by **globalisation** and information technology. Richard Florida (2002) argues that the 'three Ts' characterise creative and innovative places: *technology*, *talent* and *tolerance*. Hartley's definition of the **creative industries** emphasises the significance of 'new media technologies (ICTs) within a new knowledge economy, for the use of newly interactive citizen-consumers' (2005: 5). Nevertheless, there is surprisingly little discussion of the *nature* of the relationship between technology and the various transformations associated with the creative industries.

Mobile devices and platforms such as the iPod, iPhone (smartphone), iPad (tablet) and iTunes have dramatically transformed the music industry by changing how music is made, distributed and consumed, indicating that technologies can radically reshape media industries. Apple is now the largest distributor of music in the US market. ICTs have profound implications for the business models and organisations underpinning industries such as music and newspapers. Apps such as *Garage Band* on the iPad are also putting sophisticated cultural production and distribution tools in the hands of users (see **co-creation**). But do the devices and associated technologies, from hardware such as servers to software code and protocols, cause or determine these changes? What is the relationship between ICTs and the changes associated with the creative industries? Part of the problem here is that the neoclassical model of economics considers technology as something that can be assumed in the background of analysis. It is often approached as an 'exogenous' force that is outside of the economy but acts on market relations. This is not a case of economics disregarding the significance of technology. Instead, the *relationship* between technology and the economy is placed in the 'too hard basket'. However, key economic theorists following Joseph Schumpeter (1942) have questioned the failure of neo-classical economic theory to account for the centrality of technology to modern economic growth and change.

A significant approach in the humanities and social sciences is to question 'technological determinism' – the assumption that technology drives or determines change. Fields such as science and technology studies (STS) suggest that while technologies are most certainly important, and we therefore need carefully to consider such materials, objects and associated processes, it is a mistake to think that they directly determine economic or social outcomes. This view is called the 'social construction of technology' (SCOT) perspective (Kline and Pinch 1999; MacKenzie and Wajckman 1999). Technologies do not simply do things to us or to the social world, instead the emphasis shifts to how humans and our various competing social and economic interests shape or construct technologies. Thus, with a device such as the mobile phone, researchers may be interested in how young consumers adopt texting practices, which in turn influence the telecommunications industry's own understanding of these devices. In this approach, users and consumers are viewed as **agents** of technological change. As Kline and Pinch propose:

> SCOT emphasizes the 'interpretive flexibility' of an artifact. Different social groups associate different meanings with artifacts leading to interpretative flexibility appearing over the artifact. The same artifact can mean different things to different social groups of users. (1999: 113)

If we return to the iPhone, it would seem a fairly straightforward proposition that business users and gamers are likely to have very different understandings of the device. Is the iPhone therefore socially constructed; and when analysing it, and the industry context in which it is embedded, should we ask questions about *which* users' interests and preferred meanings become dominant and embedded in the development of such devices? But by trying to avoid and counter the problems of technological determinism we may undermine efforts to grapple with how technologies have social and economic effects and consideration of what we should do about these effects. Furthermore, in saying that technologies such as smartphones and videogames have 'effects', are we necessarily locked in to a proposition that such effects are determining rather than complex and contingent?

A starting point for a more nuanced understanding of technological change is that technology is not separate from society and the economy. Technologies provide the very materials from which society and the economy are made. This approach, associated with the work of scholars such as Latour (2005) and Callon (1998), is called actor–network theory (ANT) (see **networks**). ANT suggests that it is a mistake to think of technology and society as separate domains. Instead, they are mutually constitutive. Latour, for example, insists that social relations are made from artefacts. Just think for a moment about social network platforms such as Facebook and Google+. We need to consider how these technologies provide the material infrastructure for social relations. From this perspective, non-humans, things and objects have **agency**; in ANT terminology, they are *actants* alongside humans (Latour 2005). For ANT, a term such as 'the social' designates, if anything, the associations between entities, both human and non-human, and the kinds of actions these links and connections enable. In the economic domain, scholars such as MacKenzie (2009) and Callon (1998) focus on the materiality of **markets**. They argue that the human actors operating in markets are not disembodied calculating agents; the devices and equipment that they use, including conceptual equipment such as economic modelling tools, are fundamental to functioning as an economic agent. So, we might ask, what are the material infrastructures of social network markets (see **attention**) and how do they constitute the actions that can be taken in such emerging markets? We might want to examine how social network platforms such as Facebook and YouTube and Twitter constitute the materiality of social network markets (Potts et al. 2008a).

However, do these various discussions and debates about relations between technology and the social or economic domains get us very far with illuminating how technological change contributes to the various changes associated with the creative industries? The proposition that technology and society are mutually constitutive certainly provides a better starting position than assuming on the one hand that technology determines change or on the other that technology is merely socially constructed. But what is the nature of this dynamic between technology and domains such as the economy or wider society?

W. Brian Arthur (2009) theorises that technology evolves. Starting from a definition of technology as 'a means to fulfill a human purpose' that encompasses methods, processes and devices (Arthur, 2009: 28), he proposes that:

> Technologies, including novel ones, must descend in some way from the technologies that preceded them. This means they must link with – be 'sired' by – certain technologies that preceded them. In other words, evolution requires a mechanism of 'heredity', some detailed connection that links the present to the past. (2009: 18)

Arthur is not applying **evolution** theory *metaphorically* here. He means that technology develops and changes *literally* through an evolutionary mechanism. This mechanism is the process of combination and recombination of existing technologies to produce something new (fit for new purposes). He calls this '*combinatorial evolution*' (Arthur 2009: 22). According to Arthur, 'novel technologies arise by combination of existing technologies and that (therefore) existing technologies beget further technologies'. He continues:

> Early technologies form using existing primitive technologies as components. These new technologies in time become possible components – building blocks – for the construction of further new technologies. Some of these in turn go on to become possible building blocks for the creation of yet newer technologies. In this way, slowly over time, many technologies form from an initial few, and more complex ones form using simpler ones as components. The overall collection of technologies bootstraps itself upward from the few to the many and from the simple to the complex. We can say that technology creates itself out of itself. (2009: 21; also see 176–89)

These evolutionary processes of autopoietic (self-creating) combination and recombination are evident in the changes associated with ICTs and digital technologies, as the various components of the digital revolution – routers, code, algorithms, mainboards, processors, digital cameras, haptic display interfaces – are combined and recombined to form new devices. The iPhone for example is an innovative recombination of existing technologies. Furthermore, as Lester and Piore observe, the mobile phone emerged from 'combinatorial' logic, in 'the space created by the ambiguity about whether the product was a radio or a telephone; by playing with that ambiguity, the device became something that was different from either of them' (2004: 181). Arthur argues that profound economic change occurs when the economy 'encounters' a new body of technology such as ICTs:

> The economy reacts to the new body's presence, and in doing so changes its activities, its industries, its organisational arrangements – its structures. And if the resulting change in the economy is important enough, we call that a revolution. (2009: 146)

A new version of the economy and economic activity may emerge as technology and the economy 'mutually co-adapt and mutually create the new' (Arthur 2009: 155). Economists Erik Brynjolfsson and Andrew McAfee (2011) propose that the changes associated with the digital revolution are profoundly transforming employment and the economy. They argue that information technologies are replacing many jobs, such that in the USA we are seeing a post-GFC (Global Financial Crisis) economic recovery without significant job creation. In short, recent economic data suggest that technology may be driving unemployment in many sectors, including services industries. Nevertheless, Brynjolfsson and McAfee are not technological pessimists. Describing themselves as 'digital optimists', they propose that we need to learn how better to combine human creativity with our machines and that this especially requires *organisational* innovation. The creative industries may well be the economic sector in which we are discovering and learning these innovative responses to profound and sweeping technological change. People and organisations in the creative industries are developing the creative skills to grapple with the opportunities and risks associated with such change.

By adopting understandings of technological change such as Arthur's (2009) and Brynjolfsson and McAfee's (2011) there is a risk of falling into a technological determinism, and of overlooking the all-too-human interests that may lie at the core of these changes. However, it is difficult to avoid the transformations associated with digital technologies; and fatal to ignore the logic of technological evolution. We may well be witnessing a 'revolution' in the very fabric of our economies and of our cultural lives. At the very least these technologies are reshaping the conditions of cultural production and consumption in the creative industries.

references

Abercrombie, N. and Turner, B. (1978) 'The dominant ideology thesis', *British Journal of Sociology*, 29 (2): 149–70.

Adorno, T. and Horkheimer, M. (1979) 'The culture industry: Enlightenment as mass deception', in J. Curran, M. Gurevitch and J. Woollacott (eds), *Mass Communication and Society*. London: Verso, pp. 349–83.

Anderson, C. (2006). *The Long Tail: Why the Future of Business Is Selling Less of More*. New York, NY: Hyperion.

Anderson, C. (2008) 'The end of theory: The data deluge makes the scientific method obsolete', *Wired Magazine*, 16: 07, 23 June. Available at: www.wired.com/science/discoveries/magazine/16-07/pb_theory

Andersson, D. and Andersson, A. (2006) *The Economics of Experiences, the Arts and Entertainment*. Cheltenham: Edward Elgar.

Andrejevic, M. (2011) 'Social network exploitation', in Z. Papacharisssi (ed.), *A Networked Self: Identity, Community, and Culture on Social Network Sites*. London: Routledge, pp. 82–101.

Appadurai, A. (1996) *Modernity at Large. Cultural Dimensions of Globalization*. Minneapolis, MN: University of Minnesota Press.

Appadurai, A. and Breckenridge, P. (1988) 'Why public culture?', *Public Culture*, 1 (1): 5–9.

Arai, K., Deguchi, H. and Matsui, H. (2005) 'Agent-based modeling meets gaming simulation: Perspective on future collaborations', in K. Arai, H. Deguchi and H. Matsui (eds). *Agent-Based Modeling Meets Gaming Simulation*. Tokyo: Springer, pp. 1–13.

Arnold, M. (1869) *Culture and Anarchy*. Project Gutenberg. Available at: www.gutenberg.org/ebooks/4212

Arthur, B. (1999) 'Complexity and the economy', *Science*, 284 (5411): 107–9.

Arthur, B. (2009) *The Nature of Technology: What it is and How it Evolves*. New York, NY: Free Press.

Aspers, P. (2010) *Orderly Fashion: A Sociology of Markets*. Princeton, NJ: Princeton University Press.

Axelsson, P. and Sköld, P. (eds) (2011) *Indigenous Peoples and Demography: The Complex Relation Between Identity and Statistics*. Oxford: Berghahn Books.

Bakhshi, H., McVittie, E. and Simmie, J. (2008) *Creating Innovation: Do the Creative Industries Support Innovation in the Wider Economy?* London: Nesta.

Bakhshi, H., Freeman, A. and Potts, J. (2011) 'State of uncertainty'. Provocation paper 14. London: NESTA. Available at: www.nesta.org.uk/publications/provocations/assets/documents/State%20of%20Uncertainity.

Banks, J. (2009). 'Co-creative expertise: Auran games and *Fury* – a case study', *Media International Australia*, 130: 77–89.

Banks, J. (2012) *Co-creating Videogames*. London: Bloomsbury Academic.

Banks, J. and Deuze, M. (2009) 'Co-creative Labour?', *International Journal of Cultural Studies*, 12: 5, 419–31.

Banks, J. and Potts, J. (2010) 'Co-creating games: A co-evolutionary analysis', *New Media and Society*, 12 (2): 253–70.

Barabási, A.L. (2002) *Linked: The New Science of Networks*. Cambridge, MA: Perseus Publishing.

Barbrook, R. (2006) *The Class of the New*. Openmute. Available at: www.theclassofthenew.net

Baumol, W. and Bowen, W. (1966) *Performing Arts: The Economic Dilemma*. New York, NY: Twentieth Century Fund.

Becker, H. (2008; first published 1982) *Art Worlds*. Berkeley, CA: University of California Press.

Beer, F. and Hariman, R. (eds) (1996) *Post-Realism: The Rhetorical Turn in International Relations*. East Lansing, MI: Michigan State University Press.

Beinhocker, E. (2006) *The Origin of Wealth: Evolution, Complexity, and the Radical Remaking of Economics*. Cambridge, MA: Harvard Business Press.

Bell, D. (1973) *The Coming of Post-Industrial Society: A Venture in Social Forecasting*. New York, NY: Basic Books.

Bell, D. (1976) *The Cultural Contradictions of Capitalism*. New York, NY: Basic Books.

Bell, D. (1980) 'The social framework of the information society', in T. Forester (ed.), *Microelectronics Revolution*. Cambridge, MA: MIT Press, pp. 500–49.

Belleflamme, P., Picard, P. and Thisse, J. (2000) 'An economic theory of regional clusters', *Journal of Urban Economics*, 48 (1): 158–84.

Benkler, Y. (2006) *The Wealth of Networks*. New Haven, NJ: Yale University Press.

Benkler, Y. (2011) *The Penguin and the Leviathan: How Cooperation Triumphs over Self-Interest*. New York, NY: Crown Business.

Bennett, T. (1992) 'Putting policy into cultural studies', in L. Grossberg, C. Nelson and P. Treichler (eds), *Cultural Studies*. New York, NY: Routledge, pp. 23–37.

Bennett, T., McFall, L. and Pryke, M. (2008) 'Editorial: Culture/economy/social', *Journal of Cultural Economy*, 1: 1–7.

Bentley, R.A. (2009) 'Fashion versus reason in the creative industries', in M. O'Brien and S. Shennan (eds), *Innovation in Cultural Systems: Contributions from Evolutionary Anthropology*. Cambridge, MA: MIT Press, pp. 121–6.

Bentley, R.A., Lipo, C., Herzog, H. and Hahn, M. (2007) 'Regular rates of popular culture change reflect random copying', *Evolution and Human Behavior*, 28 (3): 151–8.

Bentley, R.A., Earls, M., O'Brien, M. and Maeda, J. (2011) *I'll Have What She's Having: Mapping Social Behavior*. Cambridge, MA: MIT Press.

Berger, P. and Luckmann, T. (1966) *The Social Construction of Reality*. New York, NY: Doubleday.

Bernstein, W. (2008) *A Splendid Exchange: How Trade Shaped the World*. London: Atlantic Books.

Bharucha, R. (2010) 'Creativity: alternative paradigms to the "creative economy"', in H. Anheier and Y. Isar (eds), *Cultural Expression, Creativity and Innovation: The Culture and Globalization, Series 3*. Thousand Oaks, NY: Sage, pp. 21–36.

Bianchini, F. (1993) 'Culture, conflict and cities: issues and prospects for the 1990s', in F. Bianchini and M. Parkinson (eds), *Cultural Policy and Urban Regeneration: The West European Experience*. Manchester: Manchester University Press, pp. 1–20.

Bilton, C. (2007) *Management and Creativity: From Creative Industries to Creative Management*. Oxford: Blackwell.

Bilton, C. (2010) 'Manageable creativity', *International Journal of Cultural Policy*, 16 (3): 255–69.

Bird, S.E. (2011) 'Are we all produsers now?', *Cultural Studies*, 25 (4–5): 502–16.

Boden, M. (2004/1990) *The Creative Mind: Myths and Mechanisms*. London: Routledge.

Bohm, D. (1996) *On Creativity*. London: Routledge.

Bohm, D. and Peat, D. (2011) *Science, Order and Creativity*. London: Routledge.

Boldrin, M. and Levine, K. (2008) *Against Intellectual Monopoly*. Cambridge: Cambridge University Press.

Bordwell, D., Staiger, J. and Thompson, K. (1985) *The Classic Hollywood Cinema: Film Style and Mode of Production to 1960*. New York, NY: Routledge.

Bourdieu, P. (1984) *Distinction: A Social Critique of the Judgment of Taste*. Cambridge, MA: Harvard University Press.

Bourdieu, P. (1998) *Practical Reason: On the Theory of Action*. London: Polity.

Boyd, B. (2009) *The Origin of Stories: Evolution, Cognition and Fiction*. Cambridge MA: Harvard University Press.

Boyd, D. and Crawford, K. (2011) 'Six provocations for big data', *A Decade in Internet Time: Symposium on the Dynamics of the Internet and Society*, September. Available at SSRN: ssrn.com/abstract=1926431

Boyd, R. and Richerson, P. (2004) *The Origin and Evolution of Cultures*. Oxford: Oxford University Press.

Brown, J. and Duguid, P. (2000) *The Social Life of Information*. Cambridge, MA: Harvard Business School Press.

Bruns, A. (2008) *Blogs, Wikipedia, Second Life and Beyond: From Production to Produsage*. New York, NY: Peter Lang.

Bryman, A. (2004) *The Disneyization of Society*. London: Sage.

Brynjolfsson, E. and McAfee, A. (2011) *Race Against the Machine: How the Digital Revolution is Accelerating Innovation, Driving Productivity, and Irreversibly Transforming Employment and the Economy*. Lexington, MA: Digital Frontier Press.

Burgess, J. and Green, J. (2009) *YouTube: Online Video and Participatory Culture*. Cambridge: Polity Press.

Caldwell J. (2003) 'Second-shift media aesthetics: Programming, interactivity, and user flows', in A. Everett and J. Caldwell (eds), *New Media: Theories and Practices of Digitextuality*. New York, NY: Routledge, pp. 127–44.

Callon, M. (ed.) (1998) *The Laws of Markets*. Oxford: Blackwell.

Camagni, R. (1991) *Innovation Networks: Spatial Perspectives*. London: Belhaven Press.

Carey, J. (1992) *The Intellectuals and the Masses*. London: Faber & Faber.

Carr, N. (2011) *What the Internet is Doing to Our Brains: The Shallows*. New York, NY: W.W. Norton.

Carruthers, M. (2008) *The Book of Memory: A Study of Memory in Medieval Culture*, 2nd edn. Cambridge: Cambridge University Press.

Castells, M. (1996) *The Rise of the Network Society*. Malden MA: Wiley-Blackwell.

Castells, M. and Aoyama, Y. (1994) 'Paths towards the informational society: Employment structure in G-7 countries, 1920–90', *International Labour Review* 133 (1): 5–33.

Caves, R. (2000) *Creative Industries: Contracts between Art and Commerce*. Cambridge, MA: Harvard University Press.

Chai, A., Earl, P. and Potts, J. (2007) 'Fashion, growth and welfare: An evolutionary approach', in M. Bianchi (ed.), *The Evolution of Consumption – Advances in Austrian Economics*, vol. 10. Oxford: Elsevier, pp. 187–207.

Chandler, D. (2007) *Semiotics: The Basics*, 2nd edn. London: Routledge. Available at: www.aber.ac.uk/media/Documents/S4B/semiotic.html

Chapain, C., Cooke, P., De Propris, L., MacNeill, S. and Mateos-Garcia, J. (2010) *Creative Clusters and Innovation: Putting Creativity on the Map*. London: NESTA.

Choi, J. (2010) *Playpolis: Transyouth and Urban Networking in Seoul*. Unpublished PhD dissertation, QUT, Brisbane.

Chomsky, N. and Herman, E. (1988) *Manufacturing Consent: The Political Economy of the Mass Media*. New York, NY: Pantheon.

Clunas, C. (2004) *Superfluous Things: Material Culture and Social Status in Early Modern China*. Honolulu: University of Hawai'i Press.

Coase, R. (1937) 'The nature of the firm', *Economica*, 4: 386–405.

Collins, H. and Evans, R. (2002) 'The third wave of science studies: Studies of expertise and experience', *Social Studies of Science*, 32 (2): 235–96.

Collins, H. and Evans, R. (2007) *Rethinking Expertise*. Chicago, IL: University of Chicago Press.

Collins, R. (1998) *The Sociology of Philosophies: A Global Theory of Intellectual Change*. Cambridge, MA: Harvard University Press.

Collis, C., Felton, E. and Graham, P. (2010) 'Beyond the inner city: real and imagined places in creative place policy and practice', *Information Society*, 26 (2): 104–12.

Commons, J. (1931) *Institutional Economics*. New York, NY: Macmillan.

Cope, B. and Kalantzis, M. (2010) 'By design', in Dan Araya and M. Peters (eds), *Education in the Creative Economy: Knowledge and Learning in the Age of Innovation*. New York, NY: Peter Lang, pp. 587–612.

Couldry, N. (2011) 'More sociology, more culture, more politics', *Cultural Studies*, 25 (4–5): 487–501.

Cowen, T. (1996) 'Why I do not believe in the cost-disease', *Journal of Cultural Economics*, 20 (3): 207–14.

Cowen, T. (1998) *In Praise of Commercial Culture*. Cambridge, MA: Harvard University Press.

Cowen, T. (2002) *Creative Destruction: How Globalization is Changing the World's Cultures*. Princeton, NJ: Princeton University Press.

Cowen, T. (2009) *Create Your Own Economy: The Path to Prosperity in a Disordered World*. New York, NY: Dutton.

Cowen, T. and Kaplan, B. (2004) 'Why do people underestimate the benefits of cultural competition?', *American Economic Review*, 94: 402–7.

Cox, G. (2006) *Cox Review of Creativity in Business: Building on the UK's Strengths*. London: HMSO. Available at: www.hm-treasury.gov.uk/coxreview_index.htm

Coyle, D. (1997) *The Weightless World*. London: Capstone.

Craik, J. (2007) *Re-Visioning Arts and Cultural Policy: Current Impasses and Future Directions*. Canberra: ANU Press.

Craik, J., Davis, G. and Sunderland, N. (2000) 'Cultural policy and national identity', in G. Davis and M. Keating (eds), *The Future of Governance: Policy Choices*. Sydney: Allen & Unwin, pp. 177–202.

Crawford, K. and Lumby, C. (2011) *The Adaptive Moment: A Fresh Approach to Convergent Media in Australia*. Sydney: University of New South Wales. Available at: www.sprc.unsw.edu.au/media/File/The_Adaptive_Moment_Convergent_media1.pdf

Cunningham, S. (2009) 'Creative industries as a globally contestable policy field', *Chinese Journal of Communication*, 2 (1): 13–24.

Cunningham, S. (2011) 'Developments in measuring the creative workforce', *Cultural Trends*, 20 (1): 25–40.

Cunningham, S. and Turner, G. (eds) (2010). *The Media and Communications in Australia*, 3rd edn. Sydney: Allen & Unwin.

Currid, E. (2007) *The Warhol Economy*. Princeton, NJ: Princeton University Press.

Curtin, M. (2007) *Playing to the World's Biggest Audience: The Globalisation of Chinese Film and Television*. Berkeley, CA: University of California Press.

Davidsson, P. (2008) *The Entrepreneurship Research Challenge*. Cheltenham: Edward Elgar.

Davies, S., Higgins, K., Hopkins, R., Stecker, R. and Cooper, D. (eds) (2009) *A Companion to Aesthetics*, 2nd edn. Malden, MA: Wiley-Blackwell.

De Vany, A. (2004) *Hollywood Economics*. London: Routledge.

Dean, M. (1999) *Governmentality: Power and Rule in Modern Society*. London: Sage.

Department of Culture, Media and Sport (DCMS) (1998; revised edn 2001) *Creative Industries Mapping Document*. London: HMSO.

Department of the Prime Minister and Cabinet (DPMC) (2011) *National Cultural Policy: Discussion Paper*. Canberra: Office of the Arts.

Department of Trade and Industry (DTI) (2005) *Creativity, Design and Business Performance*. London: Department of Trade and Industry. Available at: www.dti.gov.uk/files/file13654.pdf

Design Institute of Australia (DIA) (2010) *What is a Designer?* Available at: www.dia.org.au/index.cfm?id=186

Dicken, P. (2007) 'Economic globalization: corporations', in G. Ritzer (ed.), *The Blackwell Companion to Globalization*. Malden, MA: Blackwell, pp. 291–306.

Dirlik, A. (2003) 'Global modernity? Modernity in an age of global capitalism', *European Journal of Social Theory*, 6 (3): 275–92.

Dopfer, K. (2004) 'The economic agent as rule maker and rule user: Homo sapiens Economicus', *Journal of Evolutionary Economics*, 14 (2): 177–95.

Dopfer, K. (ed.) (2005) *The Evolutionary Foundations of Economics*. Cambridge: Cambridge University Press.

Dopfer, K. and Potts, J. (2008) *The General Theory of Economic Evolution*. London: Routledge.

Drucker, P. (1959; republished 1996) *Landmarks of Tomorrow: A Report on the New*. New Brunswick, NJ: Transaction Publishers.

Du Gay, P. and Pryke, M. (eds) (2002) *Cultural Economy: Cultural Analysis and Commercial Life*. London: Sage.

Dunn, R. (2008) *Identifying Consumption: Subjects and Objects in Consumer Society*. Philadelphia, PA: Temple University Press.

Dutton, D. (2009) *The Art Instinct: Beauty, Pleasure and Human Evolution*. Oxford: Oxford University Press.

Dyer, R. (1992) *Only Entertainment*. London: Routledge.

Dyson, J. (2010) *Ingenious Britain: Making the UK the Leading High Tech Exporter in Europe*. A report by James Dyson. Available at: media.dyson.com/images_resize_sites/inside_dyson/assets/UK/downloads/IngeniousBritain.PDF

Earl, P. (2003) 'The entrepreneur as a constructor of connections', in R. Koppl (ed.), *Austrian Economics and Entrepreneurial Studies – Advances in Austrian Economics*, No. 6. Oxford: JAI/Elsevier, pp. 117–34.

Eco, U. (1976) *A Theory of Semiotics*. Bloomington: Indiana University Press.

EDB (Economic Development Board) (1992) *Film, Video, and Music Industries*. Singapore: Economic Development Board.

Edgar, A. (2008) 'Culture industry', in A. Edgar and P. Sedgwick (eds), *Cultural Theory: The Key Concepts*. London: Routledge.

Eisenstein, E. (1979) *The Printing Press as an Agent of Change: Communications and Cultural Transformations in Early Modern Europe*. Cambridge: Cambridge University Press.

Enzensberger, H-M. (1973) *The Consciousness Industry*. New York, NY: Continuum.

European Commission (2009) *Design as a Driver of User-Centred Innovation*. Brussels: European Commission.

European Commission (2010) *Green Paper: Unlocking the Potential of the Cultural and Creative Industries*. Brussels: European Commission.

Evans, G. (2009) 'Creative cities, creative spaces and urban policy', *Urban Studies*, 46 (5/6): 1003–40.

Fingleton, B., Igliori, D., Moore, B. and Odedra, R. (2007) 'Employment growth and cluster dynamics of creative industries in Great Britain', in K. Polenske (ed.), *The Economic Geography of Innovation*. Cambridge: Cambridge University Press, pp. 60–85.

Fitzgerald, B., Fitzgerald, A., Middleton, G., Clark, E. and Lim, Y.F. (eds) (2011) *Internet and e-Commerce Law: Business and Policy*. Sydney: Thomson Reuters

Flew, T. (2010) 'New media policies', in M. Deuze (ed.), *Managing Media Work*. London: Sage, pp. 59–72.

Flew, T. (2012) *The Creative Industries, Culture and Policy*. London: Sage.

Flew, T. and McElhinney, S. (2006) 'Globalization and the structure of new media industries', in L. Lievrouw and S. Livingstone (eds), *The Handbook of New Media – Updated Student Edition*. London: Sage, pp. 287–306.

Florida, R. (2002) *The Rise of the Creative Class and How It's Transforming Work Leisure, Community and Everyday Life*. New York, NY: Basic Books.

Florida, R. (2005) *Cities and the Creative Class*. New York, NY: Routledge.

Florida, R. (2006) *The Flight of the Creative Class: The New Global Competition for Talent*. New York, NY: Harper Business.

Florida, R. (2011) 'The creative class is alive', *The Atlantic: Cities (Place Matters)*. Available at: www.theatlanticcities.com/jobs-and-economy/2011/10/creative-class-alive/252/

Foray, D. (2000) *The Economics of Knowledge*. Cambridge, MA: MIT Press.

Foucault, M. (1982) *The Archaeology of Knowledge*. New York, NY: Pantheon.

Foucault, M. (1991) 'Governmentality', in G. Burchell, C. Gordon and P. Miller (eds), *The Foucault Effect: Studies in Governmentality*. London: Harvester Wheatsheaf, pp. 87–104.

Foucault, M. (2008) *The Birth of Biopolitics: Lectures at the Collège de France 1978–1979*. Basingstoke: Palgrave Macmillan.

Free Software Foundation (2009) 'Amazon's CEO jeff Bezos apologizes for Kindle ebook deletion. Free Software Foundation calls upon Amazon to free the ebook reader'. Media Release: Available at: www.fsf.org/news/amazon-apologizes.

Frey, B. and Pommerehne, W. (1989) *Muses and Markets: Explorations in the Economics of the Arts.* Oxford: Blackwell.

Friedman, T. (2005) *The World is Flat: A Brief History of the Twenty-First Century.* New York, NY: Farrar, Strauss and Giroux.

Frow, J. (1995) *Cultural Studies and Cultural Value.* Oxford: Oxford University Press.

Gallegati, M. and Richiardi, M. (2011) 'Agent based models in economics and complexity', in R. Meyers (ed.), *Complex Systems in Finance and Economics.* New York, NY: Springer, pp. 30–53.

Garnham, N. (1987) 'Public policy and the cultural industries', *Cultural Studies*, 1 (1): 23–37.

Garnham, N. (1990) *Capitalism and Communication.* London: Sage.

Garnham, N. (2005) 'From cultural to creative industries: An analysis of the implications of the "creative industries" approach to arts and media policy making in the United Kingdom', *International Journal of Cultural Policy*, 11: 15–29.

Garnham, N. (2011) 'The political economy of communication revisited', in J. Wasko, G. Murdock and H. Souza (eds), *The Handbook of Political Economy of Communications.* Malden, MA: Wiley-Blackwell, pp. 41–61.

Gauntlett, D. (2011a) *Making is Connecting: The Social Meaning of Creativity, from DIY and Knitting to YouTube and Web 2.0.* Cambridge: Polity Press.

Gauntlett, D. (2011b) *Media Studies 2.0, and Other Battles around the Future of Media Research.* Online: Kindle e-book. Available at: www.theory.org.uk/david/kindle.htm

Gibson, C. and Kong, L. (2005) 'Cultural economy: a critical review', *Progress in Human Geography*, 29 (5): 541–6.

Gibson, M. (2007) *Culture and Power: A History of Cultural Studies.* Oxford: Berg.

Giddens, A. (1979) *Central Problems in Social Theory: Action, Structure and Contradiction in Social Analysis.* Berkeley, CA: University of California Press.

Giddens, A. (1990) *The Consequences of Modernity.* Oxford: Polity Press.

Giddens, A. (2003) *Runaway World: How Globalization is Reshaping Our Lives.* New York, NY: Routledge.

Gitlin T. (1998) 'Public sphere or public sphericules?', in T. Liebes and J. Curran (eds), *Media, Ritual and Identity.* London: Routledge, pp. 175–202.

Goldhaber, M. (1997) 'Attention Shoppers! The currency of the New Economy won't be money, but attention – A radical theory of value.' *Wired*, December. Accessible at: www.wired.com/wired/archive/5.12/es_attention.html

Golding, P. and Murdock, G. (2005) 'Culture, communication and political economy', in J. Curran and M. Gurevitch (eds), *Mass Media and Society*, 4th edn. London: Arnold, pp. 60–83.

Goody, J. (2010) *Renaissances: The One or the Many?* Cambridge: Cambridge University Press.

Govender, K. (2008) 'South Africa's creative industry: Exporting design', *Frontier Market Intelligence.* Available online: www.tradeinvestsa.co.za/feature_articles/336584.htm

Gray, J. (2008) *Television Entertainment.* London: Routledge.

Gray, J. (2010a) *Show Sold Separately: Promos, Spoilers, and Other Media Paratexts.* New York, NY: NYU Press.

Gray, J. (2010b) 'Entertainment and media/cultural/communication etc. studies', *Continuum: Journal of Media and Cultural Studies*, 24 (6): 811–17.

Green, J. and Jenkins, H. (2011) 'Spreadable media: How audiences create value and meaning in a networked economy', in V. Nightingale (ed.), *The Handbook of Media Audiences.* Germany: Wiley-VCH.

Gwee J. (2009) 'Innovation and the creative industries clusters: a case study of Singapore's creative industries', *Innovation: Management, Policy and Practice*, 11 (2): 240–52.

Hagel, J. and Seeley Brown, J. (2006) *Creation Nets, Harnessing the Potential of Open Innovation.* Working Paper. Available at: www.edgeperspectives.com

Hall, P. (1998) *Cities in Civilization: Culture, Innovation and Urban Order*. London: Phoenix Giant.

Hall, S. (1985) 'Signification, representation, ideology: Althusser and the post-structuralist debates', *Critical Studies in Mass Communication*, 2 (2): 91–114.

Hammett, J. and Hammett, K. (eds) (2007) *The Suburbanization of New York: Is the World's Greatest City Becoming Just Another Town?* New York, NY: Princeton Architectural Press.

Handke, C. (2006a) 'Plain destruction or creative destruction – copyright erosion and the evolution of the record industry', *Review of Economic Research on Copyright Issues*, 3 (2): 29–51.

Handke, C. (2006b) *Surveying Innovation in the Creative Industries*. Berlin: Humboldt University; and Rotterdam: Erasmus University.

Harding. S. (1986) *The Science Question in Feminism*. Ithaca, NY: Cornell University Press.

Hardt, M. and Negri, A. (2000) *Empire*. Cambridge, MA: Harvard University Press.

Hargreaves, I. (2011) *Digital Opportunity: A Review of Intellectual Property and Growth. An Independent Report by Prof Ian Hargreaves for the UK Government*. Available at: www.ipo.gov.uk/ipreview-finalreport.pdf

Hartley, J. (1992) *Tele-ology: Studies in Television*. London: Routledge.

Hartley, J. (2003) *A Short History of Cultural Studies*. London: Sage.

Hartley, J. (2005) 'Introduction', in J. Hartley (ed.), *Creative Industries*. Malden, MA: Wiley-Blackwell.

Hartley, J. (2008a) *Television Truths*. Malden, MA: Wiley-Blackwell.

Hartley, J. (2008b) 'Cultural science: Where money and meanings meet. Intersecting art and business in the creative economy'. Melbourne: Deakin University, November.

Hartley, J. (2009) *The Uses of Digital Literacy*. St. Lucia: University of Queensland Press and New Brunswick, NJ: Transaction Publishers.

Hartley, J. (2011) *Communication, Cultural and Media Studies: The Key Concepts*. London: Routledge.

Hartley, J. (2012a) *Digital Futures for Cultural and Media Studies*. Malden, MA: Wiley-Blackwell.

Hartley, J. (2012b) 'Authorship and the narrative of the self', in J. Gray and D. Johnson (eds), *A Companion to Media Authorship*. Malden, MA: Wiley-Blackwell.

Hartley, J. and Montgomery, L. (2009) 'Fashion as consumer entrepreneurship: Emergent risk culture, social network markets, and the launch of *Vogue* in China', *Chinese Journal of Communication*, 2 (1): 61–76.

Hartley, J., Potts, J., MacDonald, T. with Erkunt, C. and Kufleitner, C. (2012) 'CCI creative city index', *Cultural Science Journal*, 5 (1). Available at: www.cultural-science.org/journal/index.php/culturalscience/issue/view/10/showToc

Harvey, D. (2001) *Spaces of Capital: Towards a Critical Geography*. Edinburgh: Edinburgh University Press.

Harvey, D. (2005) *A Brief History of Neoliberalism*. Oxford: Oxford University Press.

Hawkes, T. (1977) *Structuralism and Semiotics*. London: Routledge.

Hawkins, G. (2009) 'The politics of bottled water: Assembling bottled water as brand, waste and oil', *Journal of Cultural Economy*, 2 (1/2): 183–95.

Hayek, F. (1945) 'The use of knowledge in society', *American Economic Review*, 35(4): 519–30. Available at: www.econlib.org/library/Essays/hykKnw1.html

Healy, K. (2002) 'What's new for culture in the new economy?' *Journal of Arts Management, Law, and Society*, 32 (2): 86–103.

Held, D. and McGrew, A. (2002) *Globalisation/Anti-Globalisation*. Cambridge: Polity Press.

Herrmann-Pillath, C. (2010) *The Economics of Identity and Creativity: A Cultural Science Approach*. St. Lucia: University of Queensland Press and New Brunswick, NJ: Transaction Publishers.

Hesmondhalgh, D. (2007) *The Cultural Industries*, 2nd edn. London: Sage.

Hesmondhalgh, D. and Pratt, A. (2005) 'Cultural industries and cultural policy', *International Journal of Cultural Policy*, 11: 1–13.

Higgs, P., Cunningham, S., Hearn, G., Adkins, B. and Barnett, K. (2005) *The Ecology of Queensland Design*. Brisbane: CIRAC.

Higgs, P., Cunningham, S. and Bakhshi, H. (2008) *Beyond the Creative Industries*. London: NESTA. Available at: www.nesta.org.uk/publications/reports/assets/features/beyond_the_creative_industries

Hill, T. (2011) *Pageantry and Power: A Cultural History of the Early Modern Lord Mayor's Show 1585–1639*. Manchester: Manchester University Press.

Hindess, B. (1996) *Discourses of Power: From Hobbes to Foucault*. Oxford: Blackwell.

Hirst, P., Thompson, G. and Bromley, S. (2009) *Globalization in Question*, 3rd edn. Cambridge: Polity Press.

Hodgson, G. (1999) *Economics and Utopia: Why the Learning Economy Is Not the End of History*. London: Routledge.

Hodgson, G. (2006) 'What are institutions?' *Journal of Economic Issues*, 40 (1): 2–4.

Hodgson, G. and Knudsen, T. (2010) *Darwin's Conjecture: The Search for General Principles of Social and Economic Evolution*. Chicago, IL: Chicago University Press.

Hoggart, R. (1957) *The Uses of Literacy*. London: Chatto & Windus.

Holden, J. (2007) *Publicly-Funded Culture and the Creative Industries*. London: Demos. Available at: www.demos.co.uk/files/Publicly_Funded_Culture_and_the_Creative_Industries.pdf

Holden, J. (2009) 'How we value arts and culture', *Asia Pacific Journal of Arts and Cultural Management*, 6 (2): 447–56.

Howkins, J. (2001) *The Creative Economy: How People Make Money from Ideas*. London: Penguin.

Howkins, J. (2005) 'The mayor's commission on the creative industries', in J. Hartley (ed.), *Creative Industries*. Malden, MA: Blackwell, pp. 117–23.

Hutter, M. (2011) 'Experience goods', in R.Towse (ed.), *Handbook of Cultural Economics*. Cheltenham: Edward Elgar.

Innis, H. (1950/2007) *Empire and Communications*. Toronto: Dundurn Press.

Internet World Stats (2011) *The Internet Big Picture: World Internet Users and Population Stats*. Available at: www.internetworldstats.com/stats.htm

Jacobs, J. (1961) *The Death and Life of Great American Cities*. New York, NY: Random House.

Jenkins, H. (2003) '*Transmedia Storytelling: Technology Review*', Cambridge, MA: MIT. Available at: www.technologyreview.com/biotech/13052

Jenkins, H. (2004) 'The cultural logic of media convergence', *International Journal of Cultural Studies*, 7 (1): 33–43.

Jenkins, H. (2006) *Convergence Culture: Where Old and New Media Collide*. New York, NY: NYU Press.

Jenkins, H. (2009) 'What happened before YouTube', in J. Burgess and J. Green (eds), *YouTube: Online Video and Participatory Culture*. Cambridge: Polity Press, pp. 109–25.

Jenkins, H. (2010) 'Transmedia storytelling and entertainment: An annotated syllabus', *Continuum: Journal of Media and Cultural Studies*, 24 (6): 943–58.

Johnson, J. (2010) 'The future of the social sciences and humanities in the science of complex systems', *Innovation: European Journal of Social Science Research*, 23 (2): 115–34.

Johnson, S. (2010) *Where Good Ideas Come From: The Natural History of Innovation*. New York, NY: Riverhead Books.

Jones, J., Gray, J. and Thompson, E. (2009) *Satire TV: Politics and Comedy in the Post-Network Era*. New York, NY: NYU Press.

Karaganis, J. (ed.) (2011) *Media Piracy in Emerging Economies*. Social Science Research Council. New York: Available at: http://piracy.ssrc.org/

Karpik, L. (2010) *Valuing the Unique*. Princeton, NJ: Princeton University Press.

Kauffman, S. (1995) *At Home in the Universe: The Search for the Laws of Self-Organization and Complexity*. Oxford: Oxford University Press.

Kauffman, S. (2000) *Investigations*. Oxford: Oxford University Press.

Kaufman, P. and Mohan, J. (2008) *The Economics of Independent Film and Video Distribution in the Digital Age*. New York, NY: Tribeca Film Institute, Intelligent Television.

Keane, M. (2007) *Created in China: The Great New Leap Forward*. London: Routledge.

Keane, M. (2012*) China's New Creative Clusters: Governance, Human Capital, and Investment*. London: Routledge.

Keen, A. (2008). *The Cult of the Amateur: How Blogs, MySpace, YouTube, and the Rest of Today's User-Generated Content are Destroying Our Economy, Our Culture, and Our Values*. New York, NY: Bantam Dell Publishing Group.

Kellner, D. (1984) *Herbert Marcuse and the Crisis of Marxism*. London: Macmillan.

Kline, R. and Pinch, T. (1999) 'The social construction of technology', in D. MacKenzie and J. Wajckman (eds), *The Social Shaping of Technology*, 2nd edn. Buckingham: Open University Press, pp. 113–16.

Knopper, S. (2009) *Appetite for Self-Destruction: The Spectacular Crash of the Record Industry in the Digital Age*. New York, NY: Free Press.

Kong, L. (2009) 'Beyond networks and relations: Towards rethinking creative cluster theory', in L. Kong and J. O'Connor (eds), *Creative Economies, Creative Cities: Asian-European Perspectives*. Dordrecht: Springer, pp. 61–76.

Kong, L., Gibson, C., Khoo, L.M. and Semple, A.L. (2006) 'Knowledges of the creative economy: towards a relational geography of diffusion and adaptation in Asia'. *Asia Pacific Viewpoint*, 47 (2): 173–94.

Korvenmaa, P. (2009) 'Design, research and policies of innovation: Case Finland', in *International Congress of Research in Design*, Bauru, Brazil. Available at: www.faac.unesp.br/ciped2009/anais/Introdu%E7%E3o/Design,%20Research.pdf

Krugman, P. (1991) 'Increasing returns and economic geography', *Journal of Political Economy*, 99: 483–99.

Krugman, P. (1992) *The Age of Diminished Expectations*. Cambridge, MA: MIT Press.

Kumar, K. (1995) *From Post-Industrial to Post-Modern Society*. Oxford: Blackwell.

Lamberton, D. (2006) 'New media and the economics of information', in L. Lievrouw and S. Livingstone (eds), *The Handbook of New Media* – Updated Student Edition. London: Sage, pp. 364–85.

Landry, C. (2000) *The Creative City: A Toolkit for Urban Innovators*. London: Earthscan.

Lanham, R. (2006) *The Economics of Attention: Style and Substance in the Age of Information*. Chicago, IL: University of Chicago Press.

Lanier, J. (2011) *You Are Not a Gadget: A Manifesto*. New York, NY: Vintage Books.

Lash, S. and Urry, J. (1994) *Economies of Signs and Space*. London: Sage.

Lasswell, H. (1948) 'The structure and function of communication in society', in L. Bryson (ed.), *The Communication of Ideas*. New York, NY: Harper.

Latour, B. (2004) 'Why has critique run out of steam? From matters of fact to matters of concern', *Critical Inquiry*, 30 (2): 225–48.

Latour, B. (2005) *Reassembling the Social: An Introduction to Actor-Network Theory*. Oxford: Oxford University Press.

Latour, B. (2011) 'Networks, societies, spheres: Reflections of an actor-network theorist', *International Journal of Communication*, 5: 796–810. Available at: http://ijoc.org/ojs/index.php/ijoc/article/viewFile/1094/558

Leadbeater, C. (1999) *Living on Thin Air: The New Economy*. London: Viking.

Leadbeater, C. (2005) *Arts Organisations in the 21st Century: Ten Challenges*. Arts Council England. Online: Available at: www.charlesleadbeater.net/cms/xstandard/Ten%20Challenges5.pdf

Leadbeater, C. (2008) *We Think: Mass Innovation, Not Mass Production*. London: Profile Books.

Leadbeater, C. (2009) *The Art of With*. Manchester: Cornerhouse. Available at: www.charlesleadbeater.net/cms/xstandard/The%20Art%20of%20With%20PDF.pdf

Leadbeater, C. (2011) *Cloud Culture*. London: Counterpoint. Available at: http://counterpoint.uk.com/2011/07/cloud-culture/

Leadbeater, C. and Miller, P. (2004) *The Pro-Am Revolution*. London: Demos. Available at: www.demos.co.uk/files/proamrevolutionfinal.pdf?1240939425

Leadbeater, C. and Oakley, K. (1999) *The Independents: Britain's New Cultural Entrepreneurs*. London: Demos.

Leibowitz, J. (2009) 'Creative destruction or just destruction – how will journalism survive the internet age?', *Federal Trade Commission News Media Workshop*. Available at: www.ftc.gov/speeches/leibowitz/091201newsmedia.pdf

Lessig, L. (2001) *The Future of Ideas: The Fate of the Commons in a Connected World*. New York, NY: Random House.

Lester, R. and Piore, M. (2004) *Innovation: The Missing Dimension*. Cambridge, MA: Harvard University Press.

LeVay, S. (1997) *Queer Science: The Use and Abuse of Research into Homosexuality*. Boston, MA: MIT Press.

Levi-Strauss, C. (1963) *Structural Anthropology*, vol. 1. New York, NY: Basic Books.

Levin, J. (2009) 'An industry perspective: Calibrating the velocity of change', in J. Holt and A. Perren (eds), *Media Industries: History, Theory, and Method*. Malden, MA: Wiley-Blackwell, pp. 256–63.

Levy, S. (2011) *In the Plex: How Google Thinks, Works and Shapes our Lives*. New York, NY: Simon and Schuster.

Li, W. (2011) *How Creativity is Changing China*. London: Bloomsbury Academic.

Liao, H.T. and Petzold, T. (2010) 'Analysing geo-linguistic dynamics of the world wide web: The use of cartograms and network analysis to understand linguistic development in wikipedia', *Cultural Science Journal*, 3: 2. Available at: http://cultural-science.org/journal/index.php/culturalscience/article/viewArticle/44

Loasby, B. (1999) *Knowledge, Institutions, and Evolution in Economics*. London: Routledge.

Lobato, R. (2010) 'Creative industries and informal economies: Lessons from Nollywood', *International Journal of Cultural Studies*, 13 (4): 337–54.

Looseley, S. (1995) *The Politics of Fun: Cultural Policy and Debate in Contemporary France*. Oxford: Berg.

Lotan, G., Graeff, E., Ananny, M., Gaffney, D., Pearce, I. and Boyd, D. (2011) 'The revolutions were tweeted; information flows during the 2011 Tunisian and Egyptian revolutions', *International Journal of Communication*, 5: 1375–405. Available at: http://ijoc.org/ojs/index.php/ijoc/article/view/1246/643

Lotman, Y. (1990) *Universe of the Mind: A Semiotic Theory of Culture*. Bloomington, IN: Indiana University Press.

Lundvall, B.A., Johnson, B., Andersen, E.S. and Dalum, B. (2007) 'National systems of production, innovation, and competence-building', in K. Polenske (ed.), *The Economic Geography of Innovation*. Cambridge: Cambridge University Press, pp. 213–40.

MacKenzie, D. (2009) *Material Markets: How Economic Agents are Constructed*. New York, NY: Oxford University Press.

MacKenzie, D. and Wajckman, J. (eds) (1999) *The Social Shaping of Technology*, 2nd edn. Buckingham: Open University Press.

Machlup, F. (1993) 'Uses, value, and benefits of knowledge', *Science Communication*, 14 (4): 448–66.

Magee, G. (2005) 'Rethinking invention: cognition and the economics of technological creativity', *Journal of Economic Behavior and Organization*, 57: 29–48.

Malbon, J. (2003) 'Taking formats seriously', in M. Keane, A. Moran and M. Ryan (eds), *Audiovisual Works, TV Formats and Multiple Markets*. Brisbane: Griffith University.

Marcuse, H. (1964) *One Dimensional Man*. Boston, MA: Beacon Press.

Marshall, A. (1890) *The Principles of Economics*. Philadelphia, PA: Porcupine. Accessible at: www.econlib.org/library/Marshall/marP.html

Marvin, C. (2008) *When Old Technologies Were New: Thinking About Electric Communication in the Late Nineteenth Century*. Oxford: Oxford University Press.

Marx, K. (1852) *The Eighteenth Brumaire of Louis Bonaparte*. Available at: www.marxists.org/archive/marx/works/1852/18th-brumaire/ch01.htm

Marx, K. and Engels, F. (1848) *The Communist Manifesto*. Available at: www.anu.edu.au/polsci/marx/classics/manifesto.html

Masuda, Y. (1990) *Managing in the Information Society: Releasing Synergy Japanese Style*. Oxford: Blackwell.

Mattelart, A. (1994) *Mapping World Communication: War, Progress, Culture*. Minneapolis, MN: University of Minnesota Press.

Mattelart, A. (2003) *The Information Society: An Introduction*. London: Sage.

McCarthy, E. (1996) *Knowledge as Culture: The New Sociology of Knowledge*. London: Routledge.

McChesney, R. and Schiller, D. (2003) *The Political Economy of International Communication: Foundations for the Emerging Global Debate about Media Ownership and Regulation*. United Nations Research Institute for Social Development. Technology, Business and Society Programme Paper No. 11, October.

McCraw, T. (2007) *Prophet of Innovation: Joseph Schumpeter and Creative Destruction*. Cambridge, MA: Harvard University Press.

McKee, A., Collis, C. and Hamley, B. (eds) (2011) *Entertainment Industries: Entertainment as a Cultural System*. London: Routledge.

McKnight, L., Vaaler, P. and Katz, R. (2001) *Creative Destruction: Business Survival Strategies in the Global Internet Economy*. Cambridge, MA: MIT Press.

McLuhan, M. (1962) *The Gutenberg Galaxy: The Making of Typographic Man*. Toronto: University of Toronto Press.

McNair, B. (2006) *Cultural Chaos: Journalism, News and Power in a Globalised World*. London: Routledge.

McPhail, T. (2010) *Global Communication: Theories, Stakeholders and Trends*, 3rd edn. Malden, MA: Wiley-Blackwell.

McRobbie, A. (2005) 'Clubs to companies', in J. Hartley (ed.), *Creative Industries*. Malden, MA: Wiley-Blackwell, pp. 375–90.

Meikle, G. and Young, S. (2012). *Media Convergence: Networked Digital Media in Everyday Life*. Basingstoke: Palgrave Macmillan.

Miège, B. (1989) *The Capitalization of Cultural Production*. New York, NY: International General.

Miège, B. (2011) 'Theorizing the cultural industries: Persistent specificities and reconsiderations', in J. Wasko, G. Murdock and H. Souza (eds), *The Handbook of Political Economy of Communications*. Malden, MA: Blackwell, pp. 83–108.

Miliband, R. (1973) *The State in Capitalist Society*. London: Merlin.

Miller, D. (ed.) (1995) *Acknowledging Consumption*. London: Routledge.

Miller, G. (2009) *Spent: Sex, Evolution and Consumption*. New York, NY: Viking Press.

Miller, J. and Page, S. (2007) *Complex Adaptive Systems: An Introduction to Computational Models of Social Life*. Princeton, NJ: Princeton University Press.

Miller, T. (2009) 'From creative to cultural industries', *Cultural Studies*, 23 (1): 88–99.

Miller, T. (2010a) *Television Studies: The Basics*. London: Routledge.

Miller, T. (2010b) 'A future for media studies: Cultural labour, cultural relations, cultural politics', in B. Beaty, D. Briton, G. Filax and R. Sullivan (eds), *How Canadians Communicate III: Contexts of Canadian Popular Culture*. Canada: Althabasca University Press, pp. 35–53.

Miller, T. and Yúdice, G. (2002) *Cultural Policy*. Thousand Oaks, CA: Sage.

Miller, T., Govil, N., McMurria, J., Maxwell, R. and Wang, T. (2005) *Global Hollywood 2*. London: British Film Institute.

Mills, C.W. (1956) *The Power Elite*. Oxford: Oxford University Press.

Ministry of Economic Affairs (MEA) (2006) *Our Creative Potential: Paper on Culture and Economy*. Netherlands: Ministry of Economic Affairs and Ministry of Education, Culture and Science. Available at: www.minocw.nl/documenten/creative_potential.pdf

Mitchell, W., Inouye, A. and Blumenthal, M. (eds) (2003) *Beyond Productivity: Information Technology, Innovation, and Creativity*. Washington, DC: The National Academies Press.

Mitleton-Kelly, E. (2006) 'A complexity approach to co-creating an innovative environment', *World Futures: The Journal of General Evolution*, 62 (3): 223–39.

Mockros, C. and Csikszentmihali, M. (1999) 'The social construction of creative lives', in A. Montuori and R. Purser (eds), *Social Creativity*, vol. 1. New Jersey: Hampton Press.

Mody, B. (2010) *The Geopolitics of Representation in Foreign News: Explaining Darfur*. Lanham, MD: Lexington Books.

Mokyr, J. (2004) *The Gifts of Athena: The Historical Origins of the Knowledge Economy*. Princeton, NJ: Princeton University Press.

Mommaas, H. (2009) 'Spaces of culture and economy: Mapping the cultural-creative cluster landscape', *Creative Economies, Creative Cities. GeoJournal Library*, 98 (2): 45–59.

Montgomery, J. (2007) *The New Wealth of Cities: City Dynamics and the Fifth Wave*. Aldershot: Ashgate.

Montgomery, L. (2010) *China's Creative Industries: Copyright, Social Networks and the Business of Culture in a Digital Age*. Cheltenham: Edward Elgar.

Moran, S. (2009) 'Creativity: a systems perspective', in T. Rickards, M. Runco and S. Moger (eds), *The Routledge Companion to Creativity*. London: Routledge, pp. 292–301.

Mou, B. (2009) *Chinese Philosophy A–Z*. Edinburgh: Edinburgh University Press.

Mulhern, F. (1979) *The Moment of 'Scrutiny'*. London: New Left Books.

Müller, K., Rammer, C. and Truby, J. (2009) 'The role of creative industries in industrial innovation', *Innovation: Management, Policy and Practice*, 11 (2): 148–68.

Mumford, L. (1961) *The City in History: Its Origins, its Transformations, and its Prospects*. New York, NY: Harcourt, Brace and World.

Negus, K. (2002) *Producing Pop: Culture and Conflict in the Popular Music Industry*. London: Arnold.

Negus, K. (2006) 'Rethinking creative production away from the cultural industries', in J. Curran and D. Morley (eds), *Media and Cultural Theory*. London: Routledge, pp. 197–208.

Nelson, R. (ed.) (1993) *National Innovation Systems*. Cambridge, MA: Harvard University Press.

Nelson, R. and Winter, S. (1982) *An Evolutionary Theory of Economic Change*. Cambridge, MA: Harvard University Press.

NESTA (2006) *Creating Growth: How the UK can Develop World Class Creative Businesses*. London: NESTA. Available at: www.nesta.org.uk/library/documents/Creating-Growth.pdf

Nielsen, M. (2011) *Reinventing Discovery: The New Era of Networked Science*. Princeton, NJ: Princeton University Press.

Nora, S. and Minc, A. (1980) *The Computerisation of Society*. Cambridge, MA: MIT Press.

North, D. (1990) *Institutions, Institutional Change and Economic Performance*. Cambridge: Cambridge University Press.

Nowotny, H. (2004) 'The Potential of Transdisciplinarity', *Interdisciplines*. Available at: helga-nowotny.eu/downloads/helga_nowotny_b59.pdf.

Oakley, K. (2004) 'Not so cool Britannia: The role of the creative industries in economic development', *International Journal of Cultural Studies*, 7 (1): 67–77.

Oakley, K. (2009) 'The disappearing arts: Creativity and innovation after the creative industries', *International Journal of Cultural Policy*, 15 (4): 403–13.

Oakley, K., Sperry, B. and Pratt, A. (2008) *The Art of Innovation: How Fine Arts Graduates Contribute to Innovation*. London: NESTA.

O'Connor, J. (2011) *Arts and Creative Industries: Historical Overview and an Australian Conversation*. Sydney: Australia Council for the Arts.

O'Connor, J. and Banks, M. (2009) 'Introduction: after the creative industries', *International Journal of Cultural Policy*, 15 (4): 365–73.

OECD (Organisation for Economic Co-operation and Development). (2007) *Participative Web: User-Created Content*. OECD Working Party on the Information Economy. Available at: www.oecd.org/dataoecd/57/14/38393115.pdf

OECD. (2008) *Global Science Forum Report on Applications of Complexity Science for Public Policy: New Tools for Finding Unanticipated Consequences and Unrealized Opportunities*. Available at: www.oecd.org/dataoecd/44/41/43891980.pdf

Ong, W. (2012; first published 1982) *Orality and Literacy: The Technologizing of the Word*. 30th Anniversary Edition with additional chapters by John Hartley. London: Routledge.

Ormerod, P. (2005) *Why Most Things Fail: Evolution, Extinction and Economics*. London: Faber & Faber.

Ormerod, P. and Bentley, R.A. (2010) 'Modelling creative innovation', *Cultural Science Journal*, 3: 1. Available at: http://cultural-science.org/journal/index.php/culturalscience/article/view/37/114

Ostrom, E. (1990) *Governing the Commons*. Princeton, NJ: Princeton University Press.

Page, S. and Bednar, S. (2007) 'Can game(s) theory explain culture? The emergence of cultural behavior within multiple games', *Rationality and Society*, 19 (1): 65–97.

Pagel, M. (2011) 'Infinite stupidity: A talk with Mark Pagel', *Edge*. Available at: http://edge.org/conversation/infinite-stupidity-edge-conversation-with-mark-pagel

Paine, T. (1792; this edn 1906) *Rights of Man*. Ed. H.B. Bonner. London: Watts & Co. Available at: www.ushistory.org/paine/rights/

Pang, L. (2006) *Cultural Control and Globalisation in Asia: Copyright, Piracy, and Cinema*. London: Routledge.

Papacharissi, Z. (2010) *A Private Sphere: Democracy in a Digital Age*. Cambridge: Polity Press.

Peacock, A. (1993) *Paying the Piper: Culture, Music and Money*. Edinburgh: Edinburgh University Press.

Peck, J. (2005) 'Struggling with the creative class', *International Journal of Urban and Regional Research*, 29 (4): 740–70.

Perelman, M. (2002) *Steal This Idea: Intellectual Property Rights and the Corporate Confiscation of Creativity*. New York, NY: Palgrave.

Perez, C. (2010) 'Technological revolutions and techno-economic paradigms', *Cambridge Journal of Economics*, 34 (1): 185–202.

Pine, B. and Gilmore, J. (1999) *The Experience Economy*. Cambridge, MA: Harvard Business School Press.

Pope, R. (2005) *Creativity: Theory, History, Practice*. London: Routledge.

Popper, K. (1968) *Conjectures and Refutations*. New York, NY: Harper & Row.

Porter, M. (1990) *The Competitive Advantage of Nations*. New York, NY: Free Press.

Potts, J. (2009a) 'Why the creative industries matter to economic evolution', *Economics of Innovation and New Technology*, 18 (7/8): 663–73.

Potts, J. (2009b) 'Creative industries and innovation policy', *Innovation: Management, Practice and Policy*, 11 (2): 138–47.

Potts, J. (2011) *Creative Industries and Economic Evolution*. Cheltenham: Edward Elgar.

Potts, J. and Cunningham, S. (2008) 'Four models of the creative industries', *International Journal of Cultural Policy*, 14 (3): 233–47.

Potts, J., Cunningham, S., Hartley, J. and Ormerod, P. (2008a) 'Social network markets: A new definition of creative industries', *Journal of Cultural Economics*, 32 (2): 167–85.

Potts, J., Hartley, J. Banks, J. Burgess, J., Cobcroft, R., Cunningham, S. and Montgomery, L. (2008b) 'Consumer co-creation and situated creativity', *Industry and Innovation*, 15 (5): 459–74.

PwC. (2011) *Global Entertainment and Media Outlook 2011–2015*. New York: Pricewaterhouse Coopers. Available at: www.pwc.com/gx/en/global-entertainment-media-outlook/index.jhtml.

Rajan, M.T.S. (2006) *Copyright and Creative Freedom: A Study of Post-Socialist Law Reform*. London: Routledge.

Raustiala, K. and Sprigman, C. (2006) 'The piracy paradox: Innovation and intellectual property in fashion design', *Virginia Law Review*, 92 (8): 1687–777.

Rehn, A. and De Cock, C. (2009) 'Deconstructing creativity', in T. Rickards, M. Runco and S. Moger (eds), *The Routledge Companion to Creativity*. London: Routledge, pp. 222–31.

Rifkin, J. (2000) *The Age of Access*. London: Penguin.

Rogers, E. (1995) *Diffusion of Innovations*. New York, NY: Free Press.

Romer, P. (1990) 'Endogenous technological change', *Journal of Political Economy*, 98 (5): S71–S102.

Roodhouse, S. (2010) *Cultural Quarters: Principles and Practice*. 2nd edn. Bristol: Intellect.

Ross, A. (2009) *Nice Work if You Can Get It: Life and Labor in Precarious Times*. New York, NY: NYU Press.

Rowse, T. (2006) 'Towards a history of indigenous statistics in Australia', in B. Hunter (ed.), *Assessing the Evidence on Indigenous Socioeconomic Outcomes*. Canberra: CAEPR Research Monograph No. 26: ANU E-Press, pp. 1–10. Available at: http://epress.anu.edu.au/c26_citation.html

Runciman, W. (2009) *The Theory of Cultural and Social Selection*. Cambridge: Cambridge University Press.

Russell-Brown, K. (2009) *The Color of Crime*, 2nd edn. New York, NY: New York University Press.

Sachs, J. (2011) *The Price of Civilization: Reawakening American Virtue and Prosperity*. New York, NY: Random House.

Samuels, E. (2000) *The Illustrated Story of Copyright*. New York: St. Martin's Press. Online edition available at: www.edwardsamuels.com/illustratedstory/index.htm

Sassen, S. (1994) *Cities in a World Economy*. Thousand Oaks, CA: Pine Forge Press.

Saunders, D. (2010) *Arrival City: How the Largest Migration in History is Reshaping Our World*. US: Pantheon. Available at: http://arrivalcity.net/

Sayre, S. and King, C. (2010) *Entertainment and Society: Influences, Impacts, and Innovations*. New York, NY: Routledge.

Schiller, D. (1999) *Digital Capitalism: Networking the Global System*. Cambridge, MA: MIT Press.

Schön, D. (1983) *The Reflective Practitioner: How Professionals Think in Action*. New York, NY: Basic Books.

Schotter, A. (1981) *The Economic Theory of Social Institutions*. New York, NY: Cambridge University Press.

Schumpeter, J. (1942) *Capitalism, Socialism and Democracy*. New York, NY: Harper; London: George Allen & Unwin.

Scott, A. (2000) *The Cultural Economy of Cities: Essays on the Geography of Image-Producing Industries*. London: Sage.

Scott, A. (2005) *On Hollywood: The Place, The Industry*. Princeton, NJ: Princeton University Press.

Scott, A. (2006a) 'Creative cities: conceptual issues and policy questions', *Journal of Urban Affairs*, 28 (1): 1–17.

Scott, A. (2006b) 'Entrepreneurship, innovation and industrial development: Geography and the creative field revisited', *Small Business Economics*, 26 (1): 1–24.

Seaman, B. (2004) 'Competition and the non-profit arts: The lost industrial organization agenda', *Journal of Cultural Economics*, 28: 167–93.

Searle, J. (2005) 'What is an institution?', *Journal of Institutional Economics*, 1 (1): 1–21.

Sennett, R. (2008) *The Craftsman*. London: Penguin.

Sewell, W. (1992) 'A theory of structure: Duality, agency, and transformation', *American Journal of Sociology*, 98 (1): 1–29.

Shapiro, C. and Varian, H. (1999) *Information Rules: A Strategic Guide to the Network Economy*. Cambridge, MA: Harvard University Press.

Sheridan, A. (1980) *Foucault: The Will to Truth*. London: Tavistock.

Shirky, C. (2008) *Here Comes Everybody: The Power of Organizing Without Organizations*. New York, NY: Penguin.

Shirky, C. (2010) *Cognitive Surplus: Creativity and Generosity in a Connected Age*. New York, NY: Penguin.

Simon, H. (1969/1996) *The Sciences of the Artificial*, 3rd edn. Cambridge, MA: MIT Press.

Simon, H. (1971) 'Designing organizations for an information-rich world', in M. Greenberger (ed.), *Computers, Communication, and the Public Interest*. Baltimore, MD: Johns Hopkins Press.

Sinclair, J. and Cunningham, S. (2000) 'Diasporas and the media', in S. Cunningham and J. Sinclair (eds), *Floating Lives: the Media and Asian Diasporas*. St. Lucia: University of Queensland Press, pp. 1–34.

Sinclair, J., Jacka, E. and Cunningham, S. (1996) *New Patterns in Global Television: Peripheral Vision*. Oxford: Oxford University Press.

Smith, C. (1998) *Creative Britain*. London: Faber & Faber.

Smith, J. (2010) *The Creative Country: Policy, Practice and Place in New Zealand's Creative Economy 1999–2008*. Unpublished PhD dissertation. Auckland: AUT.

Stark, D. (2009) *Sense of Dissonance: Accounts of Worth in Economic Life*. Princeton, NJ: Princeton University Press.

State of Victoria. (2010) *Victorian Design Action Plan 2011–2015*. Melbourne: Department of Innovation, Industry and Regional Development.

Sternberg, R. and Lubart, T. (1999) 'The concept of creativity: prospects and paradigms', in R. Sternberg (ed.), *The Handbook of Creativity*. Cambridge: Cambridge University Press.

Storper, M. (1997) *The Regional World: Territorial Development in a Global Economy*. New York, NY: Guilford.

Storper, M. and Scott, A. (2009) 'Rethinking human capital, creativity and urban growth', *Journal of Economic Geography*, 9 (1): 147–67.

Streeter, T. (2011) *The Net Effect: Romanticism, Capitalism, and the Internet*. New York, NY: New York University Press.

Strogatz, S. (2001) 'Exploring complex networks', *Nature*, 410: 268–76.

Swann, P. and Birke, D. (2005) *How Do Creativity and Design Enhance Business Performance – A Framework for Interpreting the Evidence*. London: Department of Trade and Industry. Available at: www.dti.gov.uk/files/file14794.pdf

Swedberg, R. (2006) 'The cultural entrepreneur and the creative industries: Beginning in Vienna', *Journal of Cultural Economics*, 30: 243–61.

Taylor, C. (1984) 'Foucault on freedom and truth', *Political Theory*, 12 (2): 152–83.

TEKES. (2000) *Design 2005! The Industrial Design Technology Programme*. Strategy document for TEKES, the Finnish agency for technology and innovation.

Terranova, T. (2000) 'Free labor: Producing culture for the digital economy', *Social Text* 63, 18(2): 33–58.

Tether, B. (2005) *Think Piece on the Role of Design in Business Performance*. London: Department of Trade and Industry. Available at: www.dti.gov.uk/files/file14796.pdf

Thatcher, M. (1987) *Interview for* Woman's Own *('no such thing as society')*. Margaret Thatcher Foundation. Online: www.margaretthatcher.org/document/106689

Thomas, D. and Seely Brown, J. (2011) *A New Culture of Learning: Cultivating the Imagination for a World of Constant Change*. USA: Create Space Publishing.

Thompson, E.P. (1963) *The Making of the English Working Class*. London: Gollancz.

Thompson, J. (1990) *Ideology and Modern Culture*. Cambridge: Polity Press.

Thompson, J. (1995) *The Media and Modernity*. Cambridge: Polity Press.

Thrift, N. (2002) 'Performing cultures in the new economy', in P. Du Gay and M. Pryke (eds), *Cultural Economy: Cultural Analysis and Commercial Life*. London: Sage, pp. 201–33.

Throsby, D. (1994) 'The production and consumption of the arts', *Journal of Economic Literature*, 32: 1–29.

Throsby, D. (2001) *Economics and Culture*. Cambridge: Cambridge University Press.

Throsby, D. (2010) *The Economics of Cultural Policy*. Cambridge: Cambridge University Press.

Timberg, S. (2011) 'The creative class is a lie', *salon.com*. Available at: http://entertainment.salon.com/2011/10/01/creative_class_is_a_lie/singleton/

Tomlinson, J. (2007) 'Cultural globalization', in G. Ritzer (ed.), *The Blackwell Companion to Globalization*. Malden, MA: Blackwell, pp. 352–66.

Towse, R. (2010) *A Textbook of Cultural Economics*, Cambridge: Cambridge University Press.

Tunstall, J. (2008) *The Media Were American: U.S. Mass Media in Decline*. New York, NY: Oxford University Press.

Turner, G. (2010). *Ordinary People and the Media: The Demotic Turn*. London: Sage.

references

Turner, G. (2011) 'Surrendering the Space: Convergence, culture, cultural studies, and the curriculum', *Cultural Studies*, 25 (4/5): 685–99.

United Nations Conference on Trade and Development (UNCTAD). (2008/2010) *The Creative Economy Report*. Geneva: UNCTAD/UNDP.

Utrecht [School of the Arts] (2011) *The Entrepreneurial Dimension of the Cultural and Creative Industries*. Study commissioned by the European Commission. Available at: http://ec.europa.eu/culture/key-documents/doc3124-en.htm.

Van Tassel, J. (2006) *Digital Rights Management: Protecting and Monetizing Content*. Burlington, MA and Oxford: Focal Press.

Veblen, T. (1899) *The Theory of the Leisure Class*. Project Gutenberg. Available at: www.gutenberg.org/ebooks/833

Veblen, T. (1919) *The Place of Science in Modern Civilization and Other Essays*. New York, NY: Viking Press.

Vega-Redondo, F. (2007) *Complex Social Networks*. Cambridge: Cambridge University Press.

Verganti, R. (2009) *Design-Driven Innovation*. Cambridge, MA: Harvard Business Press.

von Hippel, E. (1988) *The Sources of Innovation*. Oxford: Oxford University Press. Available at: http://web.mit.edu/evhippel/www/sources.htm

von Hippel, E. (2005) *Democratizing Innovation*. Cambridge, MA: MIT Press. Available at: http://web.mit.edu/evhippel/www/democ1.htm

Wasserman, S. and Faust, K. (1994) *Social Network Analysis: Methods and Applications*. Cambridge: Cambridge University Press.

Watson, P. (2006) *Ideas: A History from Fire to Freud*. London: Phoenix.

Watts, D. (1999) *Small Worlds*. Princeton, NJ: Princeton University Press.

Webster, F. (2006) 'The information society revisited', in L. Lievrouw and S. Livingstone (eds), *The Handbook of New Media* – Updated Student Edition. London: Sage, pp. 443–57.

Weinberger, D. (2008) *Everything is Miscellaneous: The Power of the New Digital Disorder*. New York, NY: Holt Paperbacks.

Wellman, B. (2007) 'The network is personal', *Social Networks*, 29 (3): 349–56.

Williams, R. (1958) *Culture and Society*. London: Penguin.

Williams, R. (1960) *Border Country* [novel]. London: Chatto & Windus.

Williams, R. (1974) *Television; Technology and Cultural Form*. London: Fontana.

Williams, R. (1976) *Keywords: A Vocabulary of Culture and Society*. London: Fontana.

Williams, R. (1977) *Marxism and Literature*. Oxford: Oxford University Press.

Williams, R. (1981) *Culture*. London: Fontana.

Williams, R. (1989) *Resources of Hope: Culture, Democracy, Socialism*. London: Verso.

Williamson, O. (1985) *The Economic Institutions of Capitalism*. New York, NY: Free Press.

Winston, B. (1986) *Misunderstanding Media*. Cambridge, MA: Harvard University Press.

Wolfram, S. (2002) *A New Kind of Science*. Online: www.wolframscience.com/nksonline/toc.html.

Work Foundation (2007) *Staying Ahead: The Economic Performance of the UK's Creative Industries*. London: Work Foundation.

Yúdice, G. (2003) *The Expediency of Culture: Uses of Culture in the Global Era*. Durham, NC: Duke University Press.

Zukin, S. (2010) *Naked City: The Death and Life of Authentic Urban Places*. New York, NY: Oxford University Press.

index

index

key concepts in
creative industries